SOUP SUPPERS

MORE THAN 100 MAIN-COURSE SOUPS AND 40 ACCOMPANIMENTS

ARTHUR SCHWARTZ

HarperPerennial

A Division of HarperCollins*Publishers*

HarperCollins books may be purchased for educational, business, or sales promotional use. For information please write: Special Markets Department, HarperCollins Publishers, Inc., 10 East 53rd Street, New York, NY 10022.

Designed by Charles Kreloff

Library of Congress Cataloging-in-Publication Data

Schwartz, Arthur (Arthur R.)
    Soup suppers : more than 100 main-course soups and 40 accompaniments / by Arthur Schwartz.
      p.   cm.
    Includes index.
    ISBN 0-06-096948-2
    1. Soups. 2. Entrées (Cookery) I. Title
TX757.S36 1994
641.8'13—dc20   93-29399

98 99 00 01 02 HAD 15 14 13 12 11

FOR BOB HARNED

CONTENTS

ACKNOWLEDGMENTS

This book would not have been possible without the professional guidance and personal devotion of my dear friend and editor Susan Friedland, nor without the inestimable help and good counsel of my friend and assistant Iris Carulli.

I also must thank Andrea, Milton, Brian, and Rachel Alexander; Rozanne Gold and Michael Whiteman; Suzanne and Ned Hamlin; Andy Port; Paula Wolfert; Daniel Young; Stephen Karp; Marcos Oksenhendler; Robin Zucker; Francesco de'Rogati; and above all else, Bob Harned—my circle of cheerleaders, tasters, and life advisers.

FOREWORD

FROM SOP TO SOUP TO SUPPER

Soup: The sound of eating it must have suggested the word, which, according to the Oxford English Dictionary (OED), definitely descends from the word sop (and sip), which itself goes back to the beginnings of the Indo-European languages.

Linguistically speaking, from soup (an adaptation of the Old French *souppe*) to supper, the meal at which soup was taken, is not much of a stretch. In antique English, then, the title *Soup Suppers* would be redundant, while in modern life the idea is to make sensible, enjoyable, no-fuss food for your loved ones. Most of these soup suppers are meant to be informal meals. You can take almost any recipe in this book, add a tossed salad, bread, and fresh fruit, and either call in the family or call up some company. Under the heading "Supper Suggestions" at the beginning of each recipe you'll also find other menu recommendations for the occasions when you have the time and desire to prepare a more complex meal. After the chapters on vegetable, bean and grain, meat, chicken, fish and shellfish,

and cold soups, there are coordinated recipe chapters on breads (only one baked with yeast), on vegetable and salad appetizers and side dishes, and on desserts (mostly fruit-based). In essence, *Soup Suppers* is a world of meals unto itself.

About this word "sop": Its modern meaning is "a piece of bread, or the like, dipped or steeped in water, wine, etc., before being eaten or cooked" and, with that meaning, it came into use in English in 1100, according to the OED. In the beginning, in the days before eating tools became common, a sop was, in fact, a tool for eating soup. It wasn't until 1533 that Catherine de Medici introduced the fork to France when she married Henry II, and even then it supposedly did not catch on in England until the early 1600s. Spoons were far more common during the Middle Ages and Early Renaissance, but sops remained an important part of the meal. They were and are delicious, as anyone who has ever dunked bread will testify.

In *Food in History* (Stein & Day, 1973), Reay Tannahill, by way of explaining the four main textural categories of food served in the Middle Ages, which were largely dictated by the eating implements available, recounts this story about sops:

> The number of sops in a serving was taken by guests as an indication of their host's meanness or generosity; the more, the better. On one occasion, when the Sieur de Vandy dined at the home of the Comte de Grandpré, "they placed before him a soup in which there were only two poor sops chasing each other around. Vandy tried to take one up but, as the plate was enormous, he missed his aim; he tried again, and could not catch it. He rose from the table and called his valet de chambre.
>
> "You there! Pull off my boots."
>
> "What are you going to do?" his neighbor asked him.
>
> "Permit me to have my boots removed," said Vandy coldly, "and I propose to dive into that plate in order to seize that sop!"

A sop has also lately come to mean a dish into which you mean to dunk bread, not just the bread itself. There are many in *Soup Suppers*—a pot of red peppers with garlic, shallots, olives, and capers and their rendered juices, a saffron and garlic broth that's drunk up by bread and potatoes, a Sicilian-style fava bean purée that is nothing without garlic toast. You probably never realized that a crock of French onion soup with croutons and cheese is really a sop, probably an ancient one.

INTRODUCTION

I come from a serious soup-making, soup-eating family. My maternal grandfather, with whom my immediate family shared a house, had to have burning hot soup at every meal. My other grandfather was actually at one time a professional soup maker, selling Manhattan clam chowder and other prepared foods to New York bars and grills.

One of my father's gastronomic preoccupations was thick soup, but he loved them all. He might tell you his favorite was mushroom-barley or a split-pea soup that "you can cut with a knife," though you'd never guess it by the gusto with which he savored a bowl of clear chicken soup or cold schav thickened with nothing but sour cream.

My maternal grandfather's obsession with the temperature of soup created several memorable arguments between him and my grandmother. To this day, I can see myself sitting with him at the table in the dinette while my grandmother, only a few steps away in the adjoining kitchen, announced, at the top of her lungs, "Okay, Lou, the soup is simmering. Now I'm ladling it into the bowl. Now I'm walking toward the table. You want it hotter you'll have to eat it out of the pot."

I didn't get his point then, but I do now: When it arrives at the table, soup, if it's supposed to be a hot soup, should be hotter than is really comfortable to sip. You want to catch the soup at every level of temperature, letting it reveal its different aspects as it cools.

Had my father lived to taste his way through the recipe testing for this book he would not have been disappointed in the thickness of these soups. With the obvious exception of those soups that are broths, all these recipes have been formulated to be so thick and filling that they can serve as main courses, with only a salad and simple dessert to fill out the menu. One of the great things about soup is that it is flexible: You want it thinner? Add liquid. You want it thicker? Let the liquid evaporate more by cooking it uncovered. It needs "a little something"? Add that something.

Following are some points you should note before you begin cooking.

ON WATER

Use only cold running tap water or bottled water. Hot tap water is more likely to contain minerals (such as lead) from your plumbing.

13

ON POTS

Most of the soups in this book were cooked in either an 8-quart stainless steel boiling pot with a sandwiched aluminum and copper bottom (the kind sold by several major American cookware manufacturers), a 6-quart tin-lined copper casserole, a 5-quart aluminum Dutch oven, or a 4-quart enameled cast iron casserole. The boiled dinners were cooked in a 10-quart cast iron casserole. The important things to remember about pots are:

• All your soup pots should have heavy bottoms so that you can, if necessary, sauté vegetables or flavorings without scorching them.
• All the pots should have covers or be sized so that you can create a makeshift cover with a dinner plate (tricky, but doable).
• You should choose, if necessary, a pot that is more ample than necessary rather than filling one to the brim and risk spilling soup as it cooks or is stirred.

BOILING VS. SIMMERING

In this book, as in life, a boil is when large bubbles break the surface of the water and the water rolls. In many of the recipes, you will bring the liquid to that point, or almost to that point, then be asked to adjust the heat so that the soup simmers, either uncovered, partially covered, or covered. For the purposes of these recipes:

A gentle simmer is when small bubbles occasionally break the surface.

A steady simmer is when the small bubbles break regularly.

A brisk simmer is almost a boil, but without the rolling motion.

TO COVER OR NOT

Most recipes will call for the pot to be partially covered, which means the cover is to be left slightly askew, preventing overactive cooking due to steam pressure building up and dramatic evaporation. In addition, in the case of some broths, you are instructed to leave the cover slightly askew so that meat or poultry fat is not forced by pressure into the liquid, which would make it cloudy and greasy.

Remember, a covered pot requires less heat than an uncovered pot to cook at the same intensity, so you can adjust the cooking temperature of a soup by adjusting the cover as well as the heat.

INGREDIENT SIZES

A medium onion is here defined as three onions to a pound. A large onion is two or not quite two to the pound. Whether chopped coarse or fine, a medium onion will yield about 1 cup. In almost all of these recipes it is not important if you use slightly more or less.

The same goes for other basic soup vegetables, which is why amounts are listed primarily as number and size of vegetable, not the volume they yield when prepared for the dish. Volume amounts are given parenthetically, however, and the following are for your general information:

A large rib of celery is one of the outside ribs and will yield ½ to ¾ cup when chopped or sliced. Smaller, inner ribs yield less accordingly.

A large bell pepper—two will be just under a pound—yields about 1 cup when chopped.

A medium potato—two to the pound—yields about 1 cup when cubed.

ON CHOPPING, DICING, CUBING

The appearance and texture of soups, if not their flavor, are often determined by how neatly or haphazardly, finely or coarsely the vegetables are chopped, cubed, or diced. I've used the word chopping here when, in fact, you might call it dicing, the neater process. A "finely chopped" onion, for instance, is one that has been cut in half through the root end, placed flat side down on a cutting board, then sliced down in the direction of the root end at ¼-inch intervals, then crosswise at ¼-inch intervals: the onion will fall into ¼-inch pieces. When a recipe says "coarsely chopped," it means you can use the same technique to form ½-inch pieces or chop more haphazardly.

Use your discretion about the size of vegetable pieces. However, unless the soup is to be puréed, regular, hand-cut pieces make a better-looking soup than vegetables chopped in a food processor.

REHEATING

Once a soup has been fully cooked, be careful not to recook it when you reheat it. Bring it slowly to a simmer, then serve immediately. Some soups will actually improve after they have rested for a time, then are reheated. Some will not. Read the Advance Preparation recommendations at the end of each recipe to determine the correct procedure.

Many soups will have to be reseasoned—"refreshened" is how I put it—or thinned with either broth or water when they are reheated. Bean and grain soups in particular will thicken as they stand.

ON SOAKING BEANS

All the recipes specify overnight soaking because that is the best method. It softens the skins and plumps the beans so that the skins do not break when the beans expand in cooking and the beans will cook more quickly. After picking over the beans so you can discard stray stones or bad beans, rinse them in cold water, then let them soak in cold tap water to cover by several inches for at least 8 hours. Some people cook beans in the soaking water. I discard the soaking water and start with fresh water.

For quicker soaking, place the beans in a pot with cold water to cover by a couple of inches, bring to a rolling boil for 1 minute, remove from the heat, and let stand for 1 hour. Drain well. Cook the beans in fresh water.

Use your discretion. With fish and some vegetables, in general when elements in a dish should shine over the oil, a less assertive oil is suggested. When the oil itself is a star of the soup, use a more robustly flavored oil. Save very expensive oils for eating raw, as a final drizzle on a soup, or in salads.

ON OLIVE OIL

Today we are lucky to have an enormous selection of olive oils in our food markets. Extra-virgin olive oil, which is to say the first, low-acid, cold pressing of oil from the olive, is the preferred kind because it is the closest to the source, the olive, and its manufacture involves the least human manipulation. As a result, it is the most flavorful.

Extra-virgin olive oils from different places have different flavors, and it would not be too much of a generalization to say that the taste of a place's oil is, above all else, the taste that makes a dish taste of that place. If, for instance, you are making a Tuscan soup, such as the cannellini bean soup on page 58, use a green and peppery Tuscan oil for the most authentic flavor; not that the dish would be anything less than great if you used olive oil from Liguria, Sicily, Umbria, or Spain, Greece, Turkey, Lebanon, France, or California. Well, California has a way to go in producing world-class olive oil.

Sometimes recipes here will specify a delicately flavored oil over a full-flavored one.

ON SALT

Sea salt, because it is not as refined, has a more complex, more rounded flavor than sharp-tasting, free-running table salt, even coarse kosher salt. Sea salt also has natural trace minerals, including varying degrees of iodine, depending on the water from which it was extracted. It is available in many supermarkets now, through mail-order catalogs, and in every health food store. It is more expensive than ordinary table salt, but it makes a discernible difference in the taste of food.

In dishes where the salt has time to dissolve in a copious amount of liquid—most dishes in this book—I use coarse sea salt. When a fine grind is desirable—as in a salad dressing—I use commercially ground fine sea salt or I run the coarse salt through a salt mill, which looks like a peppermill but has a plastic grinding mechanism instead of a metal one that would rust. If you must use table salt, use slightly less than called for in the recipes.

ON HERBS

Some herbs are best used fresh. Some are as good, or even better, when dried. Do not bother with dried basil or parsley. Use fresh dill whenever possible. Fresh and dried rosemary and fresh and dried bay leaves, however, are interchangeable, and in the same amounts. Dried thyme is at least twice as strong as fresh thyme. Dried oregano is at least three times as powerful as fresh oregano, which should be reserved for seasoning salads and vegetables.

Dried herbs should be kept in a relatively cool and dark place in your kitchen, never near the stove. Even with ideal storage, their bouquet and flavor are seriously diminished after six months. If you find yourself with a fading herb, use more than called for in the recipe. Inevitably, however, you will be left with a half bottle of dusty-smelling herb. Toss it out, or save it for barbecue season, when immolating old herbs at least produces some mildly fragrant smoke.

Incidentally, do not try to save money by buying tiny jars of herbs. Their per ounce cost is much greater, so there is little or no saving if you use only half of a larger jar.

ON SOY SAUCE AND SEASONING LIQUIDS

When converting a soup flavored with meat into a vegetarian dish, it may not be enough or appropriate to simply use a vegetable stock as a base. Most vegetable broths are sweet and do not truly substitute for the savory flavor of meat. Instead, try boosting the soup's flavor with soy sauce or a seasoning liquid such as Maggi, which is a blend of water, hydrolyzed plant protein, and salt. Actually, inexpensive brands of soy sauce may be nothing more than this plus caramel color, while the best are made from fermented soybeans.

CHAPTER 1

VEGETABLE SOUPS

BROCCOLI AND SHELL MACARONI SOUP
RUSSIAN SWEET AND SOUR CABBAGE SOUP
CAULIFLOWER SOUP
CORN CHOWDER
EGGPLANT SOUP WITH FRITTATA NOODLES
SKORDOZOUMI (GREEK GARLIC SOUP)
CALDO VERDE (PORTUGUESE GREENS SOUP)
MUSHROOM SOUP WITH WILD RICE AND BROWN RICE
ITALIAN MUSHROOM SOUP WITH PARMESAN
FRENCH ONION SOUP
ONION AND GRUYÈRE SOUP
QUICK SWEET PEA SOUP
SWEET RED PEPPER SOP
POTATO, ONION, AND TOMATO SOUP
PAPPA AL POMODORO (TUSCAN TOMATO AND BREAD SOUP)
FRESH TOMATO SOUP
SAVORY TOMATO RICE SOUP
MINESTRONE
RIBOLLITA (BREAD- OR RICE-THICKENED MINESTRONE)
MINESTRONE WITH SWISS CHARD
GENOESE MINESTRONE WITH PESTO
NIKA HAZELTON'S GARDEN VEGETABLE SOUP
CHORBA (MOROCCAN VEGETABLE SOUP)
NORMAN WEINSTEIN'S CHINESE HOT AND SOUR SOUP
EGG BOUILLABAISSE
ROASTED VEGETABLE BROTH
SOUP OF THE DAY
SPRING ONION AND RED POTATO SOUP

BROCCOLI AND SHELL MACARONI SOUP

Serves 3 or 4

This is a simple, quickly made low-fat soup for everyday family meals. It is best served as soon as the pasta is cooked, hot from the pot.

SUPPER SUGGESTIONS: Precede it with a mixed salad accompanied by Parmesan aioli toast (page 160) or a plate of one or more Italian cold cuts—salami, mortadella, prosciutto, etc. Accompany the soup and cold cuts with crusty bread or garlic toast (page 159). Pears are a good fruit to follow with, perhaps with a piece of blue-veined cheese, or serve a fruit salad (page 199).

2 tablespoons extra-virgin, full-flavored olive oil
1 medium onion, chopped or sliced (about 1 cup)
3 large garlic cloves, chopped or sliced
1 large celery rib, chopped (about ¾ cup)
2 tablespoons finely chopped parsley (leaves only)
½ teaspoon dried marjoram
1 16-ounce can plum tomatoes, with their juice (1½ cups)
1 pound broccoli
6 cups chicken broth, beef broth, or water
Coarse sea salt
½ teaspoon freshly ground black pepper, or more to taste
1 cup small macaroni shells or other small macaroni

⅓ cup (approximately) freshly grated Pecorino Romano cheese

1. In a 3- to 4-quart saucepan, combine the olive oil, onion, garlic, celery, parsley, and marjoram. Place over medium heat and sauté, stirring frequently, until the celery and onion are beginning to color, about 10 minutes.

2. Add the tomatoes and their juice, breaking up the tomatoes with a wooden spoon or a potato masher. Simmer briskly for 10 minutes.

3. Meanwhile, cut the top of the broccoli into small florets, then peel the stems and cut them into ½-inch pieces. You should have about 5 cups.

4. Add the broccoli, broth, salt (the amount will depend on the saltiness of the liquid you use, and pepper. Cover and bring to a boil. Adjust heat and simmer briskly, partially covered, for 10 minutes, stirring once or twice.

5. Stir in the shells and continue to simmer until shells are tender, 8 to 10 minutes, stirring a few times.

6. Taste and correct seasoning if necessary.

7. Let rest 10 minutes, then serve in flat soup bowls and pass the grated cheese.

ADVANCE PREPARATION: Should be made just before serving. If need be, however, cook through step 4, then hold up to an hour before proceeding.

RUSSIAN SWEET AND SOUR CABBAGE SOUP

Serves 6 to 8

The peak season for this substantial soup—a slight variation on my American-born grandmother's Russian-born mother's recipe—is mid-September through early October, those few weeks when summer tomatoes and autumn cabbage overlap. My grandmother, Elsie, on the other hand, made the soup all winter with canned tomatoes and we certainly never complained. If you *do* use canned tomatoes you may not need as much sugar. Elsie always described the sweet-sour balance as "winy." When you achieve it—by tasting and correcting, tasting and correcting—you'll know it. In this version, lemon juice is used as the souring agent. My grandmother used sour salt, which is citric acid crystals. These are hard to find in some parts of the country—try your local pharmacy if you can't find them in a food store—but they do give a different, more authentic sour flavor than lemon juice. As Elsie once pointed out, "Lemons didn't grow on trees in Russia."

SUPPER SUGGESTIONS: Rye bread is the right accompaniment. For a first course, Roumanian eggplant salad (page 185) hits the spot. For dessert, the peach crostata (page 194) might still be possible in late September; the plum tart's (page 195) peak season is early fall.

2 pounds flanken or short ribs
½ teaspoon salt
2 tablespoons vegetable oil
1 large Bermuda onion, cut in half then sliced
2 to 3 pounds ripe tomatoes (3 to 5 large), cored and cut into wedges, or 1 (28- or 35-ounce) can Italian plum tomatoes
2 pounds cabbage, cored and shredded (about 10 cups)
2 quarts water
2 teaspoons salt
½ teaspoon freshly ground pepper
6 tablespoons sugar
¼ cup freshly squeezed lemon juice
2½ to 3 pounds potatoes (4 to 6 large), boiled and peeled
Snipped fresh dill (optional)

1. Sprinkle the meat on all sides with salt, then put it in a heavy 8-quart pot. Place over medium-high heat and sear until browned on both sides, turning several times. Remove to a plate and set aside.

2. Immediately add the oil and the sliced onion to the pan. Sauté for 5 minutes, until the onion is wilted.

3. Add the tomato wedges and stir with the onions for 2 or 3 minutes, until the tomato juices start bubbling.

4. Add half the cabbage. Place the meat on the cabbage, then top with the remaining cabbage. Add the water, salt, pepper, and sugar. Cover and bring to a boil.

5. Lower heat and simmer very gently for 2 to 2½ hours, stirring occasionally, until the meat is so tender it practically falls apart when prodded with a fork.

6. Stir in the lemon juice and taste for seasoning, adjusting with additional salt, pepper, sugar, or lemon juice, as desired.

7. Refrigerate the soup overnight, then skim off the hardened fat. Strip the meat into large pieces, discarding bones. Return the meat to the soup and reheat.

8. Serve piping hot in a deep bowl with a boiled potato on the side, or serve in a flat bowl with quarters or chunks of potato in the bowl with the soup. Sprinkle with dill only if you are one of those cooks who feels compelled to garnish; the mahogany-colored soup is beautiful as is.

ADVANCE PREPARATION: The soup is much better if made a day ahead and reheated. It also freezes very well. In either case, however, its flavor will require refreshing. Taste carefully for salt, pepper, and lemon juice.

CAULIFLOWER SOUP

Serves 4 to 6

Here's another very simple, quickly prepared, very low-fat soup for everyday meals. The various vegetables make it so sweet you need the lemon juice to give it some edge. Add a little more than suggested if your tastebuds cry out for more tang.

SUPPER SUGGESTIONS: This is a good soup to go with a favorite sandwich. Walnut onion muffins (page 166) go well, too. Or follow with cheese and bread and a glass of red wine, then some store-bought cookies or forgotten gianduia meringues (page 198) as a sweet.

2 medium onions, chopped (about 2 cups)
2 tablespoons butter
2 medium carrots, thinly sliced (about 1 cup)
2 medium celery ribs, thinly sliced (about 1 cup)
1 medium cauliflower, cut into small florets (about 4 cups)
2 large potatoes, cut into 1½- to 2-inch chunks (about 3 cups)
10 cups water
1 (10-ounce) package frozen peas
¼ cup finely chopped parsley (leaves and thin stems)
Juice of 1 lemon (approximately)
1 teaspoon dried mint

1. In a 4- to 5-quart pot over medium heat, sauté the onion in the butter until wilted, about 5 minutes.

(continued)

2. Add the carrots, celery, cauliflower, potatoes, and water. Increase heat to high, bring to a boil, reduce heat, and simmer gently, uncovered, stirring occasionally, until all the vegetables are very tender, about 25 minutes.

3. Stir in the peas and increase heat to high. When the soup begins to boil, the peas should be cooked enough.

4. Just before serving, stir in the parsley, lemon juice, and mint.

VARIATION: To make the soup thicker and more substantial, more like porridge, add ¼ cup white rice with the vegetables.

ADVANCE PREPARATION: The soup has a beautiful fresh, sweet vegetable flavor when freshly prepared, but I found it surprisingly more appealing after it was frozen and reheated. The freezing breaks down the vegetables without rendering them tasteless, as long cooking would.

CORN CHOWDER

Makes about 2½ quarts, serving 6

I was challenged the day I tested this recipe. One of my tasters was a friend who swears that she is such a stickler about corn that no cobs can please her except those picked moments before they go in the pot. I would not be recounting this if my chowder didn't get her enthusiastic approval. The secret is to use one of the new hybrid, so-called super-sweet varieties and not to cook it much, just heat it through. These new corn varieties are at their sweetest when raw— bite into a kernel or ear and see. They get starchy only when cooked too long. To get the corn flavor to permeate the liquid, I prepare the soup a day ahead and reheat it very gently. This also gives it a richer consistency, courtesy of the potatoes, though the rest period is not truly necessary. I've tried this recipe using butter instead of bacon, and as small as the amount of bacon is, it adds a depth of flavor that butter does not. Still, if you are a vegetarian or kosher and eschew bacon you'll be very happy with the buttered version.

SUPPER SUGGESTIONS: In the summer, at the peak of corn season, tomatoes are also in season. A bacon, lettuce, and tomato sandwich could be nearly irresistible with this soup. Or serve tomatoes for their own sake, with nothing more than a drizzle of your best olive oil, a few torn basil or parsley leaves, coarse salt, and freshly ground pepper. Or make a tomato salad (page 180).

Add string beans with garlic and sesame oil (page 187) for a more substantial meal. For dessert, pick the best summer fruits.

6 ears super-sweet-variety corn, shucked
7 cups cold water
2 to 3 ounces smoked bacon (4 to 6 strips), sliced into ¼-inch-wide strips, or 2 table-spoons butter
1 large onion, finely chopped (about 1½ cups)
1 medium red bell pepper, finely chopped (about ¾ cup)
2 medium all-purpose potatoes, peeled and cut into ¼-inch cubes (about 2½ cups)
1½ teaspoons coarse sea salt
¼ teaspoon freshly ground white pepper
¼ teaspoon cayenne
1½ cups heavy cream

1. To strip the corn, hold each ear at one end, resting the other end in a large bowl. With a sharp knife, cut the kernels close to the cob, letting them fall into the bowl. Save the stripped cobs. Set the kernels aside.

2. Place the cobs in a large pot with the cold water. Bring to a boil over high heat, lower heat, and simmer 10 minutes. Remove the cobs with tongs and reserve the cooking water, now corn broth.

3. In a 4- to 5-quart pot, cook the bacon pieces over medium heat, tossing frequently, until their fat has rendered and the bacon is crisp. With a slotted spoon, remove the bacon bits and set aside on absorbent paper to drain.

4. Pour off all but 2 tablespoons of the bacon fat. Sauté the onion in the fat (or in

butter) until well wilted, about 5 minutes.

5. Stir in the chopped pepper, lower the heat, and cook gently for 10 minutes, stirring occasionally.

6. Stir in the cubed potatoes and continue to cook over low heat for another 5 minutes.

7. Add the 7 cups reserved corn broth, salt, pepper, and cayenne. Stir well, bring to a gentle simmer, and cook about 10 minutes, stirring a couple of times, until the potatoes are tender. Remove from heat and stir in the corn kernels.

8. The soup should be made ahead to this point, and be given a night's rest in the refrigerator. If you must serve it immediately, stir in the cream, taste for seasoning, and add salt and the chopped pepper. Bring slowly to a gentle simmer and cook no more than 1 or 2 minutes.

9. If prepared ahead, bring very slowly to a gentle simmer, then stir in the cream and taste for seasoning. Serve piping hot in either deep or flat bowls. Garnish each serving with crisp bacon bits. (When prepared ahead, the bacon will lose its crispness. Re-crisp in a toaster oven or, wrapped in a paper towel, in a microwave oven).

ADVANCE PREPARATION: Best when made a day ahead and reheated gently. May be frozen, but all the firm freshness—the beauty of the soup—will be lost.

EGGPLANT SOUP WITH FRITTATA NOODLES

Makes 9 cups, serving 6

Here's how Iris Carulli, my assistant and kitchen sidekick, put the flavor of Sicily into a prized farm stand eggplant from a weekend vegetable buying and cooking spree. The frittata noodles are an elegant fillip, and a protein bonus for vegetarians—which Iris is—though you could also serve the soup with egg noodles.

SUPPER SUGGESTIONS: Schiacciata (page 162) is an ideal bread to serve with this. During the summer, for a first course, serve insalata caprese (page 181), tomato salad or bruschetta (page 160), or plain sliced tomatoes with basil, freshly ground pepper, and your best olive oil. In the winter, celery and Parmesan salad (page 175) is good, or endive with walnuts and blue cheese (page 179), or fatoush, the Middle Eastern chopped salad with pita crisps, sumac, and herbs (page 176). For dessert, if you want to fuss a little, make the amaretti ricotta cheesecake (page 196). In the winter, a wine-poached pear (page 204) hits the spot.

8 tablespoons extra-virgin, full-flavored olive oil
1 large eggplant (about 1¼ pounds), peeled and cut into ½-inch cubes
1 medium onion, finely chopped (about 1 cup)
6 garlic cloves, coarsely chopped
2 large celery ribs, finely chopped (about 1 cup)
1 large green pepper, finely chopped (about 1¾ cups)
½ teaspoon salt
Pinch of red pepper flakes
⅛ teaspoon fennel seeds
1 (16-ounce) can Italian plum tomatoes, chopped, with their juice (about 1½ cups)
1½ quarts water

For the frittata noodles:
4 large eggs
2 tablespoons fine, dry, unflavored bread crumbs
4 tablespoons freshly grated Parmesan or Pecorino
1 garlic clove, finely minced
Pinch of salt
2 teaspoons finely chopped parsley
3 tablespoons olive oil
Toasted crouton cubes (see page 158)

1. In a large skillet, heat 2½ tablespoons of the olive oil over medium-high heat and sauté half the eggplant cubes until browned. Set aside. Repeat the procedure, using another 2½ tablespoons oil and the rest of the eggplant.

2. In a 4- to 6-quart pot, heat the remaining 3 tablespoons oil over medium heat and sauté the onion until wilted, about 5 minutes.

3. Stir in the garlic and let it sizzle for 30 seconds.

4. Add the celery and green pepper and sauté until the vegetables are wilted, another 10 minutes.

5. Add the sautéed eggplant and the salt, pepper flakes, fennel seeds, tomatoes, and water. Cover and bring to a boil over high heat. Reduce heat and simmer, partially covered, for 35 minutes, stirring occasionally.

6. Meanwhile, prepare the frittata noodles: In a small bowl, beat all the ingredients together except the oil and croutons.

7. In a 10-inch skillet, preferably nonstick, heat the olive oil over medium heat and pour in the egg mixture, spreading it as thin as possible. If you do not have a large enough skillet, prepare the frittata in batches, otherwise the noodles will be too thick. Reduce the heat to low and cook about 2 minutes, or until set. The frittata should not color.

8. With a large spatula, loosen the frittata, slip it onto a plate, and flip it over, back into the pan, still over low heat, to set on the other side, another 2 minutes.

9. Remove the frittata to a plate, let cool, and slice into thin strips. Cut the strips to make noodles the length you prefer.

10. Pass the soup through a food mill, or purée in a blender or food processor, or use an immersion blender in the pot.

11. Reheat the soup and serve it piping hot in flat bowls, garnished with frittata noodles and croutons.

ADVANCE PREPARATION: The soup may be kept in the refrigerator for up to a week. The frittata noodles may be made a day in advance and reheated in the soup. The soup freezes perfectly for up to a year.

SKORDOZOUMI
(Greek Garlic Soup)

Serves 2

Every culture that relishes garlic has a garlic soup, usually a very humble broth that is said to be a restorative and, oh yes, incidentally something delicious to eat. The simplest garlic soup I know is one that the late Peruvian-born chef Felipe Rojas-Lombardi shared with me. His mother had made it for him. For each cup, sauté a couple of chopped garlic cloves in a tablespoon of olive oil until the garlic is beginning to brown. Add a cup of water and simmer a minute or so. Remove from the heat and pour the garlic broth over a beaten egg in a glass or cup, beating with a fork to blend. Drink immediately. The following is much more elaborate, an adaptation of a recipe from Nicholas Stavroulakis, an Athenian who is an ancient history scholar and teacher, and who wrote *Cookbook of the Jews of Greece* (Cadmus Press, 1986).

SUPPER SUGGESTIONS: A big salad or a steamed vegetable or mixed steamed vegetable plate, this soup, a loaf of crusty bread, and a piece of fruit is a marvelous and surprisingly filling everyday meal.

1 entire head garlic
3 cups water
2 tablespoons olive oil
Coarse sea salt and freshly ground pepper
¼ pound feta cheese

(continued)

1 cup yogurt
2 eggs

1. Separate the garlic cloves, peel them, and cut them as thin as possible.

2. In a 2-quart saucepan, bring the water and olive oil to a boil.

3. Add the garlic, salt, and pepper. Simmer 3 minutes. Remove from heat.

4. Crumble the cheese into small pieces and add to the very hot soup.

5. Stir in the yogurt. Return to very low heat and heat through for 2 to 3 minutes; do not let it boil.

6. Meanwhile, in a small bowl, beat the eggs.

7. Beat some hot soup into the eggs, then pour the egg mixture into remaining soup. Heat another minute without boiling.

8. Serve immediately in a deep bowl.

ADVANCE PREPARATION: Must be made just before serving.

CALDO VERDE
(PORTUGUESE GREENS SOUP)

Makes 2½ quarts, serving 4 to 6

This is the traditional and world-famous Portuguese soup of dark green cabbage (called *couve*), potatoes, and sausage. It is so popular in its homeland that the cabbage—similar to the *cavolo nero* of Tuscany—is sold already shredded, just waiting to be tossed into the soup pot. Actually, when shredded fine enough, the cabbage, more tender than the kale substitute suggested here and in most other American recipes, is eaten uncooked. It is merely wilted by the hot soup. The quality of olive oil you use here is all important—for the authentic taste, it should be Iberian oil.

SUPPER SUGGESTIONS: Sturdy bread or focaccia (page 161) is a must. Caesar salad (page 173) or baked eggplant and garlic mounded on bread with a diced tomato garnish (page 184) are excellent beginnings. For dessert, serve either strawberries in two liqueurs (page 200) or a berry compote (page 201), when berries are in season. Otherwise, serve a fruit salad (page 199).

4 large potatoes (2 pounds), peeled and cut
*   into ¼-inch-thick rounds*
1½ teaspoons coarse sea salt
8 cups water
¼ cup olive oil, preferably Portuguese
*   or Spanish*
¼ teaspoon freshly ground black pepper
6 ounces chorizo or Portuguese linguiça sausage

½ pound kale, washed, stemmed, and very finely shredded (about 4 cups), or 4 cups finely shredded cabbage

1. In a 4- to 6-quart pot, combine the potatoes, salt, and water. Bring to a boil, adjust the heat, and simmer, uncovered, until potatoes are mashable, about 15 minutes.

2. With a slotted spoon, transfer the potatoes to a bowl. Leave the cooking water in the pot. With a potato masher or a fork, mash the potatoes coarsely or into a purée, as your taste dictates, then return them to the pot. (Alternatively, if you have an immersion blender, purée the potatoes in the pot. Or simply break up potatoes with a wooden spoon.)

3. Stir in the olive oil and pepper.

4. Bring the soup back to a simmer over medium heat.

5. Prick the sausages in a few places, add them to the pot, and simmer for 15 minutes.

6. With tongs, remove the sausages and slice them about ¼ inch thick. Reserve.

7. Add the kale or cabbage to the simmering soup. Boil, uncovered, for 3 to 4 minutes.

8. Remove from heat and add the sliced sausage.

9. Serve piping hot in flat bowls.

ADVANCE PREPARATION: The soup can be made several days ahead through step 3; finish at the last moment. Do not freeze.

MUSHROOM SOUP WITH WILD RICE AND BROWN RICE

Serves 6

In effect, this one recipe yields two soups: the soup you get when the rices have just turned tender and the soup is served immediately; and the soup you get when you prepare it ahead and reheat it, in which case the rices expand and soften, creating a cereal-like consistency. The flavor remains the same, of course. The wild rice adds a wonderfully woodsy taste, making supermarket mushrooms taste like wild ones. I prefer the soup when the rices are still fairly firm and the broth still clear. But I've served the more porridgy version to great acclaim.

SUPPER SUGGESTIONS: Celery and parmesan salad (page 175) would be an elegant, refreshing start. A platter of prosciutto and salami isn't a bad beginning either. In either case, have plenty of sturdy bread, something like a Tuscan loaf. Follow the soup with a cheese course and a good red wine if you feel you need more substance. Or just dessert—say amaretti ricotta cheesecake (page 196) if you haven't had cheese, biscotti with a sweet wine and fresh fruit if you have.

1½ pounds mushrooms
3 tablespoons extra-virgin olive oil

(continued)

⅔ *cup finely chopped carrots*
⅔ *cup finely chopped onion*
⅔ *cup finely chopped celery*
1 garlic clove, finely chopped
½ *cup brown rice*
½ *cup wild rice*
5½ *cups chicken or beef broth, homemade or*
canned
¼ *teaspoon freshly ground pepper*
1 large bay leaf

1. By hand or in a food processor, chop 1 pound of the mushrooms very fine, stems and all, almost to a paste.

2. Slice the remaining ½ pound mushrooms, right through the stems, about ¼ inch thick.

3. In a 5- to 6-quart pot, warm the oil over medium-low heat and sauté the carrot, onion, and celery together until beginning to brown, about 15 minutes.

4. Add the garlic and sauté another minute.

5. Add the chopped mushrooms and mix thoroughly. Cook over medium heat, stirring frequently.

6. When the mushrooms exude their liquid, stir in the brown rice, wild rice, broth, pepper, and bay leaf.

7. Cover and bring to a boil over high heat. Reduce heat, stir well, cover again, and let soup simmer briskly for 35 minutes, stirring occasionally.

8. Add the sliced mushrooms, cover, and simmer another 10 minutes.

9. Serve immediately in deep or wide bowls, or, for a thicker, more porridgelike soup, let stand until serving time and reheat.

ADVANCE PREPARATION: See recipe introduction. May be held at room temperature several hours or kept refrigerated for up to a week; turns particularly porridgelike after freezing.

ITALIAN MUSHROOM SOUP WITH PARMESAN

Serves 2 or 3

This is luxuriously rich, but another quickly made potful for a rushed midweek meal or any last-minute supper, a recipe I found recently on a scrap of paper that must be twenty years old. If I remember correctly, it was prepared for me once by Vincenzo Buonassisi, the Italian food writer, as we were cleaning up odds and ends from a day of cooking together. I loved it so much that I jotted down the ingredients, though it took a couple of decades for me to actually make it.

SUPPER SUGGESTIONS: You could actually make this into an elegant supper—perhaps a romantic one—by preceding it with prosciutto and either melon or figs, or, say, a Caesar salad (page 173), or steamed asparagus or an artichoke. Accompany with focaccia (page 161) or sturdy bread. For dessert, the amaretti ricotta cheesecake (page 196) is perfect for a fussy menu, fresh fruit for a simple one.

1 tablespoon butter
1 tablespoon extra-virgin olive oil
1 garlic clove, crushed or minced
1 tablespoon finely chopped onion
1 pound mushrooms, thinly sliced (about
    6 cups)
1¾ cups chicken broth, homemade or canned
1¾ cups water
3 tablespoons tomato paste
3 egg yolks
½ cup freshly grated Parmesan cheese
¼ cup finely chopped parsley
Coarse sea salt and freshly ground pepper

I. In a 2- to 3-quart pot, warm the butter and oil over medium heat and sauté the garlic and onion until the onion is wilted, about 5 minutes.

2. Add the mushrooms and sauté, still over medium heat, until their liquid has exuded, then evaporated.

3. Add the broth, water, and tomato paste. Bring to a boil, adjust heat, and simmer gently, uncovered, for 5 minutes.

4. In a small bowl, whisk the yolks until they are thick and lemony in color. Add the grated Parmesan and parsley and beat well again.

5. With the soup barely simmering, add the yolk mixture gradually, whisking constantly and vigorously over medium heat until the yolks and soup bind together in a light cream, about 3 minutes.

6. Taste and season to taste with salt and pepper.

7. Serve immediately in deep or flat bowls.

ADVANCE PREPARATION: The point is to make it fresh on the spot, but you could cook it through step 3, then keep it refrigerated for up to a week; this base freezes perfectly. Add the eggs and cheese (steps 4 through 7) at the last moment.

FRENCH ONION SOUP

Serves 6 to 8

How could you have a soup book without French onion soup? Serve as is with only a sprinkling of Parmesan and, of course, a loaf of outstanding bread. Or with big croutons to soak it up, or with big croutons topped with melted cheese. Or go all the way and make it the world's most famous sop, the famous gratinée of Paris's Les Halles—a deep bowl full of soup-saturated bread encrusted with melted cheese.

SUPPER SUGGESTIONS: Turn it into a company meal with a generous pile of steamed asparagus (page 182) or a whole artichoke (page 183) to start, or grilled portobello mushrooms on a salad (page 178), then, for dessert, serve Swedish almond cake (page 192).

3 tablespoons butter
1 tablespoon vegetable oil
6 medium onions, thinly sliced (about 6 cups)
½ teaspoon sugar
3 tablespoons flour
2 quarts light beef broth (half canned broth, half water)
3 tablespoons dry sherry or brandy
Grated Parmesan or Asiago cheese
Toasted French or Italian bread slices

1. In a 4- to 6-quart pot, heat the butter with the oil over medium heat.

2. Add the onions and toss well to coat them well with fat. Reduce heat to low, cover, and let cook for 15 minutes, until the onions are quite wilted. There is no need to stir.

3. Uncover the pot, increase the heat to medium, and stir in the sugar. Let cook, stirring frequently, for about 40 minutes, until the onions are deep brown.

4. Stir in the flour and continue to cook until the flour turns the color of the onions, 5 to 8 minutes.

5. Stir in the broth. Cover, bring to a boil, then reduce heat, partially cover, and let simmer 30 minutes, stirring occasionally.

6. Stir in the sherry or brandy and simmer 5 minutes longer.

7. Serve piping hot in deep or flat bowls. Pass grated Parmesan or Asiago cheese and

slice-sized croutons. Or, arrange slices of toasted bread on a baking sheet, cover with shredded Gruyère, Switzerland Swiss, or Italian fontina (or other cheese that melts well, such as Cheddar) and place under a broiler until bubbling. Float the cheese-covered toasts in each bowl.

Or, in deep, ovenproof bowls, place a slice-sized crouton, then soup to cover, then another crouton or two, then more soup. Top with croutons to more or less cover the surface, then add shredded cheese. Place in a 450-degree oven until cheese has melted and become a bit crusty at the edges.

ADVANCE PREPARATION: Through step 6, can be kept refrigerated for up to a week; it freezes perfectly for about a year.

ONION AND GRUYÈRE SOUP

Serves 4

Unlike the straightforward browned onion flavor of French onion soup, dry white wine and true, nutty Swiss Gruyère give this white soup a heady quality, like good fondue. If you try to blend the cheese into the soup it will not be smooth. It comes out stringy; delightfully so, say my family of tasters. I prefer the second or third presentations suggested: Either strew the cheese over the bread and soup in the bowl or, for a festive occasion, line hollowed-out miniature breads with cheese and use the bread as a soup bowl, instructing everyone to scrape up cheese and broth-soaked bread as they finish the soup.

SUPPER SUGGESTIONS: A leafy salad is all you need before this rich soup. Since bread is part of the soup presentation, you may not want to serve more with it. For dessert, the blueberry apple crumble (page 203) is ideal when blueberries are in season. At other times of the year, also think fruit—ruby poached pears (page 204) or fresh pineapple (page 200), for example.

3 tablespoons butter
6 medium onions, thinly sliced (about 6 cups)
½ teaspoon salt
1½ cups full-flavored dry white wine, such as
  a sauvignon blanc or chardonnay
3½ cups chicken broth, homemade or canned
¼ teaspoon freshly ground white pepper
Big pinch of freshly grated nutmeg
½ pound Swiss Gruyère (or Italian fontina),
  shredded (about 2 cups)
4 large slices dense bread, toasted

1. In a large skillet, over medium-high heat, heat the butter to foaming. Add the onions and sauté for 2 to 3 minutes, tossing constantly.

2. Reduce heat to low, stir in salt, and cook slowly, stirring occasionally, until onions are very tender and golden, about 1 hour.

3. Scrape the onions into a 3-quart saucepan. Add white wine and bring to a boil.

4. Add the broth to the boiling onions and wine. Add pepper and nutmeg. Simmer very gently, uncovered, for 15 minutes, stirring occasionally.

5. To serve, there are several alternatives:

• Add the shredded cheese to the gently simmering soup and stir over low heat until melted. It will remain a little stringy. Place toasts in individual bowls and pour hot soup over the toasts.

• Alternatively, do not melt the cheese into the soup. Instead, pour the soup over the toasts, which have been placed in heat-proof bowls, then sprinkle the cheese over the top. Place the bowls in a preheated 400-degree oven until the cheese melts.

• For the most elaborate presentation, cut the domed top off small round loaves of sturdy bread—white, whole wheat, or rye—then scoop out the interior to within an inch of the outer crust. Line the inside of the loaves with slices of Gruyère or Swiss cheese—not shredded cheese. Punch the cheese into the bread so that it will stay in place. Place the cheese-lined breads in shallow bowls or on plates with high rims—just in case—and fill each loaf with hot onion soup. Serve immediately. Diners can scrape the cheese and bread into the soup as they eat, then finish the bread if they like.

ADVANCE PREPARATION: Through step 4, soup can be refrigerated for up to a week; it freezes perfectly.

QUICK SWEET PEA SOUP

Makes 4½ cups, serving 2 to 4

The late English food writer Elizabeth David's recipes are so often sketchy, yet easy to follow, that I remember not realizing at first that they were given in metric measurements. Here's one, from *Summer Cooking* (Penguin, 1955), given without many measurements at all, much less metric. I created the specifics (leaving out her ham) and it tastes great, if I say so myself. I wonder if it is at all like her soup?

SUPPER SUGGESTIONS: This is elegant and light enough to be a first course before a heavy entrée at a formal dinner. As a soup supper, I'd serve it after something substantial, like potato and shrimp salad (page 186), or mozzarella with tomatoes and/or roasted peppers (page 181). In those cases, a crusty roll or French loaf is a good bread companion. A lighter meal could start with a green salad, in which case you might want to go to the trouble of baking popovers (page 165). In early summer, when you can make this with garden peas and strawberries are also in season, forget a first course altogether and wallow in a big bowl of the soup and a large strawberry shortcake (page 205).

1¾ cups shelled peas or frozen petits pois
2 cups shredded green leaf lettuce
⅓ cup finely chopped scallions (3 scallions)

½ teaspoon coarse sea salt
Dash of freshly ground white pepper
1 quart water (approximately)
1 tablespoon butter
2 tablespoons heavy cream
4 teaspoons finely chopped fresh mint (optional)

1. In a 3- to 4-quart pot, combine the peas, lettuce, scallions, salt, and pepper. Add enough water just to cover.

2. Partially cover, bring to a boil, reduce heat, and simmer until the peas are tender and the scallions soft, about 8 minutes.

3. With a food mill, or in a blender or food processor, purée the soup and return it to the pot. Or use an immersion blender in the pot.

4. Just before serving, add the butter and cream, stirring until butter melts. Serve piping hot, garnished with a little finely chopped fresh mint, if desired.

ADVANCE PREPARATION: Can be made through step 4 several hours ahead. Should never be refrigerated or frozen.

SWEET RED PEPPER SOP

Makes 4 quarts, serving 8 to 10

Sweet red peppers can become insipid when their flavor isn't concentrated. That's why they taste best grilled, roasted, sautéed, fried—dry-cooked. And that's why, when your farm stand provides enough great, cheap sweet peppers to wallow in them, they make a better sop—a stew with juices to mop up with bread—than a soup. The peppers and shallots create so much sweet juice that there's plenty to cook the potatoes and still have some left for dunking bread.

SUPPER SUGGESTIONS: A leafy salad, with or without other vegetables, is all you'll want to start. In late summer, the ideal dessert would be peaches, out of hand if they're perfect, or sliced and macerated in red or white wine sweetened with honey if they're not, or a fresh berry compote (page 201). If you must make a fuss, bake a peach crostata (page 194) or plum tart (page 195).

⅔ cup extra-virgin olive oil
12 medium bell peppers, red and yellow,
    cut into strips (about 9 cups)
4 medium russet potatoes, peeled and cut
    into chunks (about 4 cups)
2 cups sliced shallots or onions
¾ cup oil-cured black olives, pitted if desired
3 tablespoons chopped garlic
2 tablespoons capers
1 tablespoon sea salt

1. In a large heavy pot, place ⅓ cup of the oil, one third of the cut-up peppers, one third of the potatoes, ⅔ cup shallots, ¼ cup olives, 1 tablespoon garlic, and 2 teaspoons capers. Drizzle with more oil and sprinkle with 1 teaspoon salt.

2. Repeat layers until the ingredients have been used up, for a total of three layers.

3. Cover and place over medium-low heat, increasing heat gradually and slightly as peppers give up their moisture, so that after about 10 minutes you have steadily simmering liquid in the pot. Keep covered and cook about 40 minutes, stirring occasionally, until potatoes are cooked through, but still slightly firm. The peppers will have wilted considerably.

4. Serve hot or at room temperature in wide bowls, with plenty of bread to sop up the juices.

ADVANCE PREPARATION: May be kept refrigerated for several days; reheat gently. Do not freeze. Leftovers not copious enough to serve for their own sake make a delicious sauce for macaroni.

POTATO, ONION, & TOMATO SOUP

Makes 3 quarts thick soup, serving about 6

I've had this recipe for so long that I don't remember where I got it. It could be Italian. It could be Spanish. In any case, it is thick and filling—potato lovers' food, onion lovers' food, the humblest comfort food—and requires, above all else, excellent olive oil, which is not at all humble.

SUPPER SUGGESTIONS: A light, leafy salad is called for before this, fruit or fruit salad after. Focaccia (page 161) or schiacciata (page 162) is a great accompaniment.

2 pounds potatoes, peeled and cut into chunks
1 35-ounce can plum tomatoes, with their juice, coarsely chopped (about 4 cups)
1 quart water
½ teaspoon coarse sea salt
¼ teaspoon freshly ground black pepper
3 tablespoons extra-virgin olive oil, preferably full-flavored
4 medium onions, thinly sliced (about 4 cups)

1. In a 4- to 6-quart saucepan (not aluminum), combine the potatoes, tomatoes, and water. Season with salt and pepper. Bring to a boil, reduce heat, and simmer gently, partially covered, stirring occasionally, for 1½ hours, or until potatoes are very tender.

2. Meanwhile, in a 10-inch skillet, warm the olive oil over medium-high heat and sauté the onions until well wilted, about 5 minutes.

3. Lower the heat and fry very slowly until the onions are very tender and a rich golden color. This could take as long as an hour.

4. To finish the soup, break up the potatoes, mashing them slightly in the pot with a wooden spoon or potato masher. Add the onions to the potato-tomato mixture and simmer together a few minutes, stirring occasionally. Add hot water as necessary to thin out the soup slightly.

5. Serve very hot in flat bowls, drizzled lightly with olive oil.

VARIATION: The soup is vegetarian as is. You can make it a meat eater's pleasure by serving each bowl topped with a grilled Italian sausage (sweet or hot, to your taste), or add chorizo or kielbasa slices that have been fried briefly to heat them through.

ADVANCE PREPARATION: Can be prepared several hours ahead and reheated gently. May be refrigerated for up to a week.

PAPPA AL POMODORO

(TUSCAN TOMATO AND BREAD SOUP)

Serves 4

Don't make this recipe unless you have something like Tuscan bread—dense, sturdy, thick-crusted (it would be asking too much for it to be salt-free, too, as Tuscans bake it)—and absolutely dead ripe tomatoes. With them and great olive oil this porridgelike dish is a miracle of simplicity. Without them there is no point. Tuscans consider *pappa* (as in baby's *pap*) a *minestra*, the course that includes soup, pasta, rice, and, in some places, polenta. It's too thick to call it a soup, but it is a true sop.

SUPPER SUGGESTIONS: I always think *pappa* calls for a big platter of strong-flavored cold cuts (Tuscans are famous for their salty prosciutto and powerful salami), and then you get to eat more bread. Or be light, serve a big salad, a Caesar salad (page 173), or a steamed or roasted vegetable platter, the former dressed with lemon juice and olive oil. For a sweet, any fruit dessert, such as red berry compote (page 201).

3 tablespoons extra-virgin olive oil,
  preferably Tuscan
4 large garlic cloves, coarsely chopped
Pinch of dried hot pepper flakes
1 pound very ripe plum tomatoes,
  coarsely chopped (about 3 cups)
1 pound dense bread, possibly whole wheat,
  several days old
3 cups chicken or meat broth, homemade or
  canned

Coarse sea salt and freshly ground black pepper
4 to 5 large fresh basil leaves
Extra-virgin olive oil, for garnish
Freshly ground black pepper

1. In a large saucepan, warm the oil over low heat and stir in garlic and hot pepper flakes. Cook very gently, stirring a few times, for 10 to 12 minutes. Don't let the garlic brown.

2. Stir in the tomatoes, increase heat to medium, and cook tomatoes for 15 to 20 minutes, until they get saucy.

3. Cut the bread into small pieces and add to the pot with the broth, salt, black pepper, and whole basil leaves. Stir very well and simmer for 15 minutes longer.

4. Remove from heat, cover, and let rest for at least 1 hour.

5. Just before serving, stir very well. Taste. If it needs salt, add only fine salt.

6. Serve warm in flat bowls, drizzled with extra olive oil. Pass the peppermill.

ADVANCE PREPARATION: Should be made just before serving.

FRESH TOMATO SOUP

Makes about 3 ½ quarts, serving about 8

The only time to make this is when tomatoes are at their absolute peak; when they are plentiful, inexpensive, and you are sick of gorging on them for their own sake. Some might use this purée parsimoniously as a sauce. Try serving it in soup quantity—hot with chopped fresh herbs, a mix of chives, basil, chervil, tarragon, parsley, a nasturtium and its leaf ... anything and everything from the garden. What a luxury! Or serve cold with other vegetables, such as chopped cucumbers, radishes, scallions, green peppers, a dollop of sour cream or yogurt, and a garnish of sprouts. Hot or cold, add croutons for crunch, garlic croutons for added flavor. Or use this purée as a base for the tomato-rice soup that follows.

SUPPER SUGGESTIONS: Popovers (page 165) are as all-American as tomato soup. Serve them with cottage cheese and apple butter. Or start with endive with walnuts and blue cheese (page 179) and crusty bread. Tomato soup and a favorite sandwich is a natural menu, too. For dessert, apple cranberry tart (page 195) or blueberry apple crumble (page 203) are excellent.

8 pounds tomatoes
1 teaspoon salt
2 medium onions, coarsely chopped
   (about 2 cups)

FOR EACH 1 ½-CUP SERVING:
1 teaspoon (or more) sweet butter,
   1 tablespoon finely chopped fresh herbs,
   and croutons; or ½ to ¾ cup finely
   chopped mixed raw vegetables, a rounded
   tablespoon of sour cream or yogurt, and
   croutons

1. Wash the tomatoes. There is no need to dry them. With a small knife, cut out the cores and cut the tomatoes into chunks into a 6-quart pot.

2. Add the salt and chopped onions.

3. Cover the pot and place over medium heat. Simmer until tomatoes are very soft, about 20 minutes or so, stirring occasionally.

4. Purée in a food mill, and don't be greedy about getting every last drop of flavor from the tomatoes. If you grind up the seeds, the purée will be bitter. Keep adding cooked tomatoes to the mill as the previous batch is mostly processed. Don't process sludge; stop when you see the purée becoming pale.

5. Either reheat to a simmer before serving, or chill well.

6. If serving hot, place in flat bowls and garnish with a generous curl or pat of butter, a heavy sprinkling of herbs, plus croutons. If serving cold, serve with chopped vegetables, a dollop of sour cream or yogurt (or blend the sour cream or yogurt or fresh cream into the soup), plus an herb garnish.

ADVANCE PREPARATION: Can be kept refrigerated for up to three days; freezes perfectly for up to a year.

SAVORY TOMATO RICE SOUP

Makes about 2 quarts, serving 4 to 6

Tomato rice soup was a sometime treat for me when I was a boy. I have no idea why my mother withheld it or, at any rate, prepared it only occasionally when it was something we liked so much. Heat up a can of Campbell's and pour it over rice. What could be easier? Maybe she felt guilty about the lack of work. As you can see, with tomato purée in the freezer, this version doesn't require much work either.

SUPPER SUGGESTIONS: Beyond a leafy or mixed salad, sliced avocado and onion salad (page 187) would be a good first course or accompaniment. In season, a plate of asparagus or an artichoke would be great to start. In winter, a fillet of smoked trout (or other fish) with horseradish is perfect, as is a plate of sliced Italian meats. This is a good soup to pair with a favorite sandwich, too. It is also a good foil for walnut onion muffins (page 166). For dessert, the blueberry apple crumble (page 203) is a treat.

7 cups tomato soup base (see preceding recipe), made from 4 pounds of tomatoes
¼ cup Cognac
2 teaspoons Worcestershire sauce
½ teaspoon salt
2 tablespoons brown sugar

2 to 3 cups cooked white or brown rice
Shredded Cheddar cheese, as a topping (optional)

1. In a 3-quart saucepan (not aluminum), stir together the tomato base, Cognac, Worcestershire sauce, salt, and brown sugar. Bring to a boil for 5 minutes, stirring several times.

2. To serve, place a scoop of rice in the center of wide bowls. Ladle hot soup around the rice to fill the bowl. Strew cheese on the soup and/or rice, if desired.

VARIATION: At the risk of it tasting like a sweet tomato sauce, serve the soup with fine egg noodles instead of rice.

ADVANCE PREPARATION: Must be seasoned at the last moment.

MINESTRONE

Makes 3 ½ quarts thick soup, serving about 8

This is a classic central-Italian minestrone, except that it is made without chicken or beef broth. The vegetarian trick is to use the rind from a hunk of Parmigiano Reggiano to supplement the vegetable flavors. The soup is at its best in late summer/early fall when zucchini, tomatoes, Savoy cabbage, and basil are all in their high seasons. If you have a craving for it in the winter, use canned tomatoes, plain green cabbage, and parsley instead of basil. Even in the summer I now sometimes use parsley because good-tasting basil can be hard to find.

SUPPER SUGGESTIONS: Sturdy bread with a thick crust is essential. In the summer serve a few vegetable salads first; tomato and red onion salad (page 180) or insalata caprese (page 181). For a summer dessert, serve peach crostata (page 194); in winter, wacky chocolate cake (page 191).

¼ cup extra-virgin olive oil
2 medium onions, cut into ¼-inch dice
*   (about 2 cups)*
3 medium carrots, cut into ½-inch dice
*   (about 2 cups)*
2 large celery ribs, cut into ½-inch dice
*   (about 1 cup)*
¾ pound string beans, tipped, tailed, and
*   cut into ½-inch pieces*
2 medium potatoes, cut into ½-inch dice
*   (about 2 cups)*
1 pound zucchini, cut into ½-inch dice
*   (about 3 cups)*
4 large tomatoes, cut into rough 1-inch pieces
*   (4 cups), or 4 cups canned tomatoes,*
*   drained only of packing juice, chopped*
1 pound (½ average head) Savoy cabbage,
*   finely shredded*
10 cups water
Parmigiano Reggiano cheese rind, about 3
*   by 5 inches*
1½ teaspoons coarse sea salt
½ teaspoon black pepper
¼ cup chopped basil or parsley
8 ounces dried cannellini beans, rinsed and

picked over, soaked overnight in several
*   inches of water to cover, then drained*
*   (see page 15)*

1. In an 8- to 10-quart pot, warm the olive oil over medium heat.

2. Add the vegetables as you prepare them: Sauté the onions until golden while cutting the carrots. Add the carrots and stir well to coat with oil. Let them cook while cutting the celery, stirring the carrots and onions occasionally.

3. Similarly, dice and add the string beans, potatoes, then the zucchini.

4. Finally, stir in the tomatoes, then the shredded cabbage. Cover the pot and let steam for about 10 minutes, until the cabbage has wilted.

5. Add the water, cheese rind, salt, pepper, basil, and beans. Cover and bring to a boil over high heat. Reduce heat, partially cover, and simmer gently, stirring occasionally for 2 to 2½ hours, until the beans are fully tender and the soup is thick.

VARIATION: You can use chicken or beef broth, your own or canned, in place of the water. Still use a cheese rind, if possible. It will further enhance the soup's flavor.

ADVANCE PREPARATION: Best made in the morning and left at room temperature to ripen for supper. This soup can be kept refrigerated for up to a week; it freezes very well. In either case, when reheating, you will have to add more liquid and reseason the soup, adding some fresh basil or parsley as well as salt and pepper. Leftovers may be stretched and recycled into ribollita (see the following recipe).

RIBOLLITA

(BREAD- OR RICE-THICKENED MINESTRONE)

Serves 4 to 6

The preceding minestrone is perfect for turning into either a bread or rice ribollita, which literally means "reboiled." The result of reboiling the soup with bread or rice is a thick, stewlike dish.

SUPPER SUGGESTIONS: See minestrone (page 40). Obviously, bread would be redundant with bread ribollita.

FOR BREAD RIBOLLITA:

1¾ quarts minestrone (½ recipe)
2 cups water or chicken or beef broth
6 to 8 (1-inch-thick) slices dried-out,
   firm Italian or French bread
Full-flavored olive oil

FOR RICE RIBOLLITA:

1¾ quarts minestrone (½ recipe)
2 cups water or chicken or beef broth
½ cup arborio or long-grain white rice
½ cup grated Parmesan or Asiago cheese
6 fresh basil leaves, or 12 to 15 parsley leaves,

torn or snipped into small pieces

I. In a 4- to 6-quart pot, combine the minestrone with the water or broth. Bring to a boil.

2. If making a bread ribollita:

• Place a layer of bread in the bottom of another pot. Cover with soup, then cover soup with another layer of bread. Top with soup.

• Bring the pot with the bread and soup to a boil. Lower heat, cover, and simmer briskly, without stirring, until the bread is soft.

• Let stand 5 minutes, then serve in wide bowls, drizzling each serving with olive oil.

If making a rice ribollita:

• Stir the rice into the simmering soup and let simmer briskly for 15 minutes.

• Stir in the cheese and the basil or parsley.

• Ladle into wide bowls and let stand for at least 5 minutes, or until soup reaches room temperature.

ADVANCE PREPARATION: Must be made the same day it is served.

MINESTRONE WITH SWISS CHARD

Makes about 5 quarts, serving 8 to 10

In northwestern Connecticut, where I have a weekend house, the growing season is very short. Even in late spring and early summer the only locally grown vegetables at the farm stands are radishes, beets, and greens like lettuces, spinach, and Swiss chard—a lot of Swiss chard. Here's one way I use it.

SUPPER SUGGESTIONS: This is a bowl of beans, macaroni, and green leaves, so serve a green vegetable to start—asparagus and artichokes are at their peak in spring. For dessert, there may be berries for a compote. To dress up the menu, serve Parmesan aioli toast (page 160).

½ pound dried cannellini or other large white beans, such as soldier beans, rinsed and picked over, soaked overnight in water to cover by several inches (see page 15)
¼ cup extra-virgin olive oil
2 large red onions, peeled, halved, and sliced ¼ inch thick (about 3 cups)
4 medium carrots, cubed (about 2 cups)
2 large celery ribs, sliced ½ inch thick (about 1¼ cups)
1 pound unpeeled new potatoes, cubed (about 2 cups)
3 large garlic cloves, crushed
2 quarts chicken broth
½ teaspoon freshly ground pepper
Parmesan rind or a piece of prosciutto rind (optional)
1 pound green or red Swiss chard, cut into ½-inch shreds, stems and all
½ pound small macaroni, cooked (2½ cups, uncooked; 4 cups, cooked)
Grated Parmesan or Romano cheese

1. Drain the soaked beans and place them in a pot with fresh cold water just to cover. Bring to a boil, then reduce the heat and simmer, partially covered, stirring occasionally, until tender. This could be as short a time as 30 minutes or as long as an hour. Taste along the way to catch them as soon as they become tender.

2. In a 6- to 8-quart pot, combine the olive oil and onions over medium-low heat. Let the onions cook, tossing occasionally, while you prepare the carrots, celery, and potatoes, in that order. Add each to the pot as it is ready and toss well to coat with oil.

3. Stir the garlic into the vegetables; sauté until you can smell it, about a minute.

4. Add the broth, pepper, and cheese rind or prosciutto rind, if using one of them. Bring to a boil and reduce the heat so that soup simmers gently, partially covered, for about 1½ hours. Stir occasionally.

5. Stir in the Swiss chard and the cooked beans. Increase the heat and bring to a rolling boil. Reduce heat again and simmer steadily, partially covered, another 10 minutes.

6. Serve the soup over macaroni with grated cheese on the side.

ADVANCE PREPARATION: Cooked through step 4, the soup can be refrigerated for up to a week and frozen for up to six months. Bring to a brisk simmer before proceeding.

GENOESE MINESTRONE WITH PESTO

Makes 5 quarts, serving 8 or more

I love the color of this soup—so fresh and green. It tastes best when allowed to rest for several hours or overnight.

SUPPER SUGGESTIONS: Focaccia (page 161) topped with onions is a Genoese specialty. Since there are no tomatoes in this recipe and tomatoes are in season at the same time as basil, start with a tomato salad of some sort (pages 180, 181, and 187). For dessert, serve a red berry compote or strawberry shortcake (pages 201 and 209).

2 tablespoons extra-virgin olive oil
1 medium onion, finely chopped (about 1 cup)
2 large garlic cloves, finely chopped
2 pounds green cabbage, coarsely chopped
1 cup cannellini beans (or other large white bean), rinsed and picked over, soaked overnight in water to cover by several inches (see page 15)

2 quarts cold water
1½ teaspoons salt
½ teaspoon freshly ground black pepper
2 large potatoes, peeled and cut into ½-inch dice (about 4 cups)
⅓ cup arborio or long-grain rice
1 (10-ounce) package frozen spinach, defrosted
⅓ cup pesto (see following recipe)
Grated Parmesan, Pecorino Romano, or Asiago cheese

1. In a 5- to 6-quart pot, warm the oil over medium heat and sauté the onion and garlic for about 5 minutes, until the onion is translucent.

2. Add the cabbage, the drained beans, water, salt, and pepper. Increase heat, partially cover, bring to a boil, and adjust heat so liquid simmers gently for 30 to 45 minutes, until beans are just tender. Stir occasionally.

3. Add the potatoes and rice, cover, and simmer briskly until rice is tender, about 15 minutes.

4. Add the spinach and stir well. There's no need to cook the spinach further. Remove from heat until ready to serve. It's best to let the soup sit for several hours, or even overnight.

5. Just before serving, reheat and stir in the pesto. Serve with grated cheese on the side.

ADVANCE PREPARATION: See step 4. Do not freeze.

PESTO

Makes about ¾ cup

2 tightly packed cups basil
¼ cup extra-virgin olive oil
2 large garlic cloves
1 tablespoon pignoli (pine nuts)

1. Place all the ingredients in a food processor or blender.

2. Process to a fine paste.

NOTE: If using a blender, you will have to turn the machine on and off to tamp the mixture down with the handle of a wooden spoon. If necessary to blend properly, add up to 3 tablespoons more olive oil.

(To serve with pasta, add ½ cup or more grated Parmesan or a combination of Parmesan and Pecorino Romano.)

ADVANCE PREPARATION: The pesto can be covered with a thin layer of olive oil and kept refrigerated for up to a week. If making the pesto for longer storage, it can be kept frozen for up to a year, providing you omit the nuts and cheese. Add these when you are ready to serve the pesto.

NIKA HAZELTON'S GARDEN VEGETABLE SOUP

Makes about 3 quarts, serving about 6

Nika Hazelton, who was very dear to me, died on April 15, 1992. She almost made it to eighty-four and almost to the end she had an indomitably youthful spirit. Her legacy of twenty-four cookbooks and innumerable magazine stories and columns will certainly keep her memory alive for a long time to come. For me, all I need do is prepare this soup to recall our good times together—foreign food trips, "family" meals, her famous dinner parties, and most of all, our early-morning gossip sessions on the phone. Even without its nostalgia value, however, this soup would be one of my favorite deep-summer dishes. It tastes like the essence of the season because it is made in a most peculiar way: The vegetables cook only in their own rendered juices. No broth or water is added. That is why you must follow the cooking directions exactly, and why you must expect a sop, a dish with liquid to dunk bread into, more than a soup, a bowlful with liquid to sip.

SUPPER SUGGESTIONS: Great bread and some cheese are called for on this menu. Start with insalata caprese (page 181) or put out a cheese board (a red wine opportunity) after the soup. For dessert, fresh figs or other summer fruit are perfect.

2 large tomatoes, sliced

2 medium onions, thinly sliced (about 2 cups)

1 to 3 garlic cloves, minced

2 large zucchini, sliced ¼ inch thick (about 4 cups)

1 medium head romaine lettuce, finely shredded (about 7 cups)

2 pounds fresh peas, shelled, or 1 (10-ounce) package frozen peas

1 cup finely chopped parsley

2 tablespoons finely chopped basil

2 pounds fresh fava beans, shelled, or 1 (10-ounce) package frozen lima beans

⅓ to ½ cup extra-virgin olive oil, preferably Tuscan

Salt

Freshly ground pepper

Freshly grated Parmesan cheese

1. Spread the tomatoes over the bottom of a 5- to 6-quart pot.

2. Top the tomatoes with a layer of onions.

3. Sprinkle with garlic.

4. Add a layer of zucchini.

5. Top the zucchini with the lettuce.

6. Top the lettuce with the peas.

7. Sprinkle half the parsley and all the basil over the peas.

8. Add the beans.

9. Sprinkle the remaining ½ cup parsley over the vegetables.

10. Sprinkle the olive oil over everything.

11. Cook, covered, over low to medium heat for 20 minutes, or until the vegetables start releasing their liquid. Do not remove the cover for at least 10 minutes.

12. At this point, add salt and pepper to taste, reduce the heat to low, stir, and mix the vegetables well. Cook, covered, over low heat for 20 to 30 minutes, stirring frequently, until the vegetables are tender but not mushy; do not overcook. Do not add water; the vegetables have enough water of their own.

13. Serve hot, lukewarm, or at room temperature, but do not chill. Pass the grated cheese separately.

ADVANCE PREPARATION: The soup tastes best when freshly made, but it can be kept refrigerated for up to a week; reheat gently. Do not freeze.

CHORBA
(Moroccan Vegetable Soup)

Makes 6 quarts, serving about 8

This combination of vegetables and saffron produces an unmistakably Moroccan aroma and taste. You want to know what it smells like at the inevitable soup stand at a souk in the Middle Atlas mountains? This is it, courtesy of Abdel Lotfi, who owns Lotfi's, a Moroccan restaurant in New York City's Greenwich Village.

SUPPER SUGGESTIONS: No more vegetables are needed with this, but a green salad would be fine; grilled mushrooms on a green salad (page 178) would be even finer. Schiacciata (page 162), the flat bread, is a good go-with. For dessert, a slice of pound cake (page 192) is great in cold weather. Otherwise, serve a fruit salad (page 199).

10 ounces lamb neck, cut for stew
2 large onions, finely chopped (3 cups)
2 tablespoons butter
½ gram saffron pistils: 1 abundant teaspoon, not pressed
1½ teaspoons coarse sea salt
1 teaspoon freshly ground black pepper
6 cups water
4 medium turnips, peeled, halved, and sliced ¼ inch thick (about 5⅓ cups)
2 medium sweet potatoes, peeled and sliced ¼ inch thick (about 4 cups)
5 large carrots, peeled and sliced ¼ inch thick (about 4 cups)
2 to 3 large celery ribs, coarsely chopped (about 2 cups)
4 large leeks, white and a little green, sliced ¼ inch thick (about 2 cups)
2 large zucchini, halved lengthwise and sliced ¼ inch thick (about 4 cups)
1¼ cups canned Italian plum tomatoes, drained and coarsely chopped
Parsley or coriander for garnish

1. In an 8- to 10-quart pot, place the lamb, onions, butter, saffron, salt, pepper, and water. Cover and bring to a simmer over high heat. Reduce heat, partially cover, and simmer briskly for 30 minutes, stirring occasionally.

2. Stir in all the vegetables, including the canned tomatoes, and cook at a steady simmer another hour, stirring occasionally.

3. Remove meat, strip from bones, and return to soup. Discard bones.

4. Taste and correct for salt and pepper.

5. Serve piping hot in flat bowls sprinkled with fresh parsley or coriander, finely chopped or not.

VARIATIONS: Use some chicken parts instead of lamb. Or use beef stew cubes or flanken instead of lamb. Or, for a vegetarian soup, leave out the meat altogether.

ADVANCE PREPARATION: The soup tastes best when freshly made, but can be kept refrigerated for up to a week; it freezes perfectly.

NORMAN WEINSTEIN'S CHINESE HOT AND SOUR SOUP

Serves 4 to 6

Norman Weinstein is one of the best Chinese cooking teachers (and restaurant guides) in New York. To my nose and chest, his Chinese hot and sour soup is an even better cold remedy than chicken soup. Pepper clears the sinuses. Vinegar provides a dose of vitamin C.

SUPPER SUGGESTIONS: A bowl of boiled rice is the ideal accompaniment, and you'll need it as a foil if you like your soup vinegary and spicy. Along with the soup and rice, serve string beans with garlic and sesame oil (page 187) or several steamed vegetables. For dessert, try to find a fragrantly ripe pineapple and serve it with or without rum.

3 or 4 dried black mushrooms
15 cloud ears (black fungus)
15 dried lily flowers
¼ pound boneless center cut pork loin chop
1 teaspoon plus ¼ cup thin soy sauce
1 tablespoon plus ¼ cup cornstarch
6 cups chicken broth
1 pad firm bean curd (2 × 2 inches)
6 tablespoons clear rice vinegar, or to taste
1 teaspoon (at least) freshly ground black pepper
1 egg, beaten
2 scallions, finely diced
2 tablespoons sesame oil

1. In separate bowls, soak the mushrooms, cloud ears, and lily flowers in hot water for 20 to 30 minutes.

2. Trim the fat off the pork and discard. Cut the chop into ¼-inch slices across the grain, then into thin shreds along the grain.

3. Place the pork in a bowl with 1 teaspoon soy sauce. Mix well. Add 1 tablespoon cornstarch. Mix again. Set aside.

4. Put all but 1 cup of the broth in a 3-quart pot over low heat.

5. Squeeze the mushrooms dry. Discard stems and shred caps. Drain the cloud ears. Select only the smoother parts, discarding the gnarled tips. Cut the flowers in half. Reserve along with the mushrooms and cloud ears.

6. Cut the bean curd into 2 × ¼ × ¼-inch strips.

7. Combine the ¼ cup cornstarch with the reserved cup of broth. Mix well and set aside.

8. Bring the heating broth to a lively simmer. Add the ¼ cup soy sauce, then add the vinegar to taste (some like it sour).

9. Add the bean curd, mushrooms, cloud ear, and lily flower. Simmer 3 minutes.

10. Add copious amounts of black pepper (some like it hot). Stir to mix.

11. Give the cornstarch-broth mixture a last-minute stir to blend well, then stir it into the simmering broth. When the soup has thickened to a syrupy consistency, add the pork shreds and stir to separate.

12. Reduce the heat so that the soup is barely bubbling. Slowly pour in the beaten egg in a circle. Let set for 8 to 10 seconds.

13. Stir the broth gently to bring the egg to the surface. Top the soup with the scallions and sesame oil. Serve immediately in deep or flat bowls, offering additional vinegar and pepper at the table.

VARIATION: To make a vegetarian soup, eliminate the pork, use vegetable broth instead of chicken, and bolster the flavor with a few more mushrooms and cloud ears, possibly an extra dash of soy sauce.

ADVANCE PREPARATION: Prepare through step 10 up to a couple of days ahead, then finish at the last moment. Do not freeze.

EGG BOUILLABAISSE

Serves 4

Here is a recipe that has fascinated me for years, but that I never got around to making until I started writing this book. It is adapted from Richard Olney's *Simple French Food* (Collier Books, 1974) and is a godsend to lacto-ovo vegetarians who can still taste (and crave) bouillabaisse from their fish- and flesh-eating pasts.

SUPPER SUGGESTIONS: Even with just a leafy salad, a cheese course, and fresh fruit, this would make a festive supper.

*2 medium leeks, white parts finely sliced
    crosswise (about 2½ cups), greens added
    to bouquet garni*
*1 large onion, finely chopped (about 1½
    cups)*
¼ cup extra-virgin olive oil
*3 small firm, ripe tomatoes, peeled, seeded,
    and coarsely chopped (about 2 cups), or
    1½ cups canned Italian tomatoes, drained
    well*
3 large garlic cloves, finely chopped
1 teaspoon coarse sea salt
⅛ teaspoon cayenne
¼ teaspoon saffron, or less, to taste
*Bouquet garni consisting of the leek greens,
    1 medium celery rib, ¼ cup firmly packed
    parsley leaves, 1 large bay leaf, ¼ tea-
    spoon dried thyme, ½ teaspoon dried
    oregano, ¼ teaspoon ground savory, a few
    dried fennel branches or ¼ teaspoon fennel*

seeds, a 3-inch strip of fresh or dried
   orange peel
3 tablespoons pastis (Ricard or Pernod)
About 7 cups boiling water
1½ pounds waxy, preferably yellow-fleshed
   potatoes, peeled, cut into ¼-inch slices,
   and rinsed
4 extra-large or jumbo eggs
4 large, ½-inch-thick slices dried or toasted
   bread, rubbed with a cut clove of garlic
Chopped parsley leaves
Quick Rouille (recipe follows; optional)

1. In a 5- to 6-quart pot, cook the leeks
and onion gently in the olive oil, stirring
occasionally, for 15 minutes, or until soft
and golden.

2. Add the tomatoes. (If using canned,
mash them with a potato masher in the
pot.) Add the garlic and the salt, cayenne,
saffron, bouquet garni, pastis, and boiling
water. Stir and simmer for 10 minutes.

3. Add the potatoes and simmer briskly,
partially covered, for about 20 minutes, or
until the potatoes are done.

4. Fish out and discard the bouquet garni.

5. With a slotted spoon or skimmer, remove
the potatoes to a heatproof platter. Cover
with foil and keep warm in a low oven.

6. Let the broth simmer gently.

7. Taste and correct seasoning with salt,
cayenne, and perhaps another drop of
pastis.

8. Break the eggs onto a dinner plate and
slide them into the gently simmering

broth. Let them poach until cooked to
taste, then remove them with a slotted
spoon or skimmer and place back on the
plate onto which they were broken.

9. To serve, divide the potatoes among four
deep, wide bowls. Place a garlic crouton
over the potatoes. Place a poached egg on
each crouton. Ladle on the simmering
broth. Serve immediately, sprinkled with
parsley. If desired, serve rouille on the side,
to be spooned on or in to taste.

QUICK ROUILLE

Makes about 1 cup

3 large garlic cloves
3 tablespoons extra-virgin olive oil,
   preferably full-flavored
¼ teaspoon cayenne
¾ cup Hellmann's or Best Foods mayonnaise
Juice of ½ lemon (about 1 tablespoon)

1. In the jar of a blender, combine the garlic and oil and process until the garlic is
very finely chopped.

2. Add the remaining ingredients and process again. Serve at room temperature.

ADVANCE PREPARATION: Can be prepared
through step 5 and kept refrigerated for up
to a week. Thin with water when reheating.
Do not freeze. The rouille can be kept
refrigerated for several weeks.

ROASTED VEGETABLE BROTH

Makes 9 cups

For vegetarians, this is a good broth to carry pasta or rice. You can also use it to make stracciatella (page 122), zuppa pavese (page 120), or whenever you think appropriate to replace chicken or beef broth in a recipe.

1 pound carrots, scrubbed
1 pound onions, peeled and thickly sliced (about 3 cups)
3 large celery ribs, each cut into thirds
2 medium turnips, scrubbed, trimmed, and quartered
1 or 2 leeks or 6 shallots, trimmed or peeled and sliced
3 tablespoons olive oil
10 cups boiling water

1. In a large roasting pan, combine all the vegetables, then drizzle with oil.

2. Roast in a preheated 350-degree oven for about 90 minutes, until the vegetables are well browned.

3. Transfer the vegetables to a 6- to 8-quart pot.

4. Use some of the boiling water to deglaze the roasting pan, scraping up any browned, even burned, bits. Transfer to the stockpot, with the remaining boiling water.

5. Cover, bring to a boil, reduce heat, and simmer briskly for 30 minutes.

6. Let cool to room temperature, then strain.

ADVANCE PREPARATION: May be kept refrigerated for several days, then—if brought to a boil—for a few days more. It freezes perfectly.

SOUP OF THE DAY

Serves 2

The *soupe du jour* in a French restaurant is invariably a creamed vegetable purée of indeterminate origin. I don't care if they tell me it's spinach, pea, or asparagus—it all tastes about the same: hot, rich, nourishing, and often quite good. My soup of the day has the same qualities. It starts with a potato and onion base, made with water (not broth) so the taste of the vegetables really comes through, and it gets its color and remaining character from whatever other vegetables or greenery are on hand.

With slight embellishment—a few carrots—it can become something as pretentious-sounding as crécyssoise—what restaurants have been known to call cream of carrot soup—or the famous vichyssoise—the cold, elegantly smooth version that is not, strictly speaking, French but was created by French chef Louis Diat for New York's Ritz Hotel (see page 147).

SUPPER SUGGESTIONS: This is a warming and comforting, but insubstantial, soup.

For everyday meals, serve a crusty loaf of bread and have a salad, then cheese and fruit afterward. For a more elaborate menu, start with potato and shrimp salad (page 186), or a platter of ham and salami. Asparagus or an artichoke as a first course is another idea.

2 cups coarsely chopped leeks or onions
1½ cups chunked-up potato
2 cups water
½ teaspoon salt
Freshly ground white pepper
1 tablespoon butter

1. In a 2-quart saucepan, combine the leeks, potato, water, and salt. Cover and bring to a boil. Let boil for 15 minutes, or until the potatoes are very tender.

2. Using a food mill or an immersion blender, purée the soup. Return to the saucepan.

3. Bring the puréed soup to a simmer and stir in the pepper and butter. Simmer 1 minute.

4. Serve very hot in deep or flat bowls.

VARIATIONS: For carrot soup, add 2 or 3 medium carrots and ½ cup more liquid. Or use carrot juice instead of water. Or, for that matter, any kind of vegetable juice instead of water. For cream of watercress soup, add a whole bunch of watercress, coarsely chopped, with stems, for the last 2 minutes of cooking, plus ½ cup more liquid. For cream of pea soup, add ½ package frozen petits pois for the last 5 minutes of cooking, plus a few tablespoons additional

liquid. For cream of other vegetables, such as broccoli, spinach, zucchini, string beans, fennel, winter squash, brussels sprouts, turnips, parsnips, or celery root, add 1 cup of the chopped cooked vegetable and adjust liquid according to taste. Et cetera, et cetera. Take it from there.

ADVANCE PREPARATION: Should be made just before serving.

SPRING ONION AND RED POTATO SOUP

Serves 6

This is my version of a "soup of the day" that I ate many years ago in a café in Sonoma Valley, where, it being California, the vegetables were naturally superb. If you can get true spring onions and truly new potatoes, they make a difference. And the specks of green and red (potato skin) give the soup a particularly attractive appearance.

SUPPER SUGGESTIONS: See Soup of the Day, page 50.

2 bunches tiny spring onions or scallions (including all healthy-looking green), coarsely chopped (about 3 cups)
2 pounds new red potatoes, scrubbed and cut in half
6 cups water

1 cup heavy cream
Coarse sea salt and freshly ground white
  pepper
Finely chopped parsley, chives, or other herb
  for garnish

1. In a 4- to 6-quart pot, combine the chopped scallions, potatoes, and water. Cover and simmer gently until the potatoes and scallions are very tender, at least 30 minutes.

2. In a blender or food processor, or using an immersion blender in the pot, purée the soup, in small batches if necessary. Be careful not to overwork the soup or the potatoes will become gummy.

3. Return the purée to the pot and reheat the soup to a steady simmer for 2 or 3 minutes.

4. Stir in the cream and heat through.

5. Taste and season with salt and pepper.

6. Serve hot or well-chilled in deep or flat bowls. If serving cold, check seasoning before serving; flavors are diminished in cold food. Garnish with parsley, chives, or another herb, such as dill, tarragon, or chervil.

ADVANCE PREPARATION: Not advisable; the soup loses all its freshness.

CHAPTER 2

BEAN AND GRAIN SOUPS

SENATE BEAN SOUP

Makes about 9 cups, serving about 6

According to a pamphlet handed out by the U.S. Senate, this soup has been on its restaurant's menu at least since 1901. Could this be the reason our wise legislators can be so full of hot air?

"Whatever uncertainties may exist in the Senate of the United States, one thing is sure: Bean Soup is on the menu of the Senate Restaurant every day," says the official "History of Senate Bean Soup."

"The origin of this culinary decree has been lost in antiquity," it exaggerates, "but there are several oft-repeated legends. One story has it that Senator Fred Thomas Dubois of Idaho, who served in the Senate from 1901 to 1907, when chairman of the committee that supervised the Senate Restaurant, gaveled through a resolution requiring that bean soup be on the menu every day. Another account attributes the bean soup mandate to Senator Knute Nelson of Minnesota, who expressed his fondness for it in 1903.

"In any case, Senators and their guests are always assured of a hearty, nourishing dish; they know they can rely upon its delightful flavor and epicurean qualities."

In 1993, a cup of this beige rib-sticker costs 95 cents and continues to be a popular daily seller, though that is hard to believe if the Senate Restaurant is following its own recipe. The official recipe is nothing more than pea beans cooked with water, ham hocks, and some butter-sautéed onions. There are, however, many other recipes in print purporting to be the true U.S. Senate Bean Soup—in cookbooks from the 1920s through the early 1980s. The following recipe is based on those, all of which are slightly different but almost all of which contain the following ingredients. You've probably eaten something like it at, say, a diner along a highway, because it is a classic American bean soup, at one time popular from coast to coast. With a hefty portion of celery—as well as celery leaves—it has a surprisingly fresh, unstodgy flavor. Indeed, it is as noble as any Tuscan bean soup, as well it should be if it is our Senate's.

SUPPER SUGGESTIONS: An iceberg lettuce wedge dripping with blue cheese dressing (page 180) is what I'd want to eat before this. A big square of wacky chocolate cake (page 191) and a cup of coffee is what I'd want after. With the soup, serve a sturdy whole-grain bread, or a crusty French or Italian bread, perhaps toasted and rubbed with garlic.

2 cups (1 pound) dried pea beans or other
    small white beans, rinsed and picked over
1 small smoked ham hock
3 quarts water
1 large onion, finely chopped (about 1½ cups)
6 to 8 inner celery ribs, including leafy tops,
    finely chopped (about 1½ cups)
3 large garlic cloves, coarsely chopped
1 medium potato, peeled and cut into
    ¼-inch cubes (about 1 cup)
1½ to 2 teaspoons coarse sea salt

½ teaspoon freshly ground pepper
¼ cup chopped parsley leaves

1. Soak the rinsed beans overnight in cold water to cover by several inches (see page 15).

2. In a 5- to 6-quart pot, combine the drained beans, ham hock, and water. Cover and bring to a boil; adjust the heat, partially cover, and simmer briskly until the beans are tender, 1 to 1½ hours, stirring occasionally.

3. Stir in the onion, celery, garlic, potato, salt, and pepper. Keep at a steady simmer another hour, stirring occasionally, until the beans are very tender and the soup is very thick.

4. Remove the ham hock and, if desired, strip the meat off the bones, shred it, discarding the fat, rind, and bones, and put the shredded meat in the soup.

5. Serve piping hot in deep or shallow bowls.

VARIATION: For a totally unauthentic vegetarian version, delicious nonetheless, leave out the ham hock and substitute 3 tablespoons of your most full-flavored extra-virgin olive oil.

ADVANCE PREPARATION: Can be refrigerated for up to a week; it freezes perfectly. Must be thinned with water when reheating.

KIDNEY BEAN GUMBO WITH TASSO HAM

Makes about 5 quarts, serving 10 to 12

People ask food writers, "Where do recipes come from?" This one, my quasi-vegetarian rendition of a traditional Creole-Cajun dish—as well as the chicken and shrimp gumbos on pages 111 and 140—came out of my head after I read every gumbo recipe in my cookbook collection, and a few clipped from periodicals or jotted on scraps of paper gathered over the years. Among other things, this is what I learned: There are three ways to thicken a gumbo. You can use okra, which is infamously sticky and the African-American way—the word *gumbo,* in fact, derives from a Bantu word for okra. You can use filé powder, which is ground from sassafras leaves, a technique learned from the native Choctaws. Or you can use roux, which is flour browned in fat and the Cajun's way from his French heritage. Roux and okra are sometimes found in the same gumbo, but using filé powder and either of the other two is considered an overkill of thickening and it's simply not done.

So this recipe evolved because I wanted to make a bean gumbo that was merely flavored with meat, and I didn't want an okra gumbo: It's not a popular vegetable. And I didn't want a recipe that required filé powder: It's hard to find and difficult to use—it gets gummy when overheated. That forced me to settle on a roux-thickened gumbo, though that's not settling at all. To my mind, it gives the most likable and satisfying texture and the taste that most says gumbo to me.

Too much fat is the only problem with traditional roux-thickened gumbo recipes. They all call for an equal amount of oil and flour. For 5 quarts of gumbo, you need about a cup of flour for the right, rich texture, which means you use about a cup of oil. It looks like a more frightening amount than it is—it comes to only about 1½ tablespoons of fat per pint. But why not try and reduce it? I found that a third the amount of oil is absolutely sufficient. Now the fat count is down to ½ tablespoon to a pint of gumbo. If you insist on eliminating even more fat, try a method developed in the test kitchen at *Eating Well* magazine: Toast the flour to the desired color on a baking sheet in a 350-degree oven, then dissolve it in cold liquid before adding it to the pot.

SUPPER SUGGESTIONS: This is a very filling dish, so you don't need much of a first course. In the summer, a platter of sliced tomatoes and sweet onions drizzled with your best olive oil is good. In winter, a green salad is fine, or endive with blue cheese and walnuts (page 179). You might serve hot corn bread (page 163) with the gumbo, or hot biscuits (page 164). For dessert in the summer, serve the soft fruits in season or a berry dish (pages 200 and 201). Other times, fresh pears and then forgotten gianduia meringues (page 198) with hot chicory coffee.

½ cup vegetable oil
1 cup flour
2 medium onions, finely chopped (about 2 cups)
3 large celery ribs, finely chopped (about 2 cups)
1 large green bell pepper, finely chopped (about 1 cup)
3 large garlic cloves, crushed
1 28-ounce can tomatoes, cut into chunks, with their juices (discard basil)
6 cups water
1 teaspoon dried thyme
1 tablespoon Worcestershire sauce
2 large or 3 small bay leaves
½ teaspoon cayenne
½ teaspoon freshly ground black pepper
½ pound tasso ham, cut into ¼-inch cubes
1 packed cup finely chopped parsley
2 cups dried kidney beans, picked over, rinsed, and soaked overnight in cold water to cover by several inches (see page 15)
1½ cups chopped scallions

1. In a 6-quart pot, combine the oil and flour over medium-low heat. Cook, stirring regularly, for about 1 hour, until the flour has turned a very rich brown. Be careful it does not burn.

2. Meanwhile, chop the onion, celery, and green pepper.

3. As soon as the roux is the right color, immediately add the onion, celery, and pepper. Stir well. This will turn the roux a deep mahogany brown. Cover the pot and let the vegetables sweat for 10 minutes, stirring once or twice.

(continued)

4. Stir in the crushed garlic and cook, covered, 2 more minutes.

5. Stir in the tomatoes and their juice and the water. Turn heat to high and stir until the liquid boils and is smooth, though it will still look a little granular.

6. Add the thyme, Worcestershire sauce, bay leaves, cayenne, and black pepper. Cover and simmer over low heat for 30 minutes, stirring occasionally.

7. Stir in the ham and half the parsley. Simmer another 30 minutes, stirring occasionally.

8. Drain the beans and add them to the pot, discarding their soaking liquid. Cover, return the gumbo to a simmer, and cook until the beans are barely tender, 30 to 45 minutes, stirring occasionally.

9. Just before serving, stir in the remaining parsley and 1 cup of the scallions.

10. Serve piping hot in large flat bowls with a big scoop of plain white rice, sprinkled with remaining scallions.

ADVANCE PREPARATION: Cook through step 8. Can be kept refrigerated for up to a week. Freezing is not advisable (the beans get mealy). To serve, bring to a simmer before adding the final parsley and scallions.

TUSCAN BEAN SOUP

Serves 6 to 8

Sage, garlic, peppery green olive oil, and beans—it's comfort food in Tuscany, where the greens would be leaves of black cabbage, *cavolo nero,* which is unavailable here. Kale is a good stand-in, even frozen kale. Tuscans turn this soup into ribollita, "reboiling" it with slices of their dense, salt-free bread. Finding an equivalent bread in the U.S.—even baking it yourself—is nearly impossible. So instead of compromising with less appropriate bread, I serve leftovers, sometimes the freshly made soup as well, with macaroni, preferably a tubular type, such as penne, small ziti, or cavatappi, corkscrew-shaped pasta. Drizzled with peppery Tuscan olive oil and with a glass of Chianti at its side, this is one of my favorite comfort meals.

SUPPER SUGGESTIONS: In cold months, a simple salad will do. In late summer, sliced tomatoes or a tomato salad (page 180) are welcome. Keep dessert light—fresh figs would be ideal—because the soup is very filling.

1 pound dried cannellini, rinsed and picked over
¼ cup extra-virgin olive oil, preferably Tuscan
1 medium onion, finely chopped (about 1 cup)
1 medium carrot, finely chopped (about ½ cup)

*1 medium potato, cut into ¼-inch cubes
   (about 1 cup)*
*1¾ cups chicken or beef broth,
   homemade or canned*
*2 or 3 fresh sage leaves, 2 teaspoons dried leaf
   sage, or ¼ to ½ teaspoon marjoram*
3 large garlic cloves, coarsely chopped
6 cups water
Coarse sea salt and freshly ground pepper
*½ a 10-ounce package frozen chopped
   spinach or kale, defrosted, or 2 cups finely
   shredded kale, or 2 cups finely shredded
   Savoy cabbage*
Thin croutons
Extra-virgin olive oil

1. Soak the beans overnight in cold water to cover by several inches (page 15).

2. In a 4- to 6-quart saucepan, warm the olive oil over medium-low heat and sauté the onion and carrot until tender, about 10 minutes.

3. Add the potato, broth, sage, and garlic.

4. Drain the beans and add them, along with enough water to cover, about 6 cups. Cover and bring to a boil. Reduce heat, partially cover, and simmer steadily for 40 minutes to 1 hour, until the beans are very tender.

5. Ladle out about half the beans and pass through a food mill back into the pan with the remaining beans. Or purée in a blender or food processor. Or use an immersion blender, being careful not to purée all the beans.

6. Return the soup to a simmer, stirring frequently.

7. Taste and correct seasoning with salt and pepper.

8. Add the defrosted spinach or kale, or finely shredded fresh kale or cabbage, and simmer about 15 minutes.

9. Serve in wide bowls, topped with a thin crouton and a drizzle of olive oil.

ADVANCE PREPARATION: Can be kept refrigerated for up to a week; the beans suffer if you freeze the soup.

IOTA
(FRIULAN SAUERKRAUT AND BEAN SOUP)

Makes 3½ quarts, serving about 6

The far northeast of Italy, Friuli, which was once part of the Austro-Hungarian empire, has a cooking style that often overlaps with its neighbors in Austria or Croatia. For instance, bacon is smoked here and sauerkraut is popular. This soup, an honored regional specialty for which there are many recipes, combines those two ingredients in a totally Italian way.

SUPPER SUGGESTIONS: Celery and Parmesan salad (page 175) would be a refreshing, light first course before the hearty soup. A platter of different salamis or cold cuts would bolster the heartiness. A light rye bread is a natural with the soup. For dessert, fresh fruit and biscotti with sweet wine would hit the spot. So would a chilled poached pear (page 204) or Karen's raspberry wedges (page 194).

6 ounces sliced smoked bacon, coarsely
    chopped
1 large onion, coarsely chopped
½ cup loosely packed fresh parsley leaves,
    coarsely chopped
3 large garlic cloves, coarsely chopped
3 large sage leaves, or 1½ teaspoons dried
    leaf sage
3 tablespoons vegetable oil
½ pound dried cannellini beans, rinsed and
    picked over, soaked overnight in cold
    water to cover by several inches (page 15)
3 quarts beef broth (half canned broth with
    half water)
½ pound medium barley
1 large potato, cut into ¼-inch cubes
    (about 1½ cups)
½ pound sauerkraut, with its juice
1 teaspoon coarse sea salt
½ teaspoon freshly ground pepper
About 1 tablespoon red or white wine
    vinegar, if desired

1. In a food processor or blender, combine the bacon, onion, parsley, garlic, and sage. Process until the mixture becomes very finely chopped, almost a paste.

2. In a 6-quart pot, combine the bacon mixture with the vegetable oil and sauté over medium heat, stirring and spreading the bacon mixture. Fry until mixture begins to color.

3. Drain the beans and add them. Add the broth and barley. Cover and bring to a boil over high heat.

4. Add the potato, cover partially, and adjust the heat so that the soup simmers steadily for about 1 hour, or until the beans and barley are fully tender.

5. Add the sauerkraut and stir well.

6. Taste and correct seasoning with salt and pepper and, if necessary to give the soup more bite, a tablespoon or more of white or red wine vinegar.

7. Serve piping hot in deep or flat bowls.

ADVANCE PREPARATION: Can be refrigerated for up to a week or frozen for up to six months.

IRIS'S SIRACUSAN FAVA BEAN SOP

Serves 6

Iris Carulli brought this dish for me to eat one day for lunch. It tasted like manna from heaven. Here's what she says of it:

"This soup is a staple in the cuisine of eastern Sicily and the following version is one served in Carmela Giselli's home in Canicattini Bagni, a village twenty miles inland from Siracusa. Carmela and her four sisters cook in the family's Trattoria al Carmine in nearby Noto, a town well-known for its splendid baroque architecture. I doubt that she would serve this at the trattoria—it's too humble—but at home she serves it with her own extremely compact and fine-textured bread, which remains firm when cut up in pieces and stirred into the thick soup. The pale brown crust is so smooth and hard and the shapes of her loaves are so beautiful that they look like biscuit pottery."

SUPPER SUGGESTIONS: Seek out some great "compact and fine-textured bread." Then enjoy a big salad, or, in summer, a platter of tomatoes and garlic toast (page 159), bruschetta (page 160), or insalata caprese (page 181). Figs for dessert would be a treat—a very Sicilian touch.

14 ounces dried large fava beans
1 medium onion, finely chopped (about 1 cup)
5 medium celery ribs (preferably the Chinese variety, which has a more intense flavor than California celery), finely chopped (about 2½ cups)
3 large garlic cloves, finely chopped
1 tablespoon tomato paste
1 small bay leaf
⅛ teaspoon crushed red pepper
1 teaspoon coarse sea salt
¼ cup extra-virgin olive oil, plus more oil for garnish

1. Soak the beans overnight in cold water to cover by several inches (page 15).

2. With a sharp knife, remove the black "eyes" from each fava bean.

3. In a 4- to 6-quart pot, combine the drained beans with 3 quarts of fresh cold water and the remaining ingredients, except the garnishing oil. Cover and bring

to a boil over high heat. Stir well, adjust heat, partially cover, and simmer steadily for 1½ hours, or until the insides of the beans are soft and come out easily when crushed against the sides of the pot.

4. With a skimmer or slotted spoon, remove the fava beans from the pot and place them in a bowl. Let them cool. With your fingers, press the bean pulp out of the tough skin and back into the pot, discarding the skins. This works better than passing the soup through a food mill. If you prefer a chunkier soup, leave some of the fava beans whole.

5. Stir the soup well to incorporate the bean pulp and reheat.

6. Taste and correct seasonings, adding more salt, red pepper, even tomato paste.

7. Serve piping hot in deep or flat bowls, drizzled generously with extra-virgin olive oil.

ADVANCE PREPARATION: Can be kept refrigerated for up to a week; it freezes perfectly for up to six months.

BLACK BEAN SOUP

Serves 8

My favorite way to eat this, a smooth purée, is by making it almost a sauce for rice. Heap the rice in a bowl, pour the soup around it so the rice stands like a white mountain, then strew everything with chopped onion, salsa, and cheese.

SUPPER SUGGESTIONS: A salad of tomato, avocado, and onion (page 187) is perfect, and very Cuban. Corn bread (page 163) is not Cuban, but complements the soup. For dessert, pineapple doused with rum is in keeping, and put out some oatmeal lace cookies (page 197).

1 pound dried black beans, rinsed and picked over, then soaked overnight in cold water to cover by several inches (page 15)
1 large bay leaf
1 medium green bell pepper, seeded and finely chopped

FOR THE SOFRITO:
½ cup extra-virgin olive oil, preferably Spanish
4 large garlic cloves, finely chopped
1 large onion, finely chopped (about 1½ cups)
1 large green bell pepper, seeded and finely chopped (about 1 cup)
1 tablespoon ground cumin
2 tablespoons red wine vinegar
1 teaspoon (or more) finely chopped, seeded, tiny hot green or red chili pepper
8 cups cooked white rice
Chopped raw onion

Shredded Monterey Jack, crumbled queso blanco, or American farmer cheese
Pico de gallo (page 95) or pickled, sliced jalapeños

1. Drain the beans and place in a 4- to 6-quart pot. Cover with water by about 2 inches. Add the bay leaf and green pepper. Cover and bring to a boil over high heat. Stir well, adjust the heat, partially cover, and simmer briskly until very tender, about 2 hours. Stir regularly and add more water if necessary.

2. Meanwhile, make the sofrito: In a medium skillet, heat the oil over medium heat, then add the garlic, onion, and bell pepper. Cook, stirring often, until the onion is transparent, 8 to 10 minutes. Add the cumin, vinegar, and chili pepper. Mix well and bring to a boil.

3. Add the simmering sofrito to the beans after 2 hours. Mix well, then continue to simmer gently another 30 to 40 minutes. The beans should be disintegrating at this point.

4. Taste and correct seasoning with salt, pepper, and more chili pepper, as desired. Let cool slightly.

5. In a blender or food processor, or using an immersion blender, process the beans until very smooth.

6. Reheat, adding more water if a thinner soup is desired.

7. Serve piping hot in deep or flat bowls, on or around a mound of boiled white rice. Garnish with cheese and pass the chopped onion and pico di gallo salsa and/or pickled jalapeños.

ADVANCE PREPARATION: May be refrigerated for up to a week; it freezes perfectly for up to a year. The soup must be thinned with water when reheating.

RASHTA
(LEBANESE LENTIL AND NOODLE SOUP)

Makes 2½ quarts, serving about 8

In my travels as a restaurant critic I've learned that whatever they're cooking in the kitchen of an ethnic restaurant, no matter how unpretentious a place, it is probably not the food they are cooking most humbly at home for themselves. At least, the menu doesn't tell the whole story. This soup is the perfect example. It is so simple and homey that Sonia and Sabeh Kachouh say they couldn't possibly serve it at Byblos, their Lebanese restaurant in midtown Manhattan. Still, to them (and to me and all my tasters) it is heaven on earth. It is no wonder that Esau sold his birthright for a mess of lentils. In any case, as Sonia says, the beauty of this soup is its fragrance when you add the coriander and garlic. And you have to be a family gathered in the kitchen to appreciate that.

SUPPER SUGGESTIONS: Fatoush (page 176), the Lebanese chopped salad with sumac and pita crisps, is perfect to start with. No bread is necessary. Fresh fruit or a fruit salad (page 199) is the refreshing sweet you'll want.

2 cups brown lentils, preferably the small French variety
2 quarts water
2 tablespoons extra-virgin olive oil
2 medium onions, halved and sliced (about 2 cups)
5 large garlic cloves
2 teaspoons coarse sea salt
¼ cup very finely chopped coriander or parsley leaves
4 ounces medium-width egg noodles
2 tablespoons dried mint

1. In a 3- to 4-quart pot, combine the lentils and water. Bring to a boil over high heat and boil, uncovered, until tender, about 20 minutes or so, stirring a few times.

2. Meanwhile, in a large skillet, heat the olive oil over medium-high heat and fry the sliced onions until well browned, at least 15 minutes, tossing frequently.

3. In a mortar, mash the garlic with the coarse salt until the mixture is a paste. Alternatively, use a garlic press to mash the garlic. In a small bowl with the back of a spoon, mash the garlic a few seconds longer with the salt.

4. Add the coriander and mash again.

5. When the lentils are just tender, stir the garlic and herb mixture into the onions and sauté 1 minute.

(continued)

6. Add some of the lentil liquid to the garlic and herb mixture, scraping the pan to deglaze it.

7. Scrape the mixture in the skillet into the remaining lentils, stir, and cook 2 more minutes.

8. Add the noodles to the lentils. Press them down with a spoon so they are covered with liquid. Partially cover the pot and boil the noodles for 5 minutes, stirring a couple of times after the noodles become supple. The soup should be very thick; add some boiling water if you want it thinner.

9. Add the mint and boil 1 minute longer. Taste and correct with salt and pepper.

10. Serve immediately, piping hot, in flat bowls.

ADVANCE PREPARATION: Do not make ahead. If left to stand the noodles get too soft and you will have to add more water to bring the lentils back to soupy consistency. Plus, when you keep the soup for more than a couple of hours, even without the noodles, the garlic and herb flavors diminish and the soup has to be reseasoned. If there are leftovers, they can be kept refrigerated for up to a week; reheat gently and reseason, using more chopped coriander, dried mint, and raw garlic.

ANOTHER LEBANESE LENTIL SOUP

Makes about 3 quarts, serving at least 6

I didn't quite believe this recipe when I got it, another one from a restaurateur who does not serve his home comfort food in his mostly Italian restaurant, Elizabeth's, in Pittsfield, Massachusetts. What I couldn't believe is that nearly three hours of cooking is really necessary, and that the enormous quantity of celery and onions wouldn't overwhelm everything. Well, this is one of those recipes that proves cooking can be magic, or at least alchemy. After the second hour of cooking, the soup's flavor changes dramatically—for the better, naturally—and, in the end, the onions and celery do a disappearing act.

SUPPER SUGGESTIONS: Fatoush, the Lebanese salad (page 176), is the ideal first course. Fresh fruit or a fruit salad (page 199) is what you'll want to clear your palate afterward.

6 large onions (3 pounds), peeled, halved,
*   and sliced (not particularly thin)*
4 tablespoons extra-virgin olive oil
1 whole bunch celery, with leaves, sliced
*   (about 6 cups)*
½ cup finely chopped Italian parsley, leaves
*   and fine stems*
1 pound lentils, rinsed and picked over
10 cups water
1 teaspoon ground cinnamon

2 to 3 teaspoons coarse sea salt
½ teaspoon or more freshly ground pepper
Lemon wedges

1. In two skillets, sauté the onions over medium-high heat, using 2 tablespoons of olive oil for each batch. Cook, tossing and stirring frequently, if not constantly, until the onions are dark brown, with some pieces even blackened. Lower the heat as the onions become reduced, and frequently scrape up the brown film on the bottom of the pan. Each batch will take about 30 minutes.

Alternatively, to save about 15 minutes, in the same large skillet, sauté half the onions over medium-high heat for about 5 minutes, or until well wilted and beginning to brown, then toss in another quarter of the onions. Sauté 3 or 4 minutes more. Toss in the remaining onions. When the last batch is well wilted, lower the heat slightly. In this case, it takes about 45 minutes of patient tossing, stirring, and scraping the bottom of the pot for the onions to reach the rich brown stage.

2. In a 6- to 8-quart pot, combine the celery, parsley, lentils, and 8 cups of the water.

3. Scrape the onions into the pot.

4. Use the remaining 2 cups of water to rinse out the pan in which the onions cooked: Place the pan(s) with water over high heat and scrape every bit of flavor from the pan(s) into the water. Add the water to the pot with the lentils.

5. Cover the lentils and bring to a simmer. Stir well, adjust heat, partially cover, and simmer steadily, stirring occasionally, for at least 2 hours.

6. Stir in the cinnamon, salt, and pepper. Simmer another 30 minutes, stirring a few times.

7. Serve piping hot in a deep or flat bowl topped with a lemon wedge to squeeze on (or not), to taste.

ADVANCE PREPARATION: Can be kept refrigerated for up to a week; reseason and add water when reheating; it freezes perfectly.

LENTIL SOUP WITH FENNEL AND SUN-DRIED TOMATOES

Makes about 4 quarts thick soup, serving about 8

This combination of flavors can bring warmth to a winter day.

SUPPER SUGGESTIONS: Serve with fettunta (page 159). An eggplant salad plate (page 185), also with fettunta, would be an excellent start. For dessert, create a fresh fruit salad (page 199).

¼ cup full-flavored olive oil
2 medium onions, chopped (about 2 cups)
5 large garlic cloves, chopped
1 pound lentils
4 ounces sun-dried tomatoes, cut into
*   ½-inch bits*
1 medium fennel bulb, including stalks, cut
*   into ½-inch pieces (about 4 cups); reserve*
*   the leaves for garnish*
3 quarts water
1½ teaspoons coarse sea salt, or to taste
½ teaspoon freshly ground black pepper
¼ teaspoon fennel seed

1. In a 6- to 8-quart pot, warm the olive oil over medium heat and sauté the onions until they begin to brown, about 15 minutes.

2. Add the garlic and sauté another 30 seconds.

3. Add the remaining ingredients to the pot. Cover and bring to a boil over high heat. Stir well, partially cover, and adjust heat so lentils simmer steadily for about 2 hours, or until the lentils are falling apart and soup is thick. Stir regularly and add more water if necessary.

4. Pass about 2 cups of the lentils through a food mill and return the purée to the soup. Stir well.

5. Taste and correct with salt and pepper.

6. Serve hot in deep or flat bowls with a drizzle of full-flavored extra-virgin olive oil and a sprig of fresh fennel leaves.

ADVANCE PREPARATION: Can be kept refrigerated for up to a week; it freezes perfectly. Thin with water when reheating.

JEWISH-STYLE SPLIT PEA SOUP

Makes 6 quarts, serving about 12

In her family, and among her neighbors in the Sheepshead Bay section of Brooklyn, Mabel Chernow, now well into her eighties, is famous for her "sweet pea soup." The key to its much-admired sweetness is Mabel's addition of a grated sweet potato, says her daughter and my friend, Roberta Simon. It is probably impolite to also mention the sweetness of carrots, a parsnip, and the split peas themselves.

SUPPER SUGGESTIONS: This naturally sweet purée calls for a highly contrasting salad starter or accompaniment. Easiest is a plate of pickled herring in wine sauce, bought at a specialty store or in a jar in the supermarket, and served with—as much for their juicy crispness as their flavors— red radishes, whole tiny scallions, cucumber slices, and some of the pickled onions from the herring. A perfect alternative, but a little more work, is a crunchy, sharp-tasting celery root rémoulade (see page 175). Don't forget a hearty rye bread, preferably with caraway seeds, to go with all of the above. A poached pear (page 204) is a refreshing dessert. Add a piece of cake if you really want to splurge.

¾ pound beef flanken or short ribs
10 cups water
1 pound green split peas
1 medium sweet potato, peeled and grated
 (about 2 cups)
1 large garlic clove, coarsely chopped
3 large carrots, grated (about 2½ cups)
1 large onion, chopped (about 1½ cups)
1 large parsnip, peeled and grated (about
 1 cup)
1 parsley root, scrubbed and whole (if
 available)
1 large celery rib, chopped (½ to ¾ cup)
2 tablespoons or more chopped dill
2 teaspoons or more coarse sea salt
1 teaspoon or more freshly ground pepper
Croutons (fried or baked, garlic flavored if
 desired)

1. Bring a 1- to 2-quart saucepan of water to the boil. Put the flanken in the water and count 2 minutes. Drain the flanken, discarding the water.

2. In a 6- to 8-quart pot, combine the scalded flanken, 10 cups of fresh cold water, and all the remaining ingredients, except the croutons. Cover and bring to a boil over high heat. Stir well, adjust heat, partially cover, and simmer steadily for about 2 hours, stirring occasionally.

3. The meat should be falling apart when the soup is done. The soup should be a rough, thick purée. Remove the meat and strip it from its bones. Discard the bones.

4. If you prefer a smoother soup, pass it through a food mill, or process it in a blender or food processor, or use an immersion blender.

5. Taste and add additional dill, salt, and pepper to taste.

6. Shred the meat with your fingers or a fork and either stir it into the soup or garnish each bowl with a few pieces.

7. Serve piping hot, topped with croutons, in deep or flat bowls, or in mugs.

ADVANCE PREPARATION: Can be kept refrigerated for up to a week; it freezes perfectly for up to six months.

SPICY YELLOW SPLIT PEA SOUP

Makes 2 quarts, serving 4 to 6

This is my fantasy of an Indian soup, not an authentic one. Its spicing is mild, even with the optional cayenne. That's so it has a comforting, homey feel. I'd eat it on a cold night, maybe in bed watching television, followed by a bowl of yogurt with nuts and diced dried fruit.

SUPPER SUGGESTIONS: Papadums, which can be purchased in many supermarkets, are thin crackers made from lentil flour. They are a perfect accompaniment and can be puffed up in a microwave. For a salad or appetizer, I recommend celery root rémoulade (page 175). A fresh fruit salad (page 199) drizzled with yogurt and honey would be a perfect dessert.

3 medium onions, halved and sliced thin
  (about 3 cups)
3 tablespoons vegetable oil
1 tablespoon curry powder

FOR THE PEAS:
1 pound yellow split peas
2 teaspoons chopped fresh ginger
½ teaspoon ground coriander seeds
½ teaspoon freshly ground pepper
4 large garlic cloves, finely chopped
2 quarts water
¼ teaspoon cayenne (optional)
Fresh coriander leaves (optional)

1. In an 8- to 10-inch skillet, over medium-high heat, fry the onions in the oil, stirring occasionally, until well-browned but not burned, 45 minutes to an hour.

2. During the last 10 minutes of cooking, add the curry powder to the onions and blend well. Cook another 5 minutes, scraping the bottom of the pan with a wooden spoon or spatula. When the onions are done they will have reduced to about a cup of soft, dark strings.

3. While the onions are cooking, in a 6- to 8-quart pot, combine the peas, ginger, coriander seeds, black pepper, and garlic. Add the water, cover, and bring to a boil over high heat. Stir well, adjust heat, partially cover, and simmer briskly until the peas fall apart, about 1 hour.

4. Purée the peas in a food mill, blender, or food processor, or with an immersion blender. Return to the pot.

5. Mix the onions into the soup, taste for seasoning, and add the cayenne, if desired.

6. Serve piping hot in deep or flat bowls or mugs, garnished with fresh coriander leaves.

ADVANCE PREPARATION: Can be kept refrigerated up to a week; it freezes perfectly. Thin the soup with water when reheating.

POLISH CREAMED MUSHROOM BARLEY SOUP

Makes about 4½ quarts, serving about 8

In New York we have a kind of restaurant called a "Polish coffee shop." For some reason, these are owned mostly by American-born Jews, though the cooks, the food, and the waitresses are definitely not. Ignorant of any dietary laws except those of good home cooking, the kitchens turn out potato, cheese, and mixed sauerkraut–wild mushroom pirogi, cheese and potato blintzes, long-cooked bigos rich with pork chunks, kielbasa in various combinations and permutations, and filling, fabulous soups, not to mention tuna sandwiches, hamburgers, eggs any style, and the rest of the American coffee shop specialties. This soup, from Adam's on East 45th Street, near Second Avenue—close to the United Nations—is my favorite of its kind. That it is made with fresh mushrooms, not dried, and with cream sets it apart from the other mushroom barley soups in this book.

SUPPER SUGGESTIONS: A steamed vegetable plate is welcome; dress it with lemon juice and perhaps a drizzle of a flavorful oil, such as walnut or olive. Alternatively, a big mixed salad with a mustardy dressing (page 173) would be a fine start. The bread should be rye or pumpernickel, the dessert should be refreshing—like a poached pear (page 204) or a fruit salad (page 199).

2 quarts water
3 medium carrots, finely chopped (about 1½ cups)
3 medium celery ribs, finely chopped (about 1½ cups)
1 pound medium barley
Coarse sea salt
Freshly ground pepper
1½ pounds mushrooms, coarsely chopped
1 medium onion, coarsely chopped (about 1 cup)
2 tablespoons butter
6 cups chicken broth, homemade or canned
1 cup heavy cream (optional, but desirable)
3 teaspoons liquid Maggi, Bovril, or Kitchen Bouquet, or to taste
Finely chopped parsley for garnish

1. In a 6- to 8-quart pot, combine 2 quarts of fresh cold water with the chopped carrots and celery. Bring to a rolling boil over medium-high heat. Add the barley, salt, and pepper and boil for 25 minutes, until the barley is tender, adding more water if necessary.

2. Meanwhile, in a large skillet, over medium heat, sauté the mushrooms and onion in butter until the mushrooms exude their liquid and the liquid evaporates. Do not overcook.

3. Add the mushroom mixture to the barley and cook for another 15 minutes, stirring often.

4. Stir in the broth and return to a boil. Stir in the cream. Season with Maggi, salt, and pepper.

5. Serve very hot in deep or wide bowls, sprinkled with parsley.

ADVANCE PREPARATION: May be kept refrigerated for up to a week; it freezes perfectly for up to a year. Thin the soup with water when reheating.

JEWISH-STYLE MUSHROOM BARLEY SOUP

Serves about 12

The following combination of barley, split peas, and lima beans is what you find in the long cellophane packages of barley soup mix put out by Jewish food companies such as Goodman's and Manischewitz. I see where having them all together in the right proportions in one bag is handy, but I never understood the little packet of seasoning blend they give you. You have to add fresh vegetables and some meat anyway and the "seasonings" are mostly MSG and salt with a little mushroom dust. It's better and no more trouble to make the soup from scratch.

SUPPER SUGGESTIONS: Rye bread is a must. Start with a tossed salad or a Roumanian eggplant salad plate (page 185),

also with rye bread. For dessert, fuss with Karen's raspberry wedges (page 194) or poached pears (page 204), or keep it easy with store-bought cookies and fresh fruit.

4 tablespoons vegetable oil
2 medium onions, finely chopped (about 2 cups)
3 medium carrots, grated (about 2 cups)
6 quarts water
1½ to 2 pounds beef flanken or short ribs
2 pounds soup bones
1¼ cups barley
½ cup green and/or yellow split peas
¼ cup dried baby lima beans
2 tablespoons salt
½ teaspoon freshly ground black pepper
½ ounce dried mushrooms

1. In an 8-quart pot, warm the vegetable oil over medium heat and sauté the onion and carrots until the onion is very tender, about 10 minutes.

2. Add the water, flanken, and soup bones. Bring to a boil and skim off the foam that rises to the top until there is no more foam to skim, about 15 minutes.

3. Add the barley, split peas, limas, salt, and pepper. Return to a boil, reduce heat, and let simmer, partially covered, for about 1½ hours.

4. Add the mushrooms and continue to simmer another hour or longer, until the meat is falling off its bones and the soup has become thick.

5. Serve hot in deep or wide bowls.

VARIATION: Instead of beef, use a 3- to 4-pound chicken cut into 16 pieces. Or substitute bone-in lamb shoulder cut for stew.

ADVANCE PREPARATION: Can be refrigerated for up to a week; it freezes perfectly for up to six months. Thin the soup with water when reheating.

PORCINI, POTATO, AND BARLEY SOUP

Serves 6

This is my own Italianized version of the standard Eastern European mushroom barley soup (page 70). I once served it before a pork roast flavored with lemon peel, rosemary, and garlic, which I thought would be the real pièce de résistance of the party. Everyone filled up on the soup and garlic toast and ate the pork only to be polite. As I remember, no one asked for the pork recipe after the party, but two guests asked for the soup recipe. One of them, a soap opera actress, called several days later from Los Angeles to find out how to make it for her friend, Dame Judith Anderson. I was thrilled that a famous person was going to eat my soup. And we agreed: the soup, garlic bread (page 159), a mixed green and vegetable salad, then, for dessert, a nice slice of Gorgonzola or Roquefort drizzled with honey (page 203) was a magnificent menu to put before a Dame.

SUPPER SUGGESTIONS: See introduction to recipe.

½ ounce dried porcini mushrooms
3 tablespoons olive oil
2 medium onions, finely chopped (about 2 cups)
3 medium carrots, finely chopped (about 1½ cups)
2 large celery ribs, finely chopped (about 1 cup)
1 medium-large potato, cut into ½-inch cubes (about 1½ cups)
2 ounces prosciutto, coarsely chopped or cut into strips
½ cup barley
7 to 8 cups beef broth (may be half canned, half water)
½ teaspoon freshly ground black pepper
Coarse salt, as needed
Finely chopped fresh parsley, oregano, marjoram, or mint

1. In a small bowl or cup, combine the mushrooms with 1 cup of very hot water. Let them soak at least 20 minutes, or until you're ready to add them to the soup.

Alternatively, combine the mushrooms and tap water in a bowl or cup and microwave on HIGH for 1 minute, then let stand 1 minute.

2. In a 4- to 6-quart pot, heat the oil over medium heat and sauté the onions until tender, 8 to 10 minutes.

3. Add the carrots and celery. Sauté another 8 to 10 minutes, until the vegetables are beginning to brown.

(continued)

4. Drain the mushrooms, reserving the liquid. Coarsely chop the mushrooms.

5. Stir the mushrooms into the vegetables; sauté another 2 or 3 minutes.

6. Add the potatoes, prosciutto, barley, broth, and pepper. Add the reserved mushroom liquid, passing it through a coffee filter or fine strainer lined with cheesecloth. Raise the heat to high, cover, and bring to a boil. Adjust heat, partially cover, and simmer steadily for 1 hour, until the barley is very tender and the soup has become thick.

7. Taste and correct with salt and pepper.

8. The soup can be served immediately, but it is best after it rests a few hours, or up to a few days, and is then reheated. The soup will thicken as it stands and you will need to add more broth or water to thin it out. However, bring the soup back to a simmer before judging if it needs any more liquid. It should be a thick, not brothy, soup.

9. Serve very hot in deep or flat bowls, sprinkled with a chopped herb if desired—mint is amazingly appropriate.

ADVANCE PREPARATION: See step 8; it freezes perfectly for up to six months.

JUDY TILLINGER'S MEXICAN OATMEAL SOUP

Serves 2

I think of this as a *little* soup supper, something to make quickly when you have no time or patience at the end of a hard day, or to make on the spur of the moment when you need a light bite.

SUPPER SUGGESTIONS: A salad of sliced avocado and Bermuda onion with lemon vinaigrette would be nice to start. Fresh pineapple is an excellent dessert.

⅔ cup rolled oats (not quick-cooking)
4 tablespoons butter
1 medium onion, chopped (about 1 cup)
1 cup well-drained, canned plum tomatoes
2 large garlic cloves, crushed
1¾ cups chicken broth, homemade or canned
1 small pasilla pepper, seeded and ground in the blender
½ teaspoon salt

1. In a medium skillet, toast the oats over medium heat, tossing constantly, until light brown. Immediately remove from the skillet.

2. In a 2- to 3-quart saucepan, melt the butter over medium heat. Add the onion and sauté 5 minutes, until wilted.

3. Add the toasted oatmeal and the remaining ingredients, except the salt. Bring to a boil, uncovered, over high heat.

Reduce heat and simmer briskly for 5 minutes. Taste and add salt if necessary.

4. Serve immediately in deep bowls.

ADVANCE PREPARATION: Must be made just before serving.

GRAN FARRO

Makes 4 quarts dense soup, serving at least 8

For many years I have been intrigued by *gran farro,* a soup made in the Garfagnano hills of Lucca from beans and spelt, or *farro,* which is a primitive, low-protein form of wheat. Until recently, however, spelt was hard to come by in the U.S. Now VitaSpelt, a company that markets its products mainly to those with wheat and gluten allergies and intolerance, has made whole-grain spelt—as well as spelt flour, spelt pasta, garlic- and cheese-flavored spelt breadsticks, and spelt muffin and pancake mix—available in almost any health food store and many other specialty food markets. Spelt is a nutty-tasting grain that you should cook so that it is still a little chewy. It must be softer than Italian spelt because I have not found it necessary to soak it prior to cooking, as many Italian recipes instruct.

To get this recipe, I ran a sort of contest. I wrote to all the trattorie and restaurants in the area for which I could find addresses and asked them to send me their recipe. This is the best of five, from Vipore, a well-known restaurant in Pieve Santo Stefano, Lucca.

SUPPER SUGGESTIONS: It's a heavy soup, so only a leafy salad need be served before or with it. If you need an impressive or more substantial first course, serve grilled mushrooms (page 178). Afterward, refreshing poached pears (page 204) hit the spot.

8 ounces dried red kidney beans, rinsed and picked over, soaked overnight in cold water to cover by several inches (see page 15)
2 quarts water
4 ounces lean pork
2 garlic cloves, peeled
2 medium potatoes, peeled and quartered
2 or 3 large sage leaves, or ½ teaspoon dried leaf sage
1 teaspoon salt
⅓ cup full-flavored olive oil
1 medium onion, finely chopped (about 1 cup)
1 (2-ounce) piece of prosciutto, diced (about ⅓ cup)
1 large celery rib, finely chopped (about ¾ cup)
½ teaspoon dried rosemary
2 tablespoons tomato paste
¾ cup dry white wine
8 ounces spelt (1⅓ cups), rinsed and drained
1 quart boiling water

1. Drain the beans. In a 4- to 6-quart pot, combine them with 2 quarts of fresh cold water, the pork (in one piece), the garlic, potatoes, sage, and salt. Cover and bring to a boil. Stir well, adjust heat, partially cover, and simmer steadily, stirring occasionally, until the beans are tender, about 1½ hours.

2. Meanwhile, in a medium skillet, heat the oil and sauté the onion, prosciutto, and celery until the vegetables are tender, about 10 minutes. Set aside.

3. When the beans are just tender, remove the pork and dice it. Set aside.

4. Pass half the beans and potatoes through a food mill, or purée in a blender or food processor, being careful not to overwork the mixture (it will become gluey). Return to the pot with remaining soup.

5. Stir in the sautéed vegetables and prosciutto, the rosemary, tomato paste, and wine. Simmer 10 minutes.

6. Stir in the spelt and 1 quart boiling water, cover, and bring to a boil. Stir very well, reduce heat, and simmer steadily, partially covered, for another 1½ hours. Stir frequently because the spelt tends to stick to the bottom of the pot. Add boiling water during cooking if the soup thickens too much, about ½ cup at a time.

7. Stir in the reserved diced pork.

8. Serve hot with a drizzle of olive oil on each portion.

ADVANCE PREPARATION: May be refrigerated for up to a week; freezes perfectly for up to six months.

LORENZA DE' MEDICI'S SPELT SOUP

Serves 6

This is a much, much lighter dish than the previous recipe; much quicker to prepare, too—as elegant and contemporary as Lorenza, who my radio listeners know from her PBS television show and refer to as "the lady who cooks in Armani." And oh, those pearls! She also cooks and teaches at her family's Badia a Coltibuono, a twelfth-century monastery in Chianti that now produces wine and olive oil.

SUPPER SUGGESTIONS: Unless you want to keep the meal strictly vegetarian, start with prosciutto and melon or figs, or a platter of mixed cold cuts. In summer, tomato bruschetta (page 160) is a good starter or accompaniment. Or, more elaborately, a vegetable mixed grill. Focaccia (page 161) is a great accompaniment if you are not serving bruschetta and have the time to bake one. For dessert, in the summer, dress up the meal with a peach crostata (page 194). Anytime, a small slice of Gorgonzola drizzled with honey (page 203) and some whole-grain or crusty bread is a rich final course.

3 tablespoons extra-virgin olive oil, preferably Tuscan
1 small onion, finely chopped (about ¾ cup)
2 large garlic cloves, finely chopped
1 generous teaspoon fresh rosemary leaves, chopped

14 ounces spelt (2⅓ cups), rinsed and
  drained
1½ cups well-drained canned plum tomatoes
Big pinch of fennel seed
8 cups light chicken stock (may be half
  canned, half water)

1. In a 6-quart pot, warm the olive oil over
low heat. Add the onion, garlic, and rosemary and fry gently, stirring frequently,
until the onion is wilted, about 5 minutes.

2. Add the spelt, tomatoes, fennel seed,
and stock and bring slowly to a boil. Lower
the heat, cover, and simmer gently for 2 to
3 hours, stirring occasionally, until the
spelt is tender.

3. Serve piping hot in deep or flat bowls.

ADVANCE PREPARATION: This soup can be
kept refrigerated for up to a week; it freezes
perfectly for up to a year.

THREE-BEAN VEGETABLE CHILI

Serves 8

This recipe, one of my favorite party dishes
for several years, was devised by the well-
known food writer/cookbook author
Michael McLaughlin when he was the chef
and part owner of The Manhattan Chili
Company in Greenwich Village. It is also in
his book by that name. I always get requests
for the recipe when I make it, and this is the
second time I have had to ask Michael's per-
mission to share it in print. (I've made only
minor wording changes.) Its particular bril-
liance, besides vibrant flavor and fresh appeal,
is the addition of bulgur, which gives the chili
the appearance and texture of having been
made with ground meat. It has never fooled
me, though I love it for the conceit.

SUPPER SUGGESTIONS: A festive vegetarian
menu might feature a salad of sliced ripe
Hass avocado and onion dressed with lime
vinaigrette (page 187), hot corn bread (page
163), and, for dessert, cranberry orange
sherbet (page 202). A simpler menu might
be coleslaw (page 179), chili chips and tortilla chips, with a fruit salad (page 199) or
pineapple and rum (page 200) for dessert.

¾ cup medium or coarse bulgur
1 cup fresh orange juice
⅓ cup extra-virgin olive oil
4 medium onions, coarsely chopped (about
  4 cups)

(continued)

8 medium garlic cloves, minced

⅓ cup mild, unseasoned chili powder

3 tablespoons ground cumin

3 tablespoons dried oregano

1½ tablespoons dried thyme

1 to 2 teaspoons cayenne

¼ teaspoon ground cinnamon

1 (35-ounce) can Italian plum tomatoes, with its juice

3 cups water (or light chicken stock or half water, half canned chicken broth)

1 tablespoon coarse sea salt

½ pound green beans, ends trimmed, cut into 2-inch pieces

2 large sweet red peppers, cut into ½-inch dice

1 (10-ounce) package frozen corn, thawed and drained

1 (16-ounce) can red kidney beans, rinsed and drained

1 (16-ounce) can chick-peas, rinsed and drained

FOR THE GARNISH:

2 medium zucchini, scrubbed and coarsely shredded

3 medium tomatoes, seeded and diced

1 bunch scallions, trimmed and sliced

1 pint sour cream or yogurt

1. In a small bowl, combine the bulgur and orange juice. Let stand at room temperature, stirring occasionally, while you prepare the rest of the chili.

2. Warm the oil in a 5-quart heavy flameproof casserole or Dutch oven over medium heat. Add the onions and garlic. Lower the heat slightly and cook, stirring, for 20 minutes, or until vegetables are very tender.

3. Stir in the chili powder, cumin, oregano, thyme, cayenne, and cinnamon. Cook, stirring constantly, for 5 minutes.

4. Add the tomatoes and their juice. Break up the tomatoes with a wooden spoon. Add the water. Stir in the salt and bring to a boil. Lower heat, partially cover, and simmer, stirring once or twice, for 25 minutes.

5. Meanwhile, cook green beans in boiling water until tender but with a slight crunch, about 4 minutes after water returns to a boil. Drain and rinse under cold water.

6. Uncover the chili and stir in the diced sweet peppers and cook, uncovered, stirring once or twice, for 20 minutes.

7. Stir in the bulgur and continue to cook, stirring occasionally, for 25 minutes, or until the chili has thickened considerably. Stir in the green beans, corn, kidney beans, and chick-peas. Taste and correct seasonings; simmer 5 minutes more.

8. Serve very hot in deep or flat bowls. Either ladle chili into bowls and garnish each with the zucchini, tomatoes, scallions, and sour cream in the kitchen—easier to do in a wide, flat bowl—or arrange the vegetable garnishes on a platter and pass them with a bowl of sour cream at the table.

ADVANCE PREPARATION: Can be kept refrigerated for up to a week; it freezes well for up to a year.

MOROCCAN HARIRA WITH CHICK-PEAS, BEANS, AND LENTILS

Makes 5 dense quarts, serving at least 10

Harira is officially the soup of Ramadan, the period during the ninth month of the Islamic year in which no food may be eaten between sunrise and sunset. At dusk, harira serves as breakfast. A soup called harira is, however, eaten all year in every corner of Morocco, in as many guises as there are villages in the country. This is a particularly rich harira, as it comes from the particularly rich village of Greenwich, on Manhattan Island, where it is prepared in the kitchen of Lotfi's, a Moroccan restaurant.

SUPPER SUGGESTIONS: Though fatoush (page 176), the chopped salad with pita crisps and sumac, is Lebanese, not Moroccan, it is a fitting accompaniment. So is a plainer leafy salad. Fresh fruit salad (page 199) is a perfect dessert.

1 pound beef short ribs
8 ounces (3 cups) chick-peas, soaked
    overnight in cold water to cover by several
    inches, then drained
2 large onions, finely chopped (about 3 cups)
2½ teaspoons coarse sea salt
1 teaspoon freshly ground black pepper
½ gram saffron pistils: an abundant
    teaspoon, not pressed

4 ounces (1⅓ cups) kidney beans, rinsed and
    picked over, soaked overnight in water to
    cover by several inches, then drained
4 ounces (½ cup) French lentils
1¼ cups well-drained canned plum tomatoes,
    coarsely chopped
2 tablespoons tomato paste
1 cup long-grain white rice
Chopped coriander and parsley for garnish

I. In an 8-quart pot filled with 3 quarts of fresh water, combine the meat, chick-peas, onion, salt, pepper, and saffron. Bring to a boil, reduce heat, and simmer briskly, partially covered, for 25 to 30 minutes, stirring occasionally.

2. Stir in the kidney beans, lentils, tomatoes, and tomato paste and continue to simmer, stirring occasionally, for about another hour, or until the beans are tender.

3. At this point, how you proceed depends on whether you want the rice in the soup to be Moroccan style, which is nearly disintegrated, or firmer, which would be more to American tastes:

If firmer rice is desired, prepare the soup ahead through step 2. Twenty minutes before you plan to serve the soup, bring it to a brisk simmer, then add the rice. Cook, partially covered, for 12 to 15 minutes, or until the rice is cooked to taste.

For more authentically textured harira, let the rice cook for at least 20 minutes longer, stirring occasionally, or prepare the soup ahead with the rice cooked for 15 minutes, then reheat. The soup will thicken

(continued)

as it stands and you will need to add more broth or water to thin it out.

4. At the last minute, stir in the chopped coriander and parsley and serve piping hot in deep or flat bowls.

VARIATIONS: For a vegetarian soup, leave out the meat and perhaps add a few drops of soy sauce or Maggi liquid at the end.

Instead of beef, use lamb shoulder cut for stew, or a small chicken cut into serving pieces.

ADVANCE PREPARATION: See step 3; the soup, with or without rice, can be kept refrigerated for up to a week; it freezes perfectly for up to six months.

CHAPTER 3

MEAT SOUPS

Sausage, Mushroom, and Chick-pea Pasta Fazool
Charlotte Kovak's Gulyas Soup
Ukrainian Borscht
Scotch Broth
Polish Tripe Soup
Garbure
Kentucky Burgoo
Chili con Carne
Spiced Lentil Soup with Beef
Yemenite Lamb Soup
Armenian Meatball Soup
Mexican Meatball Soup
Chinese Meatball and Noodle Soup
Scandinavian Yellow Split Pea Soup with a Platter of Pork
Ella Weiser's Boiled Brisket and Soup
Sopa Portuguesa (Portuguese Boiled Beef Dinner)
Pozole
Cocido Madrileño
Bollito Misto
Beef Broth

SAUSAGE, MUSHROOM, AND CHICK-PEA PASTA FAZOOL

Serves 4

I use the corrupted, Italian-American name "pasta fazool" instead of the proper "pasta e fagioli" because this is a corrupt soup, a personal fantasy of pasta and beans: It takes no more than forty minutes to prepare, the beans are chick-peas, mushrooms give it a luxurious air, then a few plump sausages add a succulence that takes it over the top. If my sausage-cooking technique seems iconoclastic, that's because it is. I've found that starting them slowly in a little oil in a cold pot is a good way to keep them juicy while getting them crusty. In this case, I want all the savor of those sausages to stay in the skins and *not* to transfer to the soup. That's also the reason the sliced, cooked sausage are added at the end and not simmered in the liquid.

SUPPER SUGGESTIONS: Don't forget the crusty bread or focaccia (page 161). A Caesar salad (page 173) would begin this meal well, as would even a plainer leafy salad, or celery and Parmesan salad (page 175). For dessert, a fresh fruit salad of any kind (page 199) is refreshing, as is cranberry orange sherbet (page 202). The amaretti ricotta cheesecake (page 196) would be absolutely gala.

6 Italian sausages (about 1½ pounds)
2 tablespoons extra-virgin olive oil
1 large onion, finely chopped (about 1½ cups)
2 or 3 large garlic cloves, finely chopped or crushed
1 teaspoon fresh rosemary leaves (a 3-inch sprig)
10 ounces mushrooms, brushed off and sliced through the stems
6 cups water
2 cups canned crushed tomatoes
1 teaspoon coarse sea salt
½ teaspoon freshly ground black pepper
4 cups cooked chick-peas, or 2 (16-ounce) cans, drained
6 cups cooked small macaroni or rice

1. In a cold, 6- to 8-quart pot, combine the sausages and oil and brown the sausage on all sides over low to medium-low heat, turning often. Remove the sausages and set aside. Pour off all but 1 tablespoon of the fat.

2. Sauté the onion in the same pot, over medium heat, until it is wilted and the browned bits on the bottom of the pot have become syrupy, 3 to 5 minutes.

3. Stir in the garlic and rosemary and sauté another minute, until both smell profusely.

4. Stir in the mushrooms and sauté until mushrooms have exuded their liquid and have become limp and tender.

5. Add the water, crushed tomatoes, salt, and pepper. Stir well, cover, and bring to a boil over medium heat.

6. While waiting for the soup to boil, cut the sausages into ¼-inch-thick slices.

7. When the soup boils, reduce heat, uncover, and let it simmer gently for 5 minutes.

8. Stir in the drained chick-peas and return to a simmer.

9. Stir in the sliced sausages and turn off the heat. Or let the soup stand until serving time, then reheat gently.

10. Serve piping hot in flat bowls over macaroni or rice.

VARIATIONS: Instead of rosemary, use marjoram or oregano. Use cannellini or any other white bean instead of chick-peas. Use a small amount of chopped, reconstituted dried porcini instead of fresh mushrooms, and use their soaking water as part of the water in the recipe; along with the garlic and rosemary, sauté the porcini briefly before proceeding.

ADVANCE PREPARATION: Can be refrigerated for several days; freezes perfectly for up to six months.

CHARLOTTE KOVAK'S GULYAS SOUP

Serves 4 to 6

George Lang, in his definitive book *The Cuisine of Hungary* (Atheneum, 1971), writes that gulyas, according to a 1969 Gallup poll, was then the fifth favorite meat dish in America. And "what is usually served under that name shouldn't happen to a Roumanian."

Lang says that "lard, and bacon (either one or both) and chopped onion are absolute musts." And further, "never use any flour. Never use any other spices besides caraway. Never Frenchify it with wine. Never Germanize it with brown sauce. Never put in it any other garniture besides diced potatoes or galuska (egg dumplings)." Okay, George, it looks as if I've got a totally inauthentic gulyas recipe here—but it's deliciously light at the same time it's a substantial meal. It comes from one of my WOR radio listeners.

SUPPER SUGGESTIONS: Marinated mushrooms on endive (page 177) would be a good starter, or endive with blue cheese and walnuts (page 179), or an eggplant appetizer (pages 184 and 185). Rye bread is a must. For dessert, wacky chocolate cake (page 191) or oatmeal lace cookies (page 197), or a poached pear (page 204).

3 tablespoons vegetable oil (or lard)
2 large onions, chopped (about 3 cups)

2 tablespoons sweet paprika
2 teaspoons to 1 tablespoon caraway seeds
1½ to 2 pounds lean beef chuck, cut into
  1½-inch cubes
1 tablespoon coarse sea salt
2 teaspoons freshly ground black pepper
3 quarts water
3 tablespoons finely chopped parsley
4 medium carrots, sliced ¼ inch thick (about
  2 cups)
2 medium kohlrabi, peeled, halved, and
  sliced (about 2 cups)
4 large celery ribs, sliced ¼ inch thick
  (about 2 cups)
4 medium potatoes, cut into ½-inch cubes
  (5 to 6 cups)
Big pinch of cayenne (optional)

1. In a 5- or 6-quart pot, heat the oil over medium heat and sauté the onion until translucent, about 8 minutes.

2. Stir in the paprika and caraway seeds.

3. Add the beef, salt, pepper, and fresh cold water.

4. Cover and bring to a gentle simmer over high heat. Stir well, reduce heat, partially cover, and let simmer gently until the meat is just tender, 45 minutes to 1 hour.

5. Stir in the parsley, carrots, kohlrabi, and celery. Continue simmering on low heat for another 30 minutes.

6. Stir in the diced potatoes; bring to a boil and simmer steadily until the potatoes are tender, another 15 minutes.

7. Taste and correct seasonings—with salt, pepper, and possibly cayenne.

8. Serve piping hot in deep or flat bowls.

ADVANCE PREPARATION: Can be kept refrigerated for up to five days; it does not freeze well—the meat becomes ropy, the potatoes mealy, and the broth's fresh flavor is diminished.

UKRAINIAN BORSCHT

Serves 6

An underpinning of strong beef broth and what only seems like an overwhelming amount of barely cooked garlic is what makes a true Ukrainian borscht delicious, not the added sugar of so many recipes. Cubed root vegetables and shredded, roasted beets provide plenty of sweetness. In fact, to balance the soup's sweetness, you will want to add an acid edge with lemon juice.

SUPPER SUGGESTIONS: Roumanian eggplant salad (page 185) is a good first course. Serve it and the soup with rye bread or dark, very dense Russian-style black bread. For a midwinter meal, Swedish almond cake (page 192) is a good dessert. In fall, try the plum or apple cranberry tart (page 195).

2 pounds beef flanken or short ribs
3 quarts water
2 teaspoons coarse sea salt
1 medium carrot, scraped
1 medium celery root, peeled, one quarter cut
  out, the remaining cut into ½-inch cubes

*1 medium onion, not peeled, stuck with
several cloves*
8 whole allspice berries
*3 medium-large beets (about 1½ pounds
without tops)*
2 tablespoons butter or vegetable oil
*2 large onions, coarsely chopped (about
3 cups)*
*1 medium parsnip, peeled and cut into
½-inch cubes (about ¾ cup)*
*2 medium turnips, cut into ½-inch cubes
(about 2 cups)*
*1 large carrot, cut into ½-inch cubes (about
¾ cup)*
*2 medium potatoes, cut into ½-inch cubes
(about 2 cups)*
½ teaspoon freshly ground black pepper
1 well-rounded tablespoon tomato paste
8 to 10 large garlic cloves, crushed or pressed
Juice of ½ lemon, or more to taste
¾ to 1 cup sour cream or yogurt
3 tablespoons finely chopped dill
3 tablespoons finely chopped parsley

1. In a 4- to 6-quart pot, combine the meat
and water. Bring to a boil over high heat.
Reduce heat to a simmer and skim off the
foam. When foam stops rising to the top,
add the salt, carrot, one quarter of the celery root, the whole onion stuck with
cloves, and the allspice. Simmer gently,
partially covered, for 1½ to 2 hours, or
until the meat falls off the bone.

2. Meanwhile, preheat the oven to 400
degrees.

3. Scrub the beets and wrap them in aluminum foil. Place them in the oven for

about an hour, or until just tender. Poke
through the foil with a skewer to check for
doneness. Peel the beets and shred on the
coarse side of a grater.

4. When the meat is very tender, remove it,
strip it off the bones, and cut into small
cubes. Place in a bowl and keep covered
with foil. Strain the broth. Rinse out the
pot in which the broth was made.

5. Place the pot over medium heat, warm
the butter, and sauté the onion for 2 or 3
minutes.

6. Add the cubed celery root, parsnip,
turnips, and cubed carrot. Sauté for 5 minutes.

7. Add the strained broth, potatoes, and
shredded beets. Stir in pepper and tomato
paste. Bring to a boil. Reduce heat and simmer, uncovered, for about 10 minutes, or
until the vegetables are tender.

8. Just before serving, and while the soup is
simmering gently, stir in the crushed or
pressed garlic and the lemon juice. Remove
from heat immediately.

9. Serve piping hot in flat bowls with a
dollop of sour cream and a generous sprinkling of dill and parsley.

VARIATION: In addition to the root vegetables or as a substitute for turnips, add 2 to
4 cups coarsely chopped cabbage.

ADVANCE PREPARATION: Can be refrigerated for up to a week; do not freeze. When
reheating, bring to a simmer and add more
fresh crushed garlic just before serving.

SCOTCH BROTH

Makes about 4 quarts, serving 8

A parsimonious Scotsman would never use expensive leg of lamb for his traditional barley and split-pea-thickened broth; certainly not in the following extravagant amount. However, tender leg is much leaner than the typical neck or shoulder, it cooks more quickly, and it makes a very luxurious meal in a pot.

SUPPER SUGGESTIONS: A wedge of lettuce with creamy Roquefort dressing (page 180) is an easy first course, good especially in winter. In spring, try a plate of asparagus or a boiled artichoke (page 182 and 183). Oatmeal lace cookies (page 197) or forgotten gianduia meringues (page 198), with either fruit or ice cream, make a good dessert.

1 shank-end leg of lamb, about 3 pounds, boned
    and cut into 1-inch cubes (reserve the bone)
3 quarts water
2 teaspoons coarse sea salt
½ teaspoon freshly ground black pepper
¼ cup barley
¼ cup yellow split peas
2 medium carrots, sliced ¼ inch thick
    (about 1 cup)
1 large celery rib, sliced ½ inch thick
    (½ to ¾ cup)
1 large white turnip, peeled and cut into
    ½-inch cubes (about 2 cups)
2 large leeks (white only), halved and sliced
    (about 2 cups)
¼ cup finely chopped parsley

1. In a 5- to 7-quart pot, combine the lamb cubes, lamb bone, and water. Bring to a boil over high heat. Immediately reduce heat and skim off the foam that comes to the top. When the dark foam stops rising and only specks of meat are rising, add the salt, pepper, barley, and split peas.

2. Simmer gently, partially covered, for about 30 minutes, until the meat is tender.

3. Add the carrots, celery, turnip, and leeks. Simmer steadily until the vegetables are tender, 10 to 15 minutes more.

4. Just before serving, while the soup is simmering, stir in the parsley and remove from heat.

5. Serve piping hot in flat bowls.

ADVANCE PREPARATION: Can be kept refrigerated for up to a week. Thin with water when reheating.

POLISH TRIPE SOUP

Serves 12

Tripe, bovine stomach lining, is a specialized taste. However, when you've got the taste, you've usually got it in a big way. In Madrid, Spain, Caen, France, Florence, Italy, and San Antonio, Texas, not to mention the entire countries of Mexico and China, a particularly big deal is made about tripe. Each of those places is famous for a tripe dish, and in all—and this couldn't be a coincidence—the claim is made that their tripe dish is a hangover cure. (I've read that it's collagen in the tripe that staves off the headache.) No such claim has been made for the following soup, which is in the style served in New York's Polish coffee shops, but that doesn't mean it doesn't work to clear your head when you've drunk too much.

SUPPER SUGGESTIONS: Rye or pumpernickel is the bread you want. To go beyond a simple salad first, fresh fruit after, and to turn this into a tripe *occasion,* start with grilled mushrooms on an exotic salad (page 178), and finish with Swedish almond cake (page 192), or, for something light, cranberry orange sherbet (page 202).

10 pounds tripe
3 large leeks, white part only, quartered and
*   sliced ½ inch thick (about 2½ cups)*
3 large celery ribs, halved and sliced ½ inch
*   thick (about 2½ cups)*
3 large carrots, quartered and sliced ½ inch
*   thick (about 2½ cups)*

6 cups water
1 quart chicken broth (approximately)
1 teaspoon sweet paprika
½ teaspoon freshly ground black pepper
1 teaspoon coarse sea salt
¼ teaspoon freshly grated nutmeg
8 whole allspice berries
1 teaspoon dried marjoram
3 small bay leaves
2 tablespoons butter
1 tablespoon flour
1 tablespoon unflavored dried bread crumbs
Liquid Maggi, Bovril, or Kitchen Bouquet

1. In the largest pot you have, boil the tripe in as much water as possible, until almost soft, about 1 hour,

2. Drain the tripe and rinse it in cold water.

3. Cut the tripe into ¼- to ⅓-inch-wide strips about 3 inches long. Set aside.

4. In a 6- to 8-quart pot, combine the leeks, celery, and carrots with the 6 cups water. Cover and boil until soft, about 20 minutes.

5. Stir in the chicken broth, tripe, paprika, pepper, salt, nutmeg, allspice, marjoram, and bay leaves. Simmer briskly for 15 minutes.

6. In a small skillet, warm the butter over medium heat and cook flour and bread crumbs until lightly brown.

7. Stir the sautéed thickening into the soup and simmer 5 minutes longer, stirring constantly.

8. Taste and correct seasoning with up to a tablespoon of Maggi.

9. Serve piping hot in deep or flat bowls.

ADVANCE PREPARATION: Can be kept refrigerated for up to five days; it freezes perfectly for up to six months.

GARBURE

Makes 4 generous servings

The knowing line on garbure, the stout soup of Béarn, in southwest France, is that it must be so full of solids that a spoon can stand up in it. This one qualifies. There is also a tradition to finish the last spoonfuls of soup in your bowl by blending it with the last drops of the full-bodied red wine you'd be drinking. Try it. Maybe you'll like it. I'd rather have both the soup and the wine for their own sakes.

SUPPER SUGGESTIONS: This is a very filling soup, though of course you'll want to have some solid bread. A green salad before it or with it would be more than enough, especially if you're considering a cheese course after it. Or combine the cheese and salad in a course (with more bread). For dessert, for company, bake the Swedish almond cake (page 192) or a favorite fruit tart.

½ pound small white beans
1 pound Polish kielbasa, smoked ham, or smoked pork shoulder
1 small head cabbage, coarsely shredded

1½ tablespoons chicken fat (optional)
½ pound string beans, cut into ½-inch pieces
1 white turnip, cut into ½-inch cubes
1 onion, stuck with 4 whole cloves
2 pounds potatoes, peeled and cut into ½-inch-thick slices
½ teaspoon dried marjoram, or ¼ teaspoon dried oregano
3 to 4 parsley sprigs
½ head garlic, still attached to core and unpeeled (about 12 cloves)
½ pound chestnuts, roasted and peeled

1. Soak the beans overnight in plenty of cold water to cover. Or bring 2 quarts of water to a rolling boil in a 3-quart pot, add the beans, boil 1 minute, then let stand 30 minutes.

2. Drain beans and cover with fresh cold water. Simmer for 30 minutes, or until beans are just tender but not fully done. Drain and reserve beans.

3. In a 6- to 8-quart pot, bring 3 quarts of water to a rolling boil. Add the sausage or other meat and boil for 10 minutes.

4. Add the remaining ingredients in the order listed, starting with the reserved beans, and add them slowly enough so the water never stops boiling completely.

5. Adjust heat so soup simmers slowly, partially covered, for about 1½ hours.

6. Fish out the whole onion and the half head of garlic. Discard the onion. Squeeze the pulp out of the garlic and add it to the soup.

(continued)

7. Remove the sausage or other meat, cut it into slices or cubes, and return it to the soup.

8. Serve very hot in large flat bowls.

ADVANCE PREPARATION: The soup thickens and improves if made a day ahead, and can be kept in the refrigerator for up to a week. It suffers in the freezer, but is still acceptable.

KENTUCKY BURGOO

Serves a small army—well, at least 15

During the course of writing this book, I fortuitously met Kentuckians Curtis Balls and James White, who have a catering company and cable television show called "Bluegrass Country Cooking." They supplied me with the best corn bread recipe I have made to date (see page 163), and this classic regional soup-stew—one thick bowlful of food—that is made for Derby Day as well as other occasions when belles and good ol' boys gather for some partying. Old recipes call for coon and other game. The meats in this one have been modified to meet modern inclinations, though the incendiary spicing and lengthy cooking time have not. Say Curtis and James: "Burgoo must simmer for a minimum of seven hours, although ten to twelve is preferable." When everyone's gathered around the kettle with a bourbon in hand, time passes fast.

SUPPER SUGGESTIONS: Curtis and James would love you to have their burgoo with a sandwich of pit barbecue (either pulled pork or barbecued mutton) on the side, but they know you will more likely limit yourself to corn bread (page 163), coleslaw (page 179), and iced tea.

2 pounds lean stewing beef, cut into 1-inch cubes
½ pound boneless lamb or mutton, in one piece
1 (3- to 4-pound) chicken, cut into 16 pieces
1 pound barbecued smoked pork shoulder (optional)
4 quarts water
2 medium potatoes, cut into ½-inch dice (about 2 cups)
2 medium onions, finely chopped (about 2 cups)
2 cups small green butter beans or baby limas (fresh or frozen)
2 medium green bell peppers, cut into ¼-inch dice (about 1½ cups)
3 medium carrots, cut into ¼-inch dice (about 1½ cups)
2 cups corn kernels (fresh or frozen)
1 or more 3-inch red chilies, seeded and sliced
Coarse sea salt
Freshly ground pepper
2 cups 1-inch pieces okra (fresh or frozen)
12 medium tomatoes, peeled, cored, and coarsely chopped, or 1 quart canned California salad tomatoes
2 garlic cloves, finely chopped

¼ cup cider vinegar
*¼ cup freshly squeezed lemon juice (about
    2 lemons)*
1 cup 100-proof bourbon
2 cups chopped cabbage (optional)
1 or more tablespoons Tabasco (optional)
½ cup Worcestershire sauce (optional)

1. In a 10- to 12-quart pot, combine the beef, lamb, chicken, and the optional smoked shoulder. Add water. Cover and bring to a rolling boil. Reduce heat and simmer gently, covered, for 2 hours.

2. Remove the chicken and the meats.

3. Remove the skin and bones from the chicken and discard. Coarsely chop the chicken meat and return it to the pot.

4. Remove any gristle and fat from the meats and discard. Coarsely chop the meats and return to the pot.

5. Return the pot to a simmer.

6. Add the potatoes, onions, beans, peppers, carrots, and corn, stirring each one in before adding the next. Simmer gently, partially covered, for 3 hours, stirring occasionally and adding more water if the mixture seems too thick. (It should end up very thick.)

7. Season to taste with chilies, salt, and black pepper. Simmer 1 hour more.

8. Add the okra, tomatoes, garlic, cider vinegar, lemon juice, bourbon, optional cabbage, Tabasco, and Worcestershire sauce. Simmer for 3 hours more.

9. Serve very hot in deep or flat bowls.

ADVANCE PREPARATION: Can be kept refrigerated for up to a week; it freezes perfectly for six months.

CHILI CON CARNE

Serves 6

In the last twenty years, so much fuss has been made about authentic chili (which is to say chili without beans, according to the intimidating International Chili Society) and about original chili that I have lately had a strong urge for the chili of my childhood, which we called chili con carne whether it had meat or not (see three-bean vegetarian chili, page 75). I have no idea what recipe, if any, my mother used for our regular chili dinners, always served with saltines to crush into the bowl. When I got to college and needed chili in my life—other than the bland slop they poured on spaghetti in the cafeteria—I consulted my trusty 1959 edition of Fanny Farmer and found that chili con carne was nothing more than onion, garlic, ground beef, canned kidney beans, tomatoes, and . . . chili powder. (Speaking of bland: This recipe calls for only one clove of garlic, and it is supposed to be skewered on a toothpick so it can be removed at the end.) Without the chili powder and the beans—even sometimes with—some of my college friends' mothers spooned chili onto hamburger buns and called them Sloppy Joes. If you must, think of it as a sop.

SUPPER SUGGESTIONS: Chili with saltines, then some vanilla ice cream, is a fabulously indulgent meal to me. Corn bread (page 163) and biscuits (page 164) go great with chili. Coleslaw (page 179) is a great addition, too.

3 tablespoons vegetable oil
3 medium or 2 large onions, finely chopped
  (about 3 cups)
6 to 8 large garlic cloves, finely chopped or
  crushed
2 pounds lean ground beef
2 (28-ounce) cans plum tomatoes, with their
  juice, coarsely chopped
2 teaspoons coarse sea salt, or to taste
3 tablespoons chili powder
¼ to ½ teaspoon cayenne
1 teaspoon dried oregano
½ teaspoon ground cumin seeds
2 (16-ounce) cans kidney beans, drained
  (not rinsed)

FOR THE GARNISH:
About 1 cup sour cream
1 cup shredded Monterey Jack or Cheddar
  cheese
½ cup diced onion
¼ cup diced fresh chilies
¼ cup chopped coriander
1 cup diced avocado
6 lime wedges

1. In a 5- to 6-quart pot, heat the oil over medium heat and sauté the onions until they begin to brown, about 10 minutes.

2. Stir in the garlic and sauté another 30 seconds.

3. Add the ground beef and, with a wooden spoon, break it up and turn constantly until it loses its raw color.

4. Add the chopped tomatoes, salt, chili powder, ¼ teaspoon cayenne, oregano, and cumin. Stir well, partially cover, and let simmer gently for 30 minutes, stirring occasionally.

5. Taste and add more salt and cayenne if desired, remembering that the beans will tone it down.

6. Add the canned beans, stir well, partially cover again, and adjust heat so chili simmers gently for another 10 minutes.

7. Ladle into deep bowls and serve side bowls with garnishes.

VARIATION: If you want to take the trouble to blend your own chili powder, this is my unorthodox recipe: Place a variety of dried chilies, seeds and all, in the blender and process into flakes. If you overdo the seasoning and want to tone it down—or simply smooth out the flavor in general—melt in a 1-ounce square of unsweetened baking chocolate.

ADVANCE PREPARATION: Can be kept refrigerated for up to a week; it freezes perfectly without canned beans for up to six months. Bring to a simmer before proceeding and, if previously frozen, add the beans. When reheating, you will probably have to reseason and add more liquid.

SPICED LENTIL SOUP WITH BEEF

Makes 5 quarts, serving about 10

The seasoning in this old Sephardic Jewish recipe is intentionally intense. I like to imagine that the dish's abundance of spices was an ostentation to show off the family's wealth. The recipe was passed on to me as generically Sephardic, which refers to the Jews who settled at one time or another in Spain, but then, during the Inquisition of the late 1400s, emigrated to Turkey, Greece, Syria, and other eastern Mediterranean countries, as well as to North Africa. From the spicing, I would guess this thick, highly perfumed soup has more North African influence than anything else.

SUPPER SUGGESTIONS: For a company meal, serve fatoush (page 176), the Lebanese salad, before the soup. Crusty bread is in order for both, though pita is acceptable, too. For dessert, turn out as elaborate a fruit salad (page 199) as you can make, plus some cookies, plain or fancy, store-bought or homemade.

¼ cup extra-virgin olive oil
3 medium onions, finely chopped (about 3 cups)
2 pounds lean stew beef, cut into 1-inch chunks
2 medium carrots, sliced ¼ inch thick (about 1 cup)
2 large celery ribs, sliced (about 1½ cups)
1 (35-ounce) can Italian plum tomatoes, coarsely chopped, with their juice
2 quarts water
1 pound lentils
5 large garlic cloves, finely chopped
2 large bay leaves
1 cup finely chopped parsley leaves
1 teaspoon ground cumin
1 teaspoon ground coriander seeds
½ teaspoon ground cinnamon
1 teaspoon saffron pistils
1 teaspoon coarse sea salt
1 teaspoon freshly ground black pepper
¼ cup freshly squeezed lemon juice
Lemon slices or wedges for garnish

1. In a 6- to 8-quart pot, combine the olive oil, onions, and beef over medium heat. Cook, stirring frequently, until the onions are translucent and the meat has lost its raw color, 8 to 10 minutes.

2. Add the carrots and celery and continue to sauté another 3 minutes, tossing constantly.

3. Stir in the tomatoes with all their juices, water, lentils, garlic, bay leaves, parsley, cumin, coriander, cinnamon, saffron, and salt (not the pepper, yet). Cover and bring to a boil.

4. Reduce heat and simmer steadily, partially covered, stirring occasionally, for 1½ to 2 hours, until the lentils are very tender.

5. Add the pepper and the lemon juice. Taste and correct with salt. Add more water, if necessary, to bring the soup to desired consistency; it should be thick.

(continued)

6. Serve piping hot in flat bowls, each bowlful topped with a slice or wedge of lemon and a sprinkling of parsley.

VARIATION: A 3- to 4-pound chicken, cut into 16 serving pieces, may be substituted for the beef. Or use lamb instead of beef.

ADVANCE PREPARATION: Can be kept refrigerated at least five days; the meat gets somewhat ropy when frozen. You will have to add water or broth when reheating.

YEMENITE LAMB SOUP

Serves 6

This is a highly flavored broth with meat and potatoes. The spice mixture that makes it distinctively Yemenite—the black pepper, cardamom, cumin, cloves, and hot pepper—is called *hawaish* in Yemenite and no self-respecting cook would be without his or her own special blend of it on the shelf. As you are not likely to have much use for a jar of it in your spice collection, I've broken it down to its component parts here.

SUPPER SUGGESTIONS: Plenty of crusty bread is in order, preferably one that's at least slightly sour. A good first course is baked eggplant and garlic or Roumanian eggplant salad (pages 184, 185), or, in the summer, a platter of sliced tomatoes with olive oil, or both eggplant and tomatoes.

And fatoush (page 176), though from a different part of the Middle East, goes very well, too. Any fruit dessert is appropriate, especially strawberries in two liqueurs (page 200) or berry compote (page 201).

*1½ pounds boneless lamb shoulder, cut into
    2-inch chunks*
1 quart water
*3 medium-large potatoes (about 1¼ pounds),
    peeled and cut in half*
*1 medium onion, coarsely chopped (about
    1 cup)*
*1 medium tomato, peeled and coarsely
    chopped (about ¾ cup)*
1 teaspoon coarse sea salt
¼ cup finely chopped cilantro
½ teaspoon freshly ground black pepper
¼ teaspoon ground cardamom
½ teaspoon ground cumin
Big pinch of ground cloves
Big pinch of red pepper flakes
Big pinch of saffron threads

I. In a 3- to 4-quart pot, combine the lamb cubes and water. Bring slowly to a boil, uncovered, skimming any foam that comes to the top.

2. When the foam stops rising, add all the remaining ingredients and simmer gently, partially covered, stirring occasionally, until the meat is very tender, about 1½ hours.

3. Serve piping hot in deep bowls.

VARIATION: Five minutes before the end of the cooking, add 1 (16-ounce) can chick-peas, drained and rinsed under cold running water.

ADVANCE PREPARATION: Can be kept refrigerated for up to a week; do not freeze because the potatoes become mealy and the broth loses its punch.

ARMENIAN MEATBALL SOUP

Serves 4

E ven their enemies will tell you that the Armenians are the best cooks in the Middle East. This recipe at least proves they know some culinary sleight of hand: A fast onion chopper can turn out this substantial soup (two starches, rice, *and* potatoes!) in thirty minutes, though it tastes as if it took all afternoon to make.

SUPPER SUGGESTIONS: Bruschetta (page 160) or an eggplant salad plate (page 185) makes this homey entrée seem more festive. For dessert, fresh fruit and cookies are fine. For company, bake an apple cranberry tart (page 195) or poach pears in red wine (page 204). Pita is an appropriate bread, but better yet is a crusty loaf of merely lightly sour sourdough.

2 medium onions, finely chopped (about 2 cups)
3 tablespoons butter
2 cups canned tomato purée
5 cups water
1 pound lean ground beef

6 tablespoons finely chopped fresh dill
1 egg
1 teaspoon salt
½ teaspoon freshly ground black pepper
1 medium green pepper, diced (about ¾ cup)
2 medium potatoes, cut into ½-inch cubes (about 2 cups)
½ cup uncooked white rice

1. In a 5- to 6-quart pot, over medium heat, sauté the onions in butter until lightly browned, 10 to 12 minutes.

2. Add the tomato purée and water. Increase heat slightly, bring to a simmer, and let simmer gently, uncovered, for 10 minutes.

3. Meanwhile, using your hands, work together the beef, 2 tablespoons of the dill, the egg, salt, and pepper. Shape into 1-inch meatballs. The mixture should make at least 24.

4. Drop the meatballs into the simmering soup, then add the green pepper, potatoes, and rice. Cover and simmer gently for about 15 minutes, stirring once or twice, until the rice and potatoes are tender.

5. Serve immediately in flat bowls, with the remaining dill as garnish.

ADVANCE PREPARATION: The soup cooks so quickly it hardly pays to do it ahead and suffer soggy rice. However, to have the base ready as much as a day in advance, cook through step 3 and refrigerate the soup, meatballs, and pepper separately. Refrigerate the chopped potato in water to cover. Bring soup to a simmer before proceeding. Do not freeze.

MEXICAN MEATBALL SOUP

Makes about 2½ quarts, serving 6

This is not a real Mexican recipe, although Mexicans do make meatball soup. What gives these meatballs their Mexican character is the fresh coriander. The broth has a red chili in it for a trace of fire. Somehow these subtleties make this simple soup taste decidedly south of the border.

SUPPER SUGGESTIONS: An avocado and onion salad is a good way to start. Hot flour tortillas go with the soup, though you might also serve corn chips (fritas) to crumble into the soup, or simply boil some rice and put a heaping half cup or so into each bowl. For dessert, ice cream and cookies are sufficient.

FOR THE MEATBALLS:
⅓ cup raw white rice
1 medium red onion, finely chopped (about 1 cup)
⅓ cup finely chopped fresh coriander leaves
1 cup soft, fresh bread crumbs
1 egg
⅓ cup milk
1 teaspoon salt
3 garlic cloves, finely chopped
½ teaspoon dried oregano (preferably Mexican)
1 pound lean ground beef

FOR THE SOUP:
2 quarts beef broth

1 bay leaf
2 medium carrots, cut into ¼-inch pieces
1 (3-inch-long) red chili, seeded and thinly sliced
⅓ cup Madeira

1. In a small pot, bring 1 cup of water to the boil. Add the rice. Boil 5 minutes; drain. Place the rice in a large mixing bowl.

2. Add the chopped onion and coriander, the bread crumbs, egg, milk, salt, garlic, and oregano. With a fork, blend thoroughly.

3. Add the beef and, with the fork, or your hands, blend it into the rice and bread mixture.

4. Shape the meat into 1-inch meatballs. There should be about 30.

5. In a 4- to 6-quart pot, combine the broth, bay leaf, carrots, and chili. Bring to a boil. Add the meatballs, cover, and simmer gently for 30 minutes. Add the Madeira and simmer 1 minute longer. Remove the bay leaf before serving.

6. Serve piping hot, offering lime wedges and pico de gallo (recipe follows) to further season the soup.

ADVANCE PREPARATION: The soup can be kept refrigerated for up to a week; it freezes perfectly, for up to six months. The salsa should be made the same day it is served.

PICO DE GALLO

Makes about 4 cups salsa

2 large tomatoes, cored and cut into ¼-inch
   cubes (about 2 cups)
1 medium onion, finely chopped (about 1 cup)
2 jalapeño peppers, seeded and finely
   chopped (less than ¼ cup)
2 to 4 tablespoons finely chopped coriander
1 small green bell pepper, cut into ¼-inch
   dice (about ¾ cup)
1 or 2 large garlic cloves, finely chopped
Juice of 2 limes
½ teaspoon salt

Combine all the ingredients and let stand
at room temperature for at least 1 hour to
blend the flavors.

CHINESE MEATBALL AND NOODLE SOUP

Makes about 4 quarts, serving 6 to 8

To complete our mini international
meatball soup tour, here's a very quickly
made one with pork, plenty of vegetables, and cellophane noodles—truly a
whole meal in a pot.

SUPPER SUGGESTIONS: All you need is
stringbeans with garlic and sesame oil and
a simple dessert, such as fresh pineapple or
other fresh fruit, or ice cream.

FOR THE MEATBALLS:
12 ounces ground pork
2 tablespoons very finely chopped scallions
   (some green)
2 teaspoons very finely chopped fresh ginger
1½ teaspoons very finely chopped garlic
½ teaspoon fine sea salt

FOR THE BROTH:
8 cups light chicken broth (two 14½-ounce
   cans, plus water)
2 medium carrots, cut into julienne strips
   (about 1 cup)
1 large celery rib, sliced very thin on the
   diagonal (about ¾ cup)
1 large garlic clove, finely chopped
1 teaspoon finely chopped fresh ginger
1 cup thinly sliced scallions
1 medium head bok choy, shredded (about
   8 cups)
1 (14-ounce) can baby corn, drained, rinsed,
   and halved lengthwise
6 ounces cellophane noodles, soaked in
   boiling water for 10 minutes
1 tablespoon soy sauce
2 teaspoons sesame oil

1. In a small bowl, knead together with
your hands the ground pork, scallions, ginger, garlic, and salt.

2. Form into ¾-inch meatballs. You should
have between 26 and 30.

3. In a 4- to 6-quart pot, bring the broth to
a rolling boil. Add the meatballs and boil
for 15 minutes. With a slotted spoon or
skimmer, remove the meatballs and set
aside.

4. Add the carrots, celery, and garlic to the broth. Let boil 5 minutes, until the vegetables are barely tender.

5. Add the scallions, bok choy, and baby corn. Simmer another 5 minutes.

6. Add the soaked cellophane noodles, the soy sauce, and sesame oil. Stir well and boil 2 or 3 more minutes, until the noodles are tender.

7. Stir in the meatballs.

8. Immediately ladle into wide bowls and serve piping hot.

ADVANCE PREPARATION: The meatballs may be mixed ahead and refrigerated for one day. The soup should be prepared just before it is served.

SCANDINAVIAN YELLOW SPLIT PEA SOUP WITH A PLATTER OF PORK

Makes 4 quarts, serving 8 to 12

This is an adaptation of a recipe from Jane Grigson's *Book of European Cookery* (Atheneum, 1983). Nowhere else have I read about pea soup as a full-scale boiled dinner, though it is apparently traditional. Cleverly, the peas are cooked to a thick purée in one pot, while the pork cuts boil in another with some vegetables. Finally, the peas and the broth with the vegetables are joined for a thick first-course soup. The pork is eaten as a second course for its own sake.

SUPPER SUGGESTIONS: Though it is hardly Scandinavian, coleslaw (page 179) is a perfect accompaniment to the meats, as are mustards, both hot and sweet, plus a sauce made of grated horseradish blended with sour cream. Rye bread with everything would be appropriate. For dessert, either Norwegian pound cake (page 192) or Swedish almond cake (page 192) are thematic.

1 pound yellow split peas
2 quarts water
1 pound bacon (smoked or unsmoked),
*   in one piece*
6 cups water
3 large leeks, white part only, halved and
*   sliced ¼ inch thick (about 2½ cups)*

*3 large carrots, cut into ½-inch dice (about
    2½ cups)*
*1 large onion, coarsely chopped (about
    1 cup)*
*1 pound celery root, cut into ½-inch cubes,
    or 6 to 8 pale green, inner ribs of celery,
    chopped*
½ teaspoon dried thyme
*2 large potatoes (about 1 pound), peeled and
    cut into ½-inch cubes (3½ to 4 cups)*
*8 to 10 (¾-inch-thick) center-cut smoked
    pork chops*
*¾ to 1½ pounds knockwurst, franks, or
    kielbasa*

1. In a 3-quart pot, combine the split peas and 2 quarts of water. Simmer briskly, partially covered, until the peas are soft, about 1 hour.

2. Purée, either through a food mill, in a blender or food processor, or in the pot with an immersion blender. Set aside.

3. Meanwhile, in a 6- to 8-quart pot, combine the bacon with 6 cups of water. Cover and bring to a boil; boil for 1 hour.

4. Add all the vegetables except the potatoes and, if necessary, enough boiling water to cover them well. Cover the pot and return to a steady simmer for about 15 minutes.

5. Add the thyme, potatoes, pork chops, and sausage. Simmer very gently for about 45 minutes.

6. Remove the bacon and all the meats from the broth. Arrange on a platter, cover with foil, and keep warm in a low oven.

7. Stir the pea purée into the vegetable pot and add extra water if the soup is too thick for your taste.

8. Taste and correct seasoning. You may need to add salt and pepper.

9. Serve the soup piping hot, as a first course. Serve the meats separately.

ADVANCE PREPARATION: Not advisable; once the meats are cooked they should be eaten within an hour or so.

ELLA WEISER'S BOILED BRISKET AND SOUP

**Makes about 4 quarts broth,
serving 8 to 10 with meat**

This soup is from my friend Dalia Carmel Goldstein, whose mother, Ella Weiser, a physician, may or may not have brought the recipe to Tel Aviv from her native Latvia. Dalia's own touch, and I think the touch that really takes the dish out of the ordinary and, in fact, makes it taste Israeli, is the huge amount of parsley and dill.

Dr. Ella Weiser, her daughter says, served the soup clear, with the soup vegetables diced into it. Dalia likes to serve the vegetables puréed into the broth. Either way, and/or with noodles, the soup has a gorgeous aroma that fills the house.

(continued)

As you might guess, having the meat trimmed of almost all visible fat is a modern alteration of the recipe, too. Cooking the meat with more fat, then trimming it after it is cooked, would be more my style; it keeps the meat moister. In fact, Dalia remembers that her father's big treat was to cut thin slices of the soft, cooked fat, put them on fresh challah . . . with coarse salt and a dab of horseradish . . . there's no need to wait for the Messiah.

SUPPER SUGGESTIONS: With the broth as a first course and the meat with horseradish as a second, only dessert—say some pound cake and fresh fruit or forgotten gianduia meringues (page 198)—need be considered. On the other hand, Roumanian eggplant salad (page 185) is a great beginning to it all.

*1 (3- to 4-pound) first cut brisket, well
    trimmed*
2 to 3 marrow bones, about 1½ pounds
3 carrots, peeled
2 medium turnips, peeled and quartered
2 medium parsnips, peeled and halved
¼ large celery root or 1 small one, quartered
3 celery ribs, well washed and cut in half
*1 whole large onion, peeled and studded
    with 4 cloves*
3 whole large, unpeeled garlic cloves
2 small bay leaves
4 quarts water (approximately)
1 tablespoon coarse salt
12 black peppercorns
1 bunch flat-leaf parsley (at least 40 sprigs)
1 bunch dill (at least 40 sprigs)

1. Place the brisket and the marrow bones in an 8-quart pot. On top of it, arrange the carrots, turnips, parsnips, celery root, celery, onion stuck with cloves, garlic, and bay leaves.

2. Cover with about 4 quarts cold water and bring to a boil. Skim off the scum that rises to the surface, without stirring the contents of the pot. When the water comes to a rolling boil, reduce the heat to keep the liquid at a gentle simmer. Continue to skim until any foam that may come to the top is pure white.

3. Add the salt and pepper, then the two bunches of herbs. Cover and cook gently for 2½ to 3 hours, or until the meat is tender. Let cool about 30 minutes.

4. Remove the meat, marrow bones, and bay leaves. Either keep the meat warm or refrigerate it. Discard the bay leaves. The marrow is the "chef's share," to be spread on bread, as Dalia's father did the soft meat fat.

5. If serving the soup right away, skim it as best you can. Otherwise, chill the broth with the vegetables, then skim the fat when it has hardened on the surface of the broth.

6. Serve the broth hot as a first course, either with the vegetables diced and returned to the broth or puréed into the broth, followed by the sliced meat, reheated gently in the broth if refrigerated.

ADVANCE PREPARATION: Can be kept refrigerated for up to five days. The broth, either clear or with puréed vegetables, freezes perfectly. Do not freeze the meat or the vegetables if they are diced or still in big pieces.

SOPA PORTUGUESA
(PORTUGUESE BOILED BEEF DINNER)

**Makes about 4 quarts broth,
serving 8 to 10 with meat**

I have no idea where I got this recipe, or if it is indeed Portuguese. It says so on the scrap of paper I wrote the ingredients on twenty years ago, but there's a big question mark after the name of the recipe and no Portuguese book in my collection makes reference to such a dish, nor does any person of my acquaintance know it. In any case, the ingredient proportions were so intriguing I finally had to make it. The soup turned out so incredibly fragrant and unusual I have to share it.

SUPPER SUGGESTIONS: I didn't note what to do with the broth when I jotted down the recipe, except to add a dash of vinegar, but it seemed a natural receptacle for separately boiled winter vegetables—carrots, cabbage, turnips, celery root, parsnips, potatoes—and chick-peas. Or serve the soup with only the chick-peas and reserve the boiled vegetables for dressing the platter of meat, which is marvelous embellished with nothing more than a sprinkling of coarse sea salt. You'll want crusty bread, too. For dessert, pound cake (page 192) or a poached pear (page 204) fills the bill.

1 (4½- to 5-pound) boneless chuck roast
1 to 2 pounds beef soup bones (optional)
1½ ounces (1 full jar!) pickling spices
¼ teaspoon ground cumin
8 to 10 celery ribs, with their leaves, cut into thirds
4 large onions, peeled and cut into quarters
10 large garlic cloves, peeled and lightly crushed
1 tablespoon salt
4 quarts water (approximately)

1. In an 8- to 10-quart pot, combine all the ingredients over high heat, making sure there is enough fresh, cold water to barely cover the meat.

2. When the liquid starts to simmer, skim off the foam that comes to the top. Never let the liquid cook harder than a gentle simmer.

3. When the foam has stopped rising, reduce the heat and partially cover the pot. Simmer gently for 2½ to 3 hours, until the meat is very tender. Check it by sticking it with a two-pronged kitchen fork; when done, the fork should enter easily.

4. Remove the meat and let it rest on a platter for a few minutes.

5. Meanwhile, strain the broth, then skim it if desired.

6. Ladle the hot broth into deep or wide bowls, garnishing as desired.

7. Serve the meat hot as a separate course; keep the sliced meat hot by covering it with hot broth.

ADVANCE PREPARATION: Can be made entirely ahead the same day it is to be served, then gently reheated. Or it can be kept up to a week in the refrigerator; the broth freezes perfectly for up to a year.

POZOLE

Serves 6 to 8

Street stands selling steaming bowls of pozole are a fixture at Mexican fiestas, where the broth is flavored with a pig's head and maybe some tails and ears. You and your guests will probably appreciate this version much more. The pork shoulder or butt provides plenty of succulent meat. Hominy, the main addition to the broth, is puffed corn kernels. It is hard to find in the Northeast, dried or canned, though available in specialty stores. In the rest of the country, both dried and canned hominy are available in many supermarkets.

SUPPER SUGGESTIONS: For an impressive menu, serve potato and shrimp salad (page 186) first, hot flour tortillas with the soup, and amaretti ricotta cheesecake (page 196) for dessert.

1 (5-pound) fresh pork shoulder or butt
2 large garlic cloves, crushed
2 tablespoons coarse sea salt
4 quarts cold water
4 (14-ounce) cans whole hominy

FOR THE GARNISHES:
4 limes, cut into wedges
4 ripe Hass avocados, pitted, peeled, and cut
  into ½-inch cubes
1 large Bermuda onion, diced
Oregano
Crushed red pepper flakes
Fritas (store-bought or homemade corn chips)

I. In an 8-quart pot, combine the pork, garlic, salt, and water. Bring to a boil. Lower heat immediately so that water barely simmers. Cook gently, partially covered, until very tender, about 2½ hours.

2. Remove the meat from the liquid and let cool enough to handle.

3. Cool the broth, then skim the fat off the top.

4. Remove the meat from its bones and shred. Place the meat in a shallow casserole or gratin dish and cover with just enough broth to keep it moist.

5. About 20 minutes before serving, bring the skimmed broth to a boil and drain the hominy, reserving half the liquid from the cans. Add the hominy and reserved liquid to the broth. Simmer together 20 minutes.

6. To serve, place portions of pork in wide, deep bowls, then ladle on piping hot broth and some hominy. Serve the garnishes in separate plates and have each diner add the garnishes to taste, squeezing in lime juice, crushing in the fritas, or adding them whole.

ADVANCE PREPARATION: Can be kept refrigerated for several days; do not freeze.

COCIDO MADRILEÑO

Serves 4

My friend Eric Jan Zalis, who lived in Madrid for three years and is about to marry a Madrileña, put this recipe together from two sources: his mother-in-law-to-be and the Casa Paco restaurant in Madrid. He says "I've boiled it down to the basics, no pun intended. . . . There are very few dishes in Spain known as being explicitly from Madrid itself. Most of the cuisine was brought to Spain's capital from other regions of the country in the early 1600s by frustrated queens and kings. Spain's aristocrats demanded that food fit for royalty be brought into the capital because of the lack of diversity in Madrid's cuisine. Cocido Madrileño is as Madrileño as you can get. It is Madrid's gastronomic claim to fame. While other versions of cocido exist in other parts of the country, Madrid's version is considered the best."

SUPPER SUGGESTIONS: Only a dessert is necessary, say cranberry orange sherbet (page 202), or something more substantial, amaretti ricotta cheesecake (page 196).

3½ quarts water
1 beef marrow bone
1 ham bone (this is usually taken from what is left of the jamón Serrano; a prosciutto bone would do nicely as a substitute)
2 veal knuckles
4 ounces corned pork (1 loin chop or 2 corned ribs)

¾ pound chick-peas, soaked overnight
½ pound stewing beef
1 (4-pound) chicken
4 ounces ham in one piece (Serrano-type or prosciutto)
4 ounces chorizo
1 onion, halved
2 carrots, coarsely chopped
1 celery rib, left whole
2 medium leeks, white and light green, left whole
4 medium potatoes, peeled and whole
½ pound string beans, cut up
8 ounces fine egg noodles (fidelini are perfect)
Chopped parsley, for garnish

1. In an 8-quart pot, bring the water to a boil. Add all the bones and the corned pork.

2. With a slotted spoon, skim off the foam that rises to the surface. When the foam has stopped rising, reduce the heat to a simmer and continue simmering for several minutes.

3. Add the chick-peas, the beef, chicken, ham, chorizo, and the onion, carrots, celery, and leeks. Cover again and let simmer gently for an hour.

4. Add the potatoes and the string beans and let simmer for about 30 minutes longer, or until all the meats and vegetables are tender.

5. Remove from the heat and let the covered pot rest while you prepare the soup.

6. Strain 2½ quarts of the cooking broth into another pot, leaving just enough broth behind to keep the meats moistened. Bring the strained broth to a boil, then cook the egg noodles in it.

7. As soon as the noodles are cooked, ladle the soup and noodles into bowls and garnish with chopped parsley. Serve as a first course.

8. Drain the chick-peas, reserving any remaining broth, and place on a serving platter accompanied by the onion, carrots, celery, leeks, potatoes, and green beans. Place this dish on the table accompanied by a cruet of extra-virgin olive oil and one of red wine vinegar for those who would like to add either or both to their legumes and vegetables.

9. Place all the meats, cut into serving pieces, on a separate platter. Pass small hot green chili peppers and small pickled onions on a separate dish for those who wish to spice things up.

NOTE: The flavorful broth can be used for making other soups. Finely mince leftover meats and sausage, add egg and bread crumbs, then roll them into dumplings for the soup. Or you can fry these little balls in olive oil and serve them as an appetizer or *tapa.* The Spaniards love them that way. Leftover vegetables can be puréed with some of the broth, seasoned with nutmeg, and served a day or two later.

ADVANCE PREPARATION: For optimum succulence, the meats must be served the same day they are cooked, preferably within hours. However, leftover broth may be kept refrigerated for up to a week, or frozen for up to six months. Leftover meats can be kept refrigerated for several days, then recycled into a casserole or hash, or reheated gently in some broth.

BOLLITO MISTO

Serves 10 to 12

When not eaten in a restaurant that specializes in it, this grand Italian-style boiled dinner is reserved for special family meals. It is not difficult to do: The trick is the timing. Beef roast and tongue take about three hours; slices of veal shank (osso buco) take about two hours to achieve buttery tenderness; a typical American chicken takes no more than an hour to cook at a slow, steady simmer.

Traditionally, the meats are left in their broth all during the service of the dish so they remain moist. I prefer to serve the delicious broth first, with some fine pasta or tortellini, then to present the meats on a platter, each one sliced just enough to provide a first round for everyone. Side sauces are as much a part of a grand bollito as the meats and broth. I offer several recipes, of which you can make one or many. In addition, mustard-flavored fruits in syrup are a traditional accompaniment to bollito. These can be purchased in jars in a specialty food store.

SUPPER SUGGESTIONS: Serve crusty, light bread and add dessert, say poached pears (page 204) and oatmeal lace cookies (page 197), or amaretti ricotta cheesecake (page 196).

1 (5-pound) beef tongue
1 (4-pound) beef brisket (preferably second cut) or chuck roast
4 or 5 (1½-inch-thick) slices veal shank (osso buco)
1 (4-pound) chicken
1 (3-pound) cotechino sausage (optional)
2 large carrots
2 large celery ribs
1 large or 2 medium onions, peeled and stuck with 6 cloves

1. Cook all the meats together except the cotechino (if you are able to get one). If you don't have a pot large enough to hold them all, cook the bollito in two pots, using one of each vegetable in each pot. Place the meats in the pot (or pots) with the vegetables, then cover with freshly drawn cold water. Remove the meats and set aside.

2. Bring the water, with the vegetables, to a rolling boil.

3. Put in the tongue and the beef. When the water begins to boil again, reduce the heat so that the water simmers gently, and, with a slotted spoon, skim off any foam that rises to the surface.

4. When the foam stops rising, adjust the heat so that the water simmers gently, but steadily.

5. After 1 hour of cooking at a slow simmer, take the tongue out. Let it cool slightly, then peel it. Cut off and discard the gristle and fat at the base and return the tongue to the pot.

6. Add the veal. Cover, bring back to a simmer, and cook at a steady simmer for another hour.

7. Add the chicken to the pot and cook another hour at a steady simmer.

8. Keep the meats in the broth until ready to serve, which should be within an hour.

9. Meanwhile, cook the cotechino in an abundant amount of water, bringing the water to a boil with the cotechino already in it, for 2 to 2½ hours, depending on the size of the sausage. (Ask your butcher if his sausage needs to be presoaked, and how long he recommends it be cooked.) Do not combine the cotechino water with the meat broth. (See pages 104–5 for sauces to serve with bollito misto.)

ADVANCE PREPARATION: For optimum succulence, the meats must be served the same day they are cooked, preferably within hours. However, leftover broth may be kept refrigerated for up to a week, or frozen for up to six months. Leftover meats can be kept refrigerated for several days, then recycled into a casserole or hash, or reheated gently in some broth.

SALSA VERDE

Makes about 1 cup strong sauce

This is the most typical condiment-sauce accompaniment to a bollito misto.

1 firmly packed cup Italian parsley leaves
8 watercress sprigs
1 large garlic clove
1 scallion, with most of the green, chopped
4 anchovy fillets
2 tablespoons capers, finely chopped
1 tablespoon red wine vinegar
½ cup extra-virgin olive oil
Fine sea salt

1. In a large mortar with a pestle, or in a food processor, combine the parsley, watercress, garlic, scallion, and anchovies. Pound or process until nearly a paste.

2. Mix in the chopped capers and vinegar.

3. With a fork, gradually beat the oil into the mixture in the mortar, or, if using a processor, add it in a thin stream with the processor on.

4. Taste and add salt if necessary.

ADVANCE PREPARATION: Can be refrigerated for up to a week. Bring back to room temperature and stir thoroughly before serving.

BAGNET D'TOMATICHE

Makes about 3 cups

The name is Piedmontese dialect for "little bath of tomatoes." It is always served with the *gran bui* (bollito misto), according to Anna Del Conte in her *Gastronomy of Italy* (Prentice-Hall, 1987).

1½ pounds ripe tomatoes, skinned and
    chopped, or 1 (35-ounce) can plum
    tomatoes, drained and coarsely chopped
1 small onion, coarsely chopped (about
    ½ cup)
1 carrot, sliced ¼ inch thick (about ½ cup)
1 large celery rib, sliced (about ½ cup)
2 large sage leaves, torn into pieces
1 small fresh rosemary sprig
2 large garlic cloves, peeled and cut in half
20 to 25 parsley sprigs
¼ teaspoon dried marjoram
¼ to ½ teaspoon hot red pepper flakes
½ teaspoon coarse sea salt
½ tablespoon red wine vinegar
1 generous teaspoon tomato paste
2 teaspoons sugar
¼ teaspoon ground cinnamon

1. In a 3- to 4- quart saucepan, combine all the ingredients except the vinegar, tomato paste, sugar, and cinnamon.

2. Bring to a simmer over medium-low heat, then let simmer steadily, uncovered, for 30 minutes.

3. Remove the sage, rosemary, and parsley. Discard.

4. Purée the sauce through a food mill or sieve and return to the pan.

5. Mix in the vinegar, tomato paste, sugar, and cinnamon and cook until the sauce is thick, about 10 minutes.

6. Taste and adjust seasonings, adding more red pepper, salt, vinegar, tomato paste, sugar, and/or cinnamon.

7. Serve warm or cold.

ADVANCE PREPARATION: Can be kept refrigerated for up to five days; it freezes perfectly.

SWEET PEPPER AND TOMATO SAUCE

Makes about 3½ cups

This is another red sauce, inspired by Marcella Hazan, that is traditionally served with boiled meats.

¼ cup delicately flavored olive oil
5 medium onions, peeled and sliced thin
3 red bell peppers, cored, seeded, and peeled, then cut into ½-inch-wide strips
Pinch of hot red pepper flakes
2 cups canned imported Italian tomatoes, with their juice, or 3 cups cut-up fresh tomatoes
½ teaspoon coarse sea salt

1. In a 3-quart saucepan, warm the oil over medium heat and sauté the onions until they are wilted, about 5 minutes.

2. Stir in the peppers and continue cooking over medium heat, tossing occasionally, until the peppers and onions are very soft, about 30 minutes.

3. Stir in the hot pepper flakes, tomatoes, and salt. Reduce heat and simmer gently for about 25 minutes, until the sauce is thick.

4. Taste and correct for salt and hot pepper.

5. Serve hot or warm.

ADVANCE PREPARATION: Can be refrigerated for up to five days; it freezes perfectly.

HORSERADISH SAUCE

Freshly grated horseradish is all you need to put out with the meats—it goes especially well with the beef and tongue. However, to make it into a sauce, to each cup of horseradish, blend in ½ cup full-flavored olive oil, 1 to 2 tablespoons red wine or balsamic vinegar, and salt to taste.

BEEF BROTH

For a strong beef broth, follow steps 1 and 3 of the Ukrainian Borscht recipe (page 83), substituting a rib of celery for the celery root, a bay leaf for the allspice, and perhaps adding a few sprigs of parsley. Another good all-purpose beef broth results from Ella Weiser's Boiled Brisket and Soup recipe (page 97).

ADVANCE PREPARATION: Chill and skim off all fat. Can be kept refrigerated for up to a week, then for another few days if brought to a boil again. Either broth can be frozen for up to six months.

CHAPTER 4

CHICKEN SOUPS

THAI CHICKEN AND COCONUT SOUP

Serves 4

Don't let the exotic southeast Asian flavors lead you to believe this is a difficult dish to prepare. After making the soup once, you're likely to make it part of your regular repertoire. It scents the kitchen with a flowery perfume and the broth has a silky richness that is incredibly comforting.

SUPPER SUGGESTIONS: String beans with garlic and sesame oil (page 187) could be served with the soup and rice. For the family, fresh fruit is all you need to complete the meal. For informal company, cranberry orange sherbet (page 202), a store-bought tropical flavor sorbet, and cookies would be in order.

1 (4-pound) chicken, cut into 16 serving pieces
6 cups cold water
3 (7- or 8-inch) stalks lemongrass, bruised, then cut into 1-inch pieces
1 round tablespoon dried galanga chips
5 red or green (4-inch-long) chilies, halved and seeded
6 (double) kaffir lime leaves
10 black peppercorns
1 (13½-ounce) can thick unsweetened coconut milk (sometimes called coconut cream)
3 tablespoons finely chopped scallions (with some green)
1 (15-ounce) can straw mushrooms, drained and rinsed

Juice of 2 limes (about 3 tablespoons)
3 tablespoons Thai fish sauce (nam pla)
2 tablespoons finely chopped fresh coriander leaves
6 to 9 cups boiled white rice or cooked rice noodles

1. In a 4- to 6-quart pot, combine the chicken, cold water, lemongrass, galanga chips, chilies, kaffir lime leaves, and black peppercorns. Bring to a boil, adjust heat, cover partially, and simmer briskly for 30 minutes. Remove the white meat pieces when done, after about 15 minutes or so, and set aside in a covered tureen or casserole to keep moist. Cook leg, thigh, and wing pieces the full time, until tender.

2. Remove the remaining chicken and place in the tureen or casserole. If desired, strip the chicken off the bones in large pieces and discard the chicken skin and bones.

3. Strain the broth and discard the solids.

4. Return the broth to the rinsed-out pot and stir in the coconut milk, scallions, and mushrooms. Bring to a brisk simmer and cook for 5 minutes.

5. Add the lime juice, fish sauce, and chopped coriander. Pour the soup over the chicken and serve by ladling the broth and chicken pieces (on the bone or off) into large wide bowls that already have a portion of cooked rice or rice noodles in them. Or serve rice (but not noodles) in a side bowl.

ADVANCE PREPARATION: The whole soup may be refrigerated for up to three days and reheated; it freezes perfectly for up to six months.

CHICKEN FRICASSEE

Serves 6

My grandmother made chicken fricassee regularly, though, as a child, I never appreciated the bony chicken necks and wings, or the giblets. Nor did I understand why it was called *chicken* fricassee if the meatballs and the brown gravy were the most interesting, delicious things about it. To this day I consider chicken fricassee an excuse to dunk challah in gravy (for which, I now know, giblets and bony necks and wings are essential). Secondarily, to break the monotony of bread and gravy, you get to eat the tiny, peppery meatballs, and only incidentally are there those bony but succulent chicken pieces.

The following is an update of our family recipe. One thing that is different is that my grandmother thickened her gravy at the end with an uncooked *einbrin*—the German-Yiddish word for flour dissolved in water—which I think lightens the color of the gravy too much and can taste raw. Fat-cooked flour (roux) simmered into the gravy from the start is much better, if inauthentic. "Mamma," as I called my maternal grandmother, never browned the chicken parts either, but, messy as the job is, I think browning the chicken adds extra depth of flavor and a deeper brown color to the gravy. Even with these refinements, chicken fricassee is poor people's food of the best, most comforting kind.

SUPPER SUGGESTIONS: We never had anything *before* fricassee in my grandmother's or mother's house. We wallowed in numerous bowls of fricassee with a mindless amount of challah. Following this feast, we'd sip burning hot glasses of sweetened black Russian tea and pick at rugelach, tiny pastries filled with raisins and nuts, or babka, the Polish yeast cake spiraled with cinnamon and nuts. Nowadays, I'd poach some pears in red wine (page 204).

*2 pounds chicken wings or mixed wings and
    necks (but mostly wings)*
2 tablespoons vegetable oil
2 medium onions, chopped (about 2 cups)
½ cup flour
2 quarts water
*½ pound chicken giblets (hearts and
    gizzards, no livers), coarsely chopped*
1½ teaspoons salt
½ teaspoon freshly ground black pepper
1 large bay leaf (or 2 small)
½ teaspoon dried thyme
1 tablespoon sweet paprika

FOR THE MEATBALLS:
1 pound lean ground beef
1 egg, beaten
½ cup dry (unseasoned) bread crumbs
½ teaspoon salt
½ teaspoon freshly ground black pepper

1. With a sharp knife or poultry shears, cut the chicken wings at their joints into three pieces. Don't discard the wing tips. They have no meat to speak of, but they will add flavor to the gravy. Hack the necks in half.

2. In a 6-quart pot, warm the oil over medium heat and, without crowding the pan, cook the chicken wings and necks until browned lightly on all sides. Remove with a slotted spoon or tongs to a bowl. Reserve.

3. In the fat left in the pot (about 3 tablespoons), cook the chopped onion until wilted, about 5 minutes.

4. Stir in the flour and cook over medium heat for 5 minutes, stirring frequently and scraping up any browned bits left from the chicken.

5. Stir in the water and bring to a boil, stirring frequently.

6. Stir in the giblets and the reserved chicken wings and necks. Season with salt, pepper, bay leaf, thyme, and paprika. Adjust heat, partially cover, and let simmer steadily for about 1 hour.

7. Meanwhile, make the meatballs: In a mixing bowl, combine the beef, beaten egg, bread crumbs, salt, and pepper. With a fork or your hands, mix thoroughly. Shape into meatballs no more than 1 inch in diameter. (You should have 26 to 30.)

8. When the chicken has cooked for about an hour, add the meatballs, increase the heat, and simmer briskly another 15 minutes.

9. Taste the gravy and correct the salt and pepper.

10. Serve very hot in flat bowls, with plenty of bread to sop up the gravy.

VARIATION: Instead of browning the wings first (step 2), start by sautéing the onions in the oil, but cook them over medium heat until brown, about 15 minutes, then make the roux with the flour, also letting it brown lightly before adding the water and chicken parts.

ADVANCE PREPARATION: Can be kept refrigerated for up to a week; it freezes perfectly for to six months. When reheating, add water or broth to thin out the gravy.

CHICKEN GUMBO

Serves 6 to 8

Oysters are frequently an extra fillip in a chicken gumbo. If you can get freshly shucked ones, add a dozen or so at the final moment. For a really elaborate gumbo, combine this recipe with shrimp gumbo (page 140), then add the oysters, or even some crabmeat. In that case, use the shrimp stock outlined in the shrimp gumbo recipe instead of chicken broth.

SUPPER SUGGESTIONS: A leafy salad is all you need to start or serve with this big, rich dish. You might want to keep dessert light, too—a fresh fruit salad (page 199).

2 tablespoons vegetable oil
1 (3- to 4-pound) chicken, cut into 16 serving pieces
½ cup flour
2 medium onions, finely chopped (about
 2 cups)
4 large celery ribs, finely chopped (about
 2 cups)
1 large green bell pepper, finely chopped
 (about 1 cup)
4 large garlic cloves, crushed
1 (28-ounce) can plum tomatoes, cut in
 chunks, with their juice (discard basil)
8 cups light chicken broth (part canned, part
 water)
1¼ teaspoons dried thyme
1 tablespoon Worcestershire sauce
2 large or 3 small bay leaves
¼ to ½ teaspoon cayenne
½ teaspoon freshly ground black pepper
1½ cups finely chopped scallions
1 tightly packed cup chopped parsley leaves
6 to 8 cups cooked long-grain white rice
Tabasco or other Louisiana hot sauce

1. In a 6- to 8-quart pot, heat the oil over medium-low heat and, without crowding the pot, cook the chicken until nicely browned on all sides. Remove it as it is done and reserve on a platter, covered to keep the chicken moist.

2. Stir the flour into the fat left in the pot and cook over low heat, stirring frequently, for about 1 hour, until the flour has turned a rich brown.

3. While the roux is cooking, chop all the vegetables.

4. As soon as the roux is the right color, immediately add the onions, celery, and bell pepper. This will turn the roux a deep mahogany brown. Cover the pot and let the vegetables sweat for 10 minutes, stirring once or twice.

5. Add the crushed garlic and cook, covered, 2 more minutes.

6. Add the tomatoes with their juice and the chicken broth. Turn heat to high and stir until the liquid boils and is smooth, although it will still look a little granular.

7. Stir in the thyme, Worcestershire sauce, bay leaves, cayenne, and black pepper.

8. Add the reserved chicken pieces and mix well. Simmer, covered, over low heat, for 30 minutes longer.

9. Add half the scallions and half the parsley. Simmer another 30 minutes.

10. Either stir in or garnish with the remaining scallions and parsley.

11. To serve, mound the rice in the center of a shallow soup bowl, then ladle piping hot gumbo and chicken around it. If using the parsley and scallions as a final garnish, sprinkle it over everything. Put a bottle of Tabasco or other Louisiana hot sauce on the table.

VARIATION: With additions of seafood— shrimp, crab, scallops, oysters—the base can be extended to serve 10 to 12.

ADVANCE PREPARATION: Cook through step 9, refrigerate for up to a week; without seafood, it freezes perfectly for up to six months.

WHITE CHILI

Serves 6 to 8

This can be a relatively low-fat dish if you want it to be, but don't try to save even more fat by using skinless and boneless chicken breasts. Yes, you will save the fat, but the chicken will be dry and lifeless. If, however, you poach the chicken gently with its skin and bones, then discard the fat parts, it will be juicy and tender.

SUPPER SUGGESTIONS: For a party, you might make this part of a chili buffet, along with three-bean vegetarian chili (page 75) and chili con carne (page 89). Put out a few pans of hot corn bread (page 163), a big bowl of coleslaw (page 179), plus a platter of avocado, onion, and orange slices and you're in business. For a single-chili supper, the same side dishes apply. For dessert, serve pineapple with rum (page 200) and/or forgotten gianduia meringues (page 198)

2½ to 3 pounds chicken breasts with their skin and bones (about 3 whole breasts)
6 cups chicken broth, homemade or canned
2 tablespoons extra-virgin olive oil
2 medium onions, chopped (about 2 cups)

8 large garlic cloves, chopped or crushed
3 or 4 red or green 3-inch chilies, or any kind and/or combination of fresh chilies, finely chopped (about ¼ cup)
1 tablespoon ground cumin
1 tablespoon dried oregano, preferably Mexican
½ teaspoon ground cinnamon
1 pound small white beans ("California small white," pea, navy, Great Northern, or other), rinsed and picked over, soaked overnight in water to cover by several inches
Coarse sea salt (may be unnecessary)
Tabasco or other bottled hot sauce
3 to 4 cups grated Monterey Jack cheese (12 ounces to 1 pound)
Sour cream
Tomato salsa
Lime wedges

1. In a 5- to 6-quart pot, combine the chicken with the chicken broth. Bring to a gentle simmer and poach the chicken, uncovered, until just cooked, 18 to 20 minutes. Let the chicken cool in the broth for at least 15 minutes.

2. Remove the chicken from the broth. Pour the broth into a large bowl and skim off the fat. Set broth aside. (You should have 6 cups.)

3. Let the chicken cool, then remove and discard the skin and bones. Either shred the chicken or cut it into cubes. If doing this ahead, cover with plastic wrap to keep it moist and set aside.

4. Rinse and dry the same 5- to 6-quart pot, then warm the olive oil over medium heat and sauté the onions until beginning to brown, 8 to 10 minutes.

5. Stir in the garlic and sauté another 30 seconds.

6. Add the chopped chilies, cumin, oregano, cinnamon, beans, and the reserved broth. Stir well, partially cover the pot, and reduce the heat so the beans cook at a brisk simmer until very tender, 1 to 1½ hours, depending on the beans.

7. Stir in the cubed or shredded chicken. Let simmer gently for 2 or 3 minutes.

8. Taste and correct seasoning with salt and hot sauce, remembering that the cheese that is added next will reduce the hotness.

9. Just before serving, heat through and stir in 1 cup of the shredded cheese.

10. Serve piping hot in deep or flat bowls, with side dishes of grated cheese, sour cream, salsa, and lime wedges to dress the chili.

ADVANCE PREPARATION: Can be prepared through step 8 and kept refrigerated for several days; or can be frozen for up to six months. Proceed as directed.

JEWISH CHICKEN IN THE POT WITH CHINESE GINGER-SCALLION SAUCE

Serves 4

Is this cross-cultural, or what?

Cook up the chicken with the traditional eastern European vegetables and herbs—carrots, parsnips, dill, parsley, celery, and onion or leek. Serve the soup as a first course with fine egg noodles and diced soup vegetables, then serve the boiled-out chicken with a brassy ginger-scallion dipping sauce. The dish depends on the quality of the chicken. Only a really flavorful bird is worth eating after two hours of simmering. Only a really flavorful bird will make a rich broth. If you are using a supermarket chicken, start with chicken broth instead of water and cook the chicken only until done, 45 minutes to an hour, depending on size. Or use water, but add about a pound of chicken wings, backs, and/or necks to boost the flavor of the broth.

SUPPER SUGGESTIONS: Since this is already a two-course meal, all you'll need is a simple dessert. If you have the inclination to bake, Swedish almond cake (page 192) is as impressively homey as the soup. Now that would be crossing cultures!

1 (3½- to 4-pound) chicken, excess fat
    pulled off
2 medium carrots, peeled

1 large leek with some green, split to the top
   of the white and well washed
1 medium parsnip, peeled
5 quarts water (approximately)
1 small celery heart (4 to 6 small, light, inner
   ribs and their leaves)
At least 40 sprigs dill
At least 40 sprigs parsley
About 12 white peppercorns
2 teaspoons coarse sea salt
3 to 4 cups cooked fine egg noodles and/or 8
   matzo balls (page 124)
Chinese ginger-scallion sauce (recipe follows)

1. In a 6- to 8-quart pot, combine the chicken, carrots, leek, and parsnip. Cover with water and, uncovered, bring to a steady simmer over high heat. Lower heat and skim foam as it comes to the top until surface is nearly foam free.

2. Tie the celery heart, dill, and parsley together with a piece of string and add to the pot. Add the peppercorns and salt. Cover partially and reduce the heat so that the liquid simmers gently for 2 hours.

3. Let the chicken cool in the broth for at least 15 minutes. Remove the chicken and set aside. Remove the tied-up herbs and celery and discard. Remove the other vegetables and cut them into small or large pieces for the soup. Set aside.

4. Strain the soup—you should have about 3½ quarts—then taste. (If desired, chill the soup to facilitate skimming off the fat.) To concentrate its flavor, simmer the soup until reduced to about 2½ quarts.

5. Reheat the vegetables and the chicken, cut into quarters or smaller serving pieces, in the simmering soup.

6. To serve, ladle the soup and vegetables over fine egg noodles and/or matzo balls in wide bowls.

7. Serve the chicken separately with ginger sauce on the side.

ADVANCE PREPARATION: The soup may be kept refrigerated for up to five days; if brought to a boil then it will keep another two or three days in the refrigerator; it freezes perfectly. The chicken and vegetables should be consumed within two days. Matzoh balls may be held in their cooking water or in broth for several hours. When reheated, they get heavier.

CHINESE GINGER-SCALLION SAUCE

Makes about ⅓ cup

2 rounded teaspoons very finely minced fresh
   ginger
3 rounded tablespoons very finely minced
   scallion (white only)
1 teaspoon salt
1 teaspoon soy sauce
3 tablespoons corn or peanut oil

1. In a small heatproof bowl, combine the ginger, scallion, salt, and soy sauce.

2. In a small pot (a butter warmer or Turkish coffee pot are perfect), heat the oil just to smoking.

3. Pour the oil over the ginger-scallion mixture. It will sizzle violently. Let the sauce stand at least 10 minutes before serving.

ADVANCE PREPARATION: Ginger-scallion sauce is best prepared at the last minute and served warm.

SOUTHWESTERN CHICKEN IN THE POT

Serves 6

This is a fall dish in New England, where I do most of my cooking, and in most other parts of the country, though it has the warm flavors of the Southwest. My idea was to make a boiled chicken supper with only native American vegetables. Somehow Savoy cabbage got stuck in the pot, and onions and garlic are as Old World as the ancient Egyptians, probably older. Still, roasting the tomatoes whole gives the dish a Mexican edge, and the lovely red broth filled with colorful vegetables has both the sweetness and chili charge of American food.

SUPPER SUGGESTIONS: It's truly a meal-in-a-bowl. Poached pears (page 204), plus some plain cookies, are the perfect dessert. Or bake a plum tart (page 195).

1 (4-pound) chicken
2 large celery ribs, chopped into ½-inch pieces

1 onion with skin, poked in several places
1 head garlic with skin, poked in several places
1 tablespoon salt
12 black peppercorns
14 cups water (3½ quarts)
3 whole tomatoes
2 dried ancho chilies
1 pound winter squash, peeled and cut into large chunks
1½ pounds Savoy cabbage, cut into large chunks and pierced through the wooden skewers to keep them from falling apart while cooking
1½ pounds all-purpose potatoes, peeled and cut into chunks
3 cups fresh or frozen corn kernels, or 3 ears corn on the cob, cut into quarters or halves

OPTIONAL GARNISHES:
Chopped onion, chopped fresh green chilies, diced avocado, fried flour or corn tortilla strips (fritas)

1. In an 8- to 10-quart pot, combine the chicken, celery, onion, garlic, salt, and peppercorns. Cover with the water. Bring to the barest simmer and skim the foam until no more rises to the surface.

2. Adjust heat and partially cover so that the liquid simmers steadily.

3. Meanwhile, broil the tomatoes in an ungreased pan, 7 minutes to the side. Place some broth in the pan to "degrease" the juices and add it, with the tomatoes, still whole, to the simmering soup.

4. Cook the chicken until done, about 1 hour.

5. Remove the chicken from the pot. Cover it to keep it moist and set aside.

6. Add the chilies, squash, cabbage chunks on skewers, and potatoes. Simmer, uncovered, for 20 minutes.

7. Add the corn for the last 5 minutes.

8. Meanwhile, with poultry shears or a sharp knife, cut the chicken into serving pieces as desired.

9. Taste the broth and adjust the seasonings.

10. Serve piping hot in very large bowls, with some of every ingredient in each bowl. Pass garnishes, if desired.

ADVANCE PREPARATION: Cook the soup through step 6 and keep refrigerated for up to two days. Bring to a simmer before proceeding. The broth freezes perfectly, but the vegetables and chicken will suffer in the freezer.

GREEK CHICKEN IN THE POT

Serves 4 to 6

This is from Nicholas Stavroulakis, the Greek historian who welcomes students into his home to experience his Greek-Jewish table.

SUPPER SUGGESTIONS: Serve plenty of crusty bread, a tossed salad, and a fruit dessert.

1 (3- to 4-pound) chicken
2 to 3 quarts water
1 teaspoon ground ginger
2 large bay leaves
½ teaspoon black peppercorns
1 tablespoon coarse sea salt
Big pinch of turmeric or saffron
3 large onions, quartered
3 large tomatoes, quartered
*2 medium zucchini, ends cut off, cut into
    2-inch lengths*
3 large carrots, cut into 2-inch lengths
*1 large celery root, peeled and cut into
    wedges*
4 to 6 cups boiled white rice
Juice of 1 lemon, plus extra lemon wedges
Extra-virgin olive oil
Coarse sea salt

1. In a 6- to 8-quart pot, combine the chicken with just enough water to cover. Over high heat, bring to a boil, uncovered. Reduce heat and, with a slotted spoon, skim off the foam. When the foam has stopped rising, add the ginger, bay leaves, peppercorns, salt, and turmeric. Simmer gently, partially covered, for 30 minutes.

2. Add the onions, tomatoes, zucchini, carrots, and celery root wedges. Continue simmering gently, partially covered, for at least 30 minutes longer, or until the chicken and the vegetables are very tender.

3. Remove the chicken, cut it into serving pieces, and arrange on a platter with the vegetables. Set aside, covered with foil, in a low oven to keep warm.

4. Serve the soup first, in deep or wide bowls with plenty of rice.

5. Serve the chicken and vegetables dressed with the juice of a lemon, a drizzling of olive oil (if desired), and a sprinkle of coarse sea salt (if desired).

VARIATION: The vegetables can be changed depending on what is available: String beans and well-trimmed small, whole artichokes are excellent possibilities.

ADVANCE PREPARATION: The chicken and vegetables are best if served soon after they have finished cooking. However, leftover broth can be kept refrigerated for up to a week or frozen for up to six months. Leftover vegetables can be puréed into the broth. Leftover poultry should be stripped from the bones and either recycled into another dish or reheated in leftover broth.

MEXICAN CHICKEN SOUP WITH FRIED NOODLES

Serves 4

Aida Gabalondo is the mother of my friend Zarela Martinez, owner of Zarela restaurant in New York. It is from Aida's cookbook, *Mexican Family Cooking* (Fawcett, 1986), six years before her daughter's autobiographical *Food from the Heart* (Macmillan, 1992) was published, that I learned that the curse of Mexican chicken soup is sweet vegetables—onion, carrot, and celery in particular, the ones most of us depend on for adding flavor to our broth. A Mexican chicken broth, insists Aida, contains only the glorious chicken, tomatoes for a little color, peppercorns, and garlic. She says it never has herbs, though I know other Mexican cooks who put in a little oregano. Aida's way puts the full flavor onus on the chicken, so you'd better start shopping for an old hen that's full of flavor.

SUPPER SUGGESTIONS: This is already a two-course meal. Add corn bread (page 163), possibly avocado, onion, and tomato salad (page 187), too. Wacky chocolate cake (page 191) is a good dessert.

FOR THE BROTH:
1 (5- to 7-pound) hen
3 to 4 quarts water
2 large ripe tomatoes, cut in half
1 tablespoon black peppercorns
1 tablespoon mashed garlic

FOR THE NOODLES:
½ cup vegetable oil
4 ounces vermicelli broken into 2-inch lengths

2 tablespoons olive oil
1 small onion, chopped (about ½ cup)
1 medium ripe tomato, cut into ¼-inch cubes (about 1 cup)
1 teaspoon mashed garlic
2 tablespoons finely chopped coriander
2 cups shredded Monterey Jack cheese
Tortilla chips (optional)

1. To make the broth: In an 8- to 10-quart pot, combine the chicken with enough fresh, cold water just to cover, 3 to 4 quarts. Bring to a boil. Reduce heat and, with a slotted spoon, skim the foam.

2. When the foam stops rising, add the tomatoes, peppercorns, and garlic. Partially cover and simmer steadily for at least 2 hours, until the chicken is completely cooked and has given the broth a good flavor.

3. Remove the chicken and either let it cool—to be refrigerated for another meal or later use—or keep warm while preparing the noodle soup.

4. Measure the broth. You should have at least 3 quarts. Skim the fat (refrigerating it facilitates this) and simmer the soup until reduced to 2 strong-tasting quarts.

5. In a large skillet, heat the vegetable oil until hot but not smoking. Fry the vermicelli until golden. Remove immediately and drain on absorbent paper.

6. In a 3- to 4-quart pot, warm the olive oil over medium heat and sauté the onion and tomato for 2 minutes.

7. Add the broth, the mashed garlic, and the coriander. Bring to a boil.

8. Add the fried noodles and boil until they are tender, about 20 minutes.

9. Serve piping hot in wide bowls. Pass the shredded cheese and tortilla chips to put in the soup.

10. The chicken may be served as a separate course, with salsa and warm flour tortillas on the side.

ADVANCE PREPARATION: The broth itself (through step 4) can be kept refrigerated for up to a week, then, if it is brought to a boil, kept another several days; it freezes perfectly for up to six months. Do not add the final soup flavorings (steps 6 and 7), or the fried noodles, until the last minute.

ZUPPA PAVESE

Serves 1

According to a charming legend—the kind of tale that frequently aggrandizes dishes of obvious peasant roots—this soup was created in 1525 for Francis I of France when he was defeated, in Pavia, by the Spanish Emperor Charles V of the Holy Roman Empire. In one version of the legend, poor Francis scours the Pavese countryside for food and help. Finally he comes upon a farmer's wife who serves him, as she would her family, some broth ladled over a piece of dry bread—a sop. Upon learning that he is a king, however, she feels an understandable need to embellish the dish. So she fetches two eggs from the henhouse and breaks them into his steaming soup. Eccola! Zuppa Pavese.

SUPPER SUGGESTIONS: This is the kind of homey dish that doesn't usually come surrounded by a menu, though grilled mushrooms are a good supplement. Fresh fruit is the only finish you need, though a pear with a good piece of cheese is always welcome. With the meal, have plenty of hearty bread.

FOR EACH SERVING:
1½ to 2 tablespoons olive oil or butter, depending on the size of your bread
2 or 3 (½-inch-thick) slices Italian or French bread (however many will fit nicely in the bottom of your bowl)
1½ cups chicken, beef, or vegetable broth

1 or 2 eggs
Grated Parmesan cheese (or, less authentically, Pecorino Romano or Asiago)
Freshly ground pepper

1. In a medium skillet, heat the oil or butter over medium heat and fry the bread until golden on both sides. Place the toast in a soup bowl.

2. Bring the broth to a gentle simmer. Break the egg (or eggs) onto a small plate and slide it (or them) into the broth. When the whites have set, remove the eggs with a slotted spoon and place it (or them) in the soup bowl, on top of the toast.

3. Pour the hot broth over and serve immediately. Pass the cheese and a pepper mill.

VARIATION: For the daring, sometimes the egg is broken directly onto the toast, then cooked ever so slightly by the simmering broth that is ladled over it.

ADVANCE PREPARATION: Should be made just before serving.

CHRISTINE'S WHITE BORSCHT

Serves 6

Mellow but tart, creamy rich but briskly healthful, this blend of allspice-flavored chicken broth and, of all things, sauerkraut stock has a cult following in New York. It is served at Christine's on the corner of Second Avenue and Twenty-sixth Street, one of a new breed of so-called Polish coffee shops (see page 69). With a few slices of kielbasa floating in the broth, a boiled potato and hard-cooked egg in the bowl, and the basket of rye and pumpernickel that comes with it, it is one of the least expensive great meals in the city.

SUPPER SUGGESTIONS: Rye bread is the only accompaniment you need. A wedge of lettuce with blue cheese dressing (page 180) can go before or after.

4 cups water
2 pounds sauerkraut (not canned), not
    drained
2 or 3 chicken legs
3 small bay leaves
4 medium celery ribs
2 medium carrots
2 large leeks, white part only
2 teaspoons whole allspice
2 quarts water
Coarse sea salt and freshly ground pepper
2 teaspoons dried marjoram
4 teaspoons cornstarch

1 cup heavy cream
½ to ¾ pound kielbasa, sliced, at room
    temperature

FOR THE GARNISH:
6 medium boiled potatoes
3 hard-cooked eggs, cut into halves

1. In a 2- to 3-quart saucepan, bring the 4 cups water to a boil. Add the sauerkraut and simmer, partially covered, for about 30 minutes.

2. Strain the liquid while it is still hot and reserve. There should be about 5 cups. (The sauerkraut can be discarded; its flavor is much diminished.)

3. While preparing the sauerkraut stock, make the chicken broth: In a 3- to 5-quart saucepan, combine the chicken, bay leaves, celery, carrots, leeks, allspice, and 2 quarts of fresh cold water. Bring to a brisk simmer over high heat, reduce heat, partially cover, and let simmer steadily for 1½ hours.

4. Strain the chicken broth and reserve. There should be about 4 cups; if not, add a little water.

5. In a 4- to 6-quart pot, combine the 4 cups chicken broth with 4 cups of the sauerkraut stock. Season to taste with salt and pepper. Cover and bring to a boil. Add the marjoram.

6. In a small cup or bowl, mix the cornstarch with the remaining cup of sauerkraut stock. Whisk into the briskly boiling soup and cook for 1 minute, stirring slowly. This

(continued)

will not perceptibly thicken the soup, but it will bind it.

7. Turn off the heat and stir in the heavy cream.

8. To serve, place several rounds of kielbasa, a boiled potato, and half an egg into each wide, deep bowl. Ladle on the hot soup.

ADVANCE PREPARATION: Can be kept refrigerated for up to a week (don't worry if it separates); it freezes perfectly. Reheat to a simmer before serving.

STRACCIATELLA

Serves 3

This is Italian egg drop soup. When you have good chicken broth in the refrigerator or freezer, it's an almost instant light supper.

SUPPER SUGGESTIONS: Make yourself a salad, asparagus, or an artichoke and have plenty of crusty bread and a piece of cheese and fruit.

2 eggs, lightly beaten
3 tablespoons freshly grated Parmesan cheese
2 tablespoons bread crumbs
⅛ teaspoon freshly grated nutmeg
5 cups chicken stock
2 tablespoons finely chopped parsley

1. In a small bowl, beat together the eggs, cheese, bread crumbs, and nutmeg.

2. Stir in ½ cup of the stock.

3. In a 3- to 4-quart saucepan, bring the remaining 4½ cups of broth to a boil, covered or not.

4. Reduce the heat and add the egg mixture, stirring constantly.

5. Cook for 3 minutes, continuing to stir until the eggs take on the appearance of tiny flakes.

6. Garnish with parsley and serve immediately.

ADVANCE PREPARATION: Should be made just before serving.

AVGOLEMONO

Serves 4

This is the simple soup that a Greek mother might prepare as a restorative for her family—a first course for a simple dinner, or the focus of a light supper. As these common national dishes go, there are almost as many recipes as commoners—from flour-thickened bouillons to smooth, egg-enriched stocks with a liaison of rice; and, the one constant, lots of lemon juice. This recipe is somewhere in between the richest and the most meager.

SUPPER SUGGESTIONS: A big so-called Greek salad, which in Greek is called *horiatiki,* "country salad," is the ideal accompaniment. Dress a bowl of chopped romaine lettuce tossed with cucumber, tomato, and either sweet onions or scallions, with oil and vinegar, dried oregano, crumbled feta cheese, and Greek olives. With crusty bread, it's a feast. For dessert, serve store-bought cookies. This is, after all, a simple supper.

6 cups chicken broth
5 tablespoons white rice
4 egg yolks
⅓ to ½ cup freshly squeezed lemon juice
(2 or 3 lemons)
Freshly ground black pepper
Finely chopped parsley or dill, for garnish

1. In a small saucepan, bring the broth to a boil. Add the rice, cover completely, and reduce heat to simmer the rice briskly for 12 to 15 minutes.

2. In a small bowl, beat the eggs until well blended.

3. When the rice is tender to taste, ladle a cup or so of hot soup into the beaten eggs, stirring constantly.

4. Pour the egg mixture back into the saucepan. Add lemon juice and pepper to taste. Heat through but don't allow the soup to boil.

5. Serve immediately in deep or flat bowls, or mugs, sprinkled with dill or parsley.

ADVANCE PREPARATION: Must be made just before serving.

SUSAN FRIEDLAND'S CHICKEN SOUP WITH MATZO BALLS

Makes 5 to 6 quarts

The blandness of chicken is such these days that, to make a soup as good as our grandmothers', it takes two old fowls instead of one. The first will make a merely decent soup, especially if you remove the bird when the flesh still has some flavor and can be eaten for its own sake. The second is cooked in the first's broth to get a soup that's really rich in flavor. My dear friend Susan Friedland is the editor of this book, and she writes cookbooks herself. This is from her *Jewish-American Kitchen* (Stewart, Tabori & Chang, 1989).

SUPPER SUGGESTIONS: If serving soup with matzo balls, then the boiled chicken for its own sake, all you'll need is dessert, say pound cake (page 192), and fruit.

1 (5- to 6-pound) fowl (older chicken), including neck and giblets but without the liver
5 to 6 quarts water
2 large onions, halved but unpeeled
3 carrots, scraped and cut into large chunks
10 to 15 parsley sprigs
18 to 20 black peppercorns, crushed
Coarse sea salt and freshly ground white pepper
Matzoh balls (recipe follows)

1. Remove the fat from the cavities of the fowl and set aside for rendering for future use.

2. Place the fowl in a 10- to 12-quart pot with the cold water, the vegetables, and parsley. The vegetables and fowl should be barely covered with water. Bring to a boil and immediately lower the heat. Skim any foam that rises to the surface and adjust the heat so just the odd bubble appears on the surface.

3. Add the peppercorns, partially cover the pot, and simmer for about 2 hours, skimming occasionally. The fowl should be cooked through but not falling apart.

4. Remove the fowl to a large platter and, when it is cool enough to handle, remove the meat from the bones. Reserve the meat for sandwiches or salad—or eat as is, perhaps with salsa (pages 95 and 104) or ginger-scallion sauce (page 115).

5. Return the bones and skin to the simmering soup and cook for another hour or so. Strain the soup into a large bowl and discard everything in the strainer. Cool the soup and refrigerate overnight. Remove the fat that has hardened on the surface.

6. For a really superb soup, start again, using this broth, with a second batch of vegetables and a second fowl. You may need to add a bit more cold water to cover the fowl and vegetables.

7. Before serving, reheat the soup and taste carefully for seasoning. It will surely need

salt, and perhaps pepper. Serve with matzo balls.

VARIATIONS: I always add a few sprigs of dill with the vegetables, and Jewish cooks also use parsley root as one of the soup greens. If desired, cook some carrots and parsnips separately and put a large piece of each into each bowl with the soup and matzo balls.

ADVANCE PREPARATION: Can be kept refrigerated for up to a week, then it can be kept for several more days if brought to a boil. Or freeze for up to six months.

MATZO BALLS

Makes about 16 matzo balls

4 eggs
½ cup water or seltzer
6 tablespoons melted schmaltz
Salt
Freshly ground black pepper
1 cup matzo meal

1. Beat the eggs until whites and yolks are blended.

2. Stir in the water or seltzer, schmaltz, salt, and pepper.

3. Gradually stir in the matzo meal.

4. Cover and refrigerate for at least 1 hour.

5. Bring a large quantity of water to a boil. Form the matzo balls with moistened palms, using about 2 tablespoons for each ball.

6. Drop into the boiling water and simmer, covered, for about 30 minutes.

7. Remove with a slotted spoon and set aside until ready to serve in soup.

VARIATION: Before stirring in the matzo meal, add 2 teaspoons grated fresh ginger, a few gratings of nutmeg, and 3 tablespoons minced parsley to the egg mixture.

ADVANCE PREPARATION: Matzo balls can be prepared several hours ahead of serving time. Freezing is possible, although the balls may not be as light as when they are freshly made: Either wrap each individually in plastic before freezing, or arrange all the balls on a baking sheet and freeze until hard, then pack them into plastic bags.

CHICKEN BROTH

Makes about 2½ quarts

Although I suggest using canned chicken broth throughout this book, a homemade broth can be much superior. Use this as a cooking broth, though it is certainly flavorful enough to sip for its own sake.

3 pounds chicken wings
2 carrots, peeled
1 large onion, peeled and stuck with 4 cloves
1 large celery rib, with leaves if possible
2 or 3 parsley sprigs
12 peppercorns
Coarse sea salt (optional)
4 quarts water

1. In a 6- to 8-quart pot, combine all the ingredients. If salting, start with 2 teaspoons. Bring to a boil over high heat. As soon as the water boils, reduce heat, simmer gently, and skim off the foam.

2. When the foam stops rising, partially cover and adjust heat so that water simmers gently for 3 hours.

3. Let cool about 30 minutes.

4. Strain in a large strainer or colander, then taste and add salt if necessary.

5. Refrigerate until well chilled, then skim off all fat.

ADVANCE PREPARATION: Keeps refrigerated for up to a week or in the freezer for up to six months.

CHAPTER 5

FISH AND SHELLFISH SOUPS

SUCCOTASH CHOWDER

Serves 2

This is a quickie for clam lovers who are not above using frozen corn and lima beans. It's as much a sop as a soup, so serve plenty of bread for dunking into the creamy broth.

SUPPER SUGGESTIONS: A salad of sliced tomatoes, avocado, and Bermuda onion (page 187) would be wonderful. When good tomatoes are not around, try grilled portobello mushrooms on greens (page 178). Baking powder biscuits (page 164) are good with the soup. Cookies and fruit for dessert.

2 tablespoons butter
1 small onion, finely chopped (about ½ cup)
½ cup dry white wine or dry French vermouth
2 dozen littleneck or cherrystone clams, scrubbed and soaked (see page 136)
1 (10-ounce) package frozen lima beans
1 (10-ounce) package frozen sweet corn kernels
½ cup heavy cream, or more to taste
Coarse sea salt and freshly ground black pepper
Finely chopped parsley or coriander

1. In an 8- to 10-quart pot, heat the butter over medium heat and sauté the onion until wilted, about 5 minutes.

2. Add the white wine and clams. Cover and steam over high heat until the clams open, about 5 minutes. Be careful not to overcook. Remove the clams.

3. Add the lima beans, corn, and heavy cream. Heat through until vegetables are crisp-tender.

4. Taste for salt and pepper; add a little more cream, if desired.

5. To serve, divide the clams between two large bowls, then ladle on the hot chowder. Sprinkle liberally with parsley or coriander.

ADVANCE PREPARATION: Must be made just before serving.

THAI SHRIMP SOUP

Serves 4

This is a long recipe to read, but not difficult or even time-consuming to prepare. The hardest part is finding the fresh ingredients—kaffir lime leaves and lemongrass. However, once you have them in your freezer where they'll keep for months, you'll be making this frequently. It has such a new, fresh, and satisfying flavor for most of us. Thai fish sauce is available even in supermarkets now, and I give a recipe for an easy chili paste if you can't find that.

SUPPER SUGGESTIONS: A big bowl of white rice is an absolute must. I like to put my rice in the soup, then also have extra rice in a bowl to "send down," as the Chinese would say, a variety of steamed vegetables. It's a healthful menu that can also be a triumph of textures, colors, fragrances, and flavors. Instead of steamed vegetables, also consider string beans with garlic and sesame oil (page 187). A glorious pineapple and whatever other tropical fruits you can find would be the ideal dessert. For company, add crisp cookies if you feel you need more than fruit alone.

1½ pounds large shrimp (about 36)

FOR THE CHILI PASTE (SEE NOTE):
3 (3-inch-long) hot green or red chilies
3 large shallots, unpeeled, cut in half through the root-blossom axis
6 large garlic cloves, unpeeled, cut the long way
4 tablespoons vegetable oil

FOR THE BROTH:
Shells from 1½ pounds shrimp
1 tablespoon vegetable oil
2 quarts light chicken broth (half canned, half water); or one third bottled clam juice, two thirds water; or fresh fish stock
3 stalks lemongrass (each about 7 inches), roots removed
Zest of ½ lime, julienned
4 (double) kaffir lime leaves
1 teaspoon salt
1 tablespoon chili paste

1 (15-ounce) can straw mushrooms, drained and rinsed (optional)

FOR THE FINAL FLAVORING:
1 tablespoon Thai fish sauce (nam pla)
3 tablespoons freshly squeezed lime juice
3 tablespoons finely chopped scallions (with some green)

2 tablespoons finely chopped or sliced red or green chilies
2 tablespoons coarsely chopped fresh coriander

FOR THE GARNISH:
Additional chopped scallions, chopped or sliced chilies, and chopped coriander, plus lime wedges

1. Peel the shrimp and save the shells.

2. To make the chili paste (about ⅓ cup): In a small heavy skillet (cast iron is perfect), over medium-low heat, slowly dry-fry the chilies, shallots, and garlic, turning frequently, until all are soft and spotted with brown blisters.

3. Peel the shallots and garlic. Remove the seeds from the chilies. Place shallots, garlic, and chilies in a blender with 3 tablespoons of the oil. Process into a paste, turning the motor on and off and tamping and stirring between sets of pulses.

4. Scrape from the blender jar and into a small skillet with the remaining 1 tablespoon of oil. Sauté, stirring frequently, until the mixture turns a dark green-brown or red-brown, depending on color of chilies. Remove from heat and scrape into a small bowl or jar. The paste can be kept refrigerated for up to a month.

5. To make the broth: In a 3-quart pot, over medium heat, sauté the shrimp shells in the 1 tablespoon of vegetable oil until pink, about a minute.

6. Add the chicken broth and bring to a simmer, uncovered.

7. Meanwhile, remove the tough outer layer of the lemongrass. On a board, using the back of a chef's knife or Chinese cleaver, badly bruise the lemongrass about every inch on several sides, rotating the grass as you pound. Then cut the grass into 2-inch lengths.

8. Add the lemongrass, lime zest, lime leaves, salt, and chili paste to the simmering broth. Cover, reduce heat, and simmer briskly for 20 minutes.

9. Strain the broth through a fine sieve.

10. Rinse the pot and pour in the strained broth.

11. When ready to serve, bring the broth to a simmer. Add the shrimp and straw mushrooms and cook 2 minutes.

12. Immediately remove from heat and add the fish sauce, lime juice, chopped scallions, sliced or chopped chilies, and coriander.

13. Ladle into wide, deep bowls and, if desired, pass lime wedges and bowls of chopped scallions, sliced chilies, and chili paste. Place a bottle or cruet of fish sauce on the table.

NOTE: If you can find bottled Thai chili paste (nam prig pow) in a specialty food store, use it. It generally contains tamarind and is truly an exotic blend of sweet, sour, and hot. If you don't want to go to the trouble of making the chili paste above,

Madhur Jaffrey suggests in *Far Eastern Cookery* (HarperPerennial, 1989) that a fair substitute is ¼ teaspoon ground red (cayenne) pepper combined with ¼ teaspoon sugar and ½ teaspoon vegetable oil. That's about the right amount for this recipe, but the chili paste recipe given here has far more dimension than the substitute.

ADVANCE PREPARATION: Can be prepared ahead through step 9, then refrigerated for up to two days, along with the raw shrimp.

ERIC JAN ZALIS'S POTAGE DE GARBANZOS CON ESPINACAS Y BACALAO

Makes 4 quarts, serving 8

This recipe was the winner in an olive oil cooking contest I ran on my radio show. It won because olive oil is the unbilled star of the dish, because it uses a small amount of high-quality oil to great advantage, and because it is so simple to prepare—representative of the best kind of home cooking, Spanish or otherwise. Potage is a lenten dish in Madrid, where Eric, who is from New Jersey, was living for several years. It is somewhere between soup and stew. The liquid is brothy, but not copious, and, at least the way Eric makes it, it is filled with *stuff*. Be aware also that the soup tastes delicious without the salt cod, which is really the main ingredient in Spain, and with only the spinach, which is Eric's own addition. It is excellent with fresh cod (or other fish) poached in it, too, and I'm sure it would also be good with sliced chorizo instead of fish.

SUPPER SUGGESTIONS: Serve plenty of crusty bread or garlic toast (page 159). No first course is necessary, but a good dessert would be the Swedish almond cake (page 192), seeing that almonds are so Spanish.

1 pound chick-peas, picked over, soaked
   overnight, and drained (page 15)
2 quarts water
2 medium onions, chopped (about 2 cups)
1 large celery rib, sliced (½ to ¾ cup)
1 carrot, sliced (about ½ cup)
1 large parsley sprig
1 large bay leaf
4 to 6 tablespoons extra-virgin olive oil,
   preferably Spanish
1 pound fresh spinach, washed carefully and
   coarsely chopped
½ pound bacalao, soaked overnight (change
   the water twice in a 12-hour period),
   then deboned
Sea salt and freshly ground black pepper
2 large garlic cloves, finely chopped
1 cup canned, well-drained Italian tomatoes,
   coarsely chopped
Dry sherry (fino) (optional)

I. In a 6-quart pot, combine the chick-peas, water, half the onions, the celery, car-rot, parsley, and bay leaf. Slowly bring to a boil, then simmer, partially covered, over low heat for 1 hour, or until the chick-peas are tender.

2. Add 2 or 3 tablespoons of olive oil, the spinach, and the deboned and desalted bacalao to the pot. Continue simmering for another 20 minutes. Add salt and pepper to taste.

3. Meanwhile, in a small skillet, over medium-high heat, sauté the remaining onion with the garlic and tomatoes in 2 to 3 tablespoons olive oil, until the mixture becomes saucy, about 5 minutes.

4. Add the tomato mixture to the soup along with, if desired, a healthy shot of sherry. Cook 10 minutes longer.

5. Serve piping hot in wide bowls.

ADVANCE PREPARATION: Long advance preparation is not advisable, although the dish can be held for several hours and gently reheated.

FISH STEW WITH FENNEL

Serves 6

have been making this for nearly twenty years, and though I keep thinking that it should have evolved over all this time, it hasn't. One of its advantages is that you can make the base well in advance—even freeze it—then add the fresh seafood at the last moment. It's a good party dish.

SUPPER SUGGESTIONS: A big mixed salad is called for, as is plenty of crusty bread, not sourdough, then peach crostata (page 194).

¼ cup delicately flavored olive oil
2 medium onions, finely chopped (about
    2 cups)
3 large garlic cloves, finely chopped
1 cup dry vermouth
1 teaspoon fennel seed
1 (35-ounce) can tomatoes with tomato purée
2 cups bottled clam juice
3 cups water
1 teaspoon salt
Freshly ground black pepper
2 pounds firm fish fillets, such as whiting
    and monkfish, cut into serving pieces
1 pound medium or large shrimp, shelled
    (and deveined if desired)
18 littleneck or cherrystone clams, scrubbed
    and soaked, (see page 136)
⅓ cup finely chopped parsley
4 to 6 cups cooked rice or small macaroni

I. In a 3-quart saucepan or in the 8-quart pot in which you will eventually cook the whole stew, heat the oil over medium heat and sauté the onions until golden.

2. Add the garlic and sauté a minute or two longer.

3. Add the vermouth and stir over high heat for a minute. Add the fennel seed and cook a few seconds more.

4. Add the tomatoes and, with a wooden spoon or potato masher, break them up into small chunks. Add the clam juice, water, salt, and pepper to taste. Simmer gently, uncovered, for 20 to 30 minutes, or until most of the tomatoes have disintegrated.

5. Pour into an 8-quart pot if the base isn't in one already.

6. Add the fish, shrimp, clams, and parsley to the simmering base. Simmer, covered, for about 15 minutes, or until the clams open and the fish is cooked.

7. Serve piping hot ladled into wide deep bowls mounded with rice or macaroni.

ADVANCE PREPARATION: Cook through step 4; this is the stew base, essentially a sauce. It can be left at room temperature for several hours (not in aluminum), or it can be refrigerated for up to two days, or frozen for up to six months.

ZUPPA DI COZZE
(MUSSEL SOUP)

Serves 4

It used to be such an ordeal to clean mussels that I rarely cooked them, and when I did I made my friends participate in the scrub-down. Nowadays mussels are farm-raised—cultivated—and they wouldn't dare be so dirty. In any case, this dish is worth any effort. Seafood. Garlic. Hot Pepper. Heaven!

SUPPER SUGGESTIONS: Toasted Italian or French bread is a must. Or, for something more substantial, serve over linguine. A big salad is a good idea. For dessert, if it's a family meal, fruit and cookies are enough. For a more festive menu, serve biscotti and sweet wine, such as Marsala.

4 pounds mussels
3 to 4 tablespoons delicately flavored olive oil
1 whole head garlic (about 20 cloves), peeled and thickly sliced
1 (28-ounce) can Italian tomatoes with their juice
½ teaspoon coarse sea salt
Big pinch of red pepper flakes
1 cup finely chopped parsley leaves
4 large, thick slices toasted bread, or 8 to 12 friselli, Italian hardtack, often seasoned with cracked black pepper

1. Clean the mussels by scrubbing each one very well under cold running water and removing any traces of "beard" from the shells. Discard any mussels that remain open during cleaning. Let the mussels soak for 20 to 30 minutes in several changes of cold water. Rinse and drain.

2. While the mussels are soaking, make a sauce in a 6-quart pot: Warm the olive oil over medium heat and sauté the garlic until it just begins to turn golden.

3. Add the tomatoes, breaking them up in the pot with a potato masher or with a wooden spoon.

4. Add the salt and pepper flakes. Simmer uncovered over medium heat for 15 minutes, stirring occasionally.

5. Stir in the parsley, then add the drained and rinsed mussels. Cover the pot tightly to steam the mussels, shaking the pan every once in a while to mix the sauce with the mussels. The soup is done when all the mussels have opened, after 8 minutes or so. The time will vary according to the mussels.

6. To serve, place a large slice of toasted bread or a few friselli in each wide deep bowl. Evenly divide the mussels and broth among the bowls. You should have a generous ¾ cup thick broth for each serving.

ADVANCE PREPARATION: The sauce, steps 2 through 4, may be held at room temperature for several hours (not in aluminum), kept refrigerated up to two days, or frozen for up to six months. Bring to a simmer before proceeding.

PAULA WOLFERT'S SALMON SOLIANKA

Serves 4

The word *solianka* is used for a group of Russian soups that have as a common denominator a sour broth flavored and garnished with capers and olives. Paula Wolfert developed this recipe for an early edition of Cuisinart's now-defunct *Cooking* magazine.

SUPPER SUGGESTIONS: A Roumanian eggplant salad plate (page 185) would be a terrific first course. Serve it and the soup with Russian black bread or Westphalian pumpernickel—at any rate a dark, dense, rye-based bread. For an easy dessert, ice cream on pound cake (page 192).

2 pounds fish trimmings: heads, tails, and bones of a sole, bass, red snapper, or any other white-fleshed fish
2 tablespoons butter
2 medium onions, sliced (about 2 cups)
2 large celery ribs with leaves, sliced (about 1 cup)
1 medium carrot, thinly sliced (about ½ cup)
½ teaspoon coarse sea salt
1 teaspoon cracked peppercorns
2 parsley sprigs
5 dill sprigs
1½ quarts water
1½ tablespoons tomato paste
½ teaspoon sugar
Juice of 1 lemon
1 cup sauerkraut juice, drained from 2 (16-ounce) packages
1 pound (or more) fresh salmon or sturgeon, boned, skinned, and cut into 4 portions
12 capers, rinsed and drained
4 black olives, halved
¼ cup diced dill pickle
4 thin lemon slices
4 teaspoons chopped fresh dill

1. Wash the fish trimmings under cool running water; cut away any traces of blood, liver, intestines, or eggs; set aside.

2. In a heavy 4-quart saucepan, melt the butter over medium heat and sauté the onions, celery, and carrot for a few minutes, stirring. Add the fish trimmings, salt, peppercorns, parsley, and dill sprigs. Moisten with the water and stir over high heat until it comes to a boil. Skim. Stir in the tomato paste and the sugar. Simmer, covered, for 30 minutes, skimming when needed.

3. Strain. Add the lemon and sauerkraut juice.

4. Return the strained soup to a clean saucepan and reheat to a simmer. Poach the fish pieces in the soup for about 5 minutes (7 minutes if the pieces are thick), but not longer. The fish should just barely flake. If the soup is too sour to your taste, add 1 teaspoon of sugar.

5. Using a slotted spoon, arrange 1 piece of fish in each wide flat bowl. Add to each bowl 3 capers, 2 olive halves, 1 tablespoon diced pickle, 1 lemon slice, and 1 teaspoon chopped dill. Ladle in the hot soup and serve at once.

VARIATION: For an original summer soup or to make use of any leftover broth, strain the broth and chill until set. Beat with a fork, serve jellied, and top with chopped fresh dill.

ADVANCE PREPARATION: Cook through step 3 and refrigerate for up to two days.

ZUPPA BIANCA DI VONGOLE

(CLAM SOUP WITH WHITE WINE AND GARLIC)

Serves 3 or 4

If you like your linguine with clam sauce with lots of little brown nubbies of garlic, you will love this. You could, in fact, serve this broth over spaghetti or linguine instead of toast or *friselli*, the hardtack that is traditionally put in the bottom of the soup bowl in southern Italy. Choose wide, deep bowls for serving.

SUPPER SUGGESTIONS: For a start, try endive and mushroom salad; for dessert, store-bought sorbet or granita with biscotti.

4 dozen littleneck clams (be sure to buy only the smallest size of this variety)
10 large garlic cloves, coarsely chopped
¼ cup delicately flavored olive oil
1 cup dry white wine
½ cup finely chopped parsley
Big pinch of hot red pepper flakes
3 or 4 large slices toasted Italian or French bread (or friselli)

I. Clean the clams by scrubbing each one very well under cold running water, removing any traces of sand from the shells. Discard any clams that remain open during cleaning. Let the clams soak for 20 to 30 minutes in several changes of cold water. Rinse and drain.

2. In a 4- to 6-quart pot, combine the garlic and oil and place over low heat. Let the garlic sizzle gently until it turns pale golden.

3. Immediately add the white wine and let it evaporate a minute. Stir in the parsley, then add all the clams. Cover the pot and let steam about 8 minutes, until all the clams open.

4. To serve, place a slice or two of toasted bread or *friselli* in the bottom of each bowl. Distribute the hot clams in their shells and the broth evenly among the bowls.

ADVANCE PREPARATION: Must be made just before serving.

DOWN EAST CLAM CHOWDER

Makes about 2 quarts, serving 4 to 6

I got this recipe many years ago from a woman who grew up in Falmouth, Massachusetts, on Cape Cod. I figured if she didn't know how to make a great creamy "chowda," as they say Down East, then no one knew. I was surprised to see evaporated milk in the mix, which this cook insisted was authentic, but the real trick to a great chowder, she said, is grinding the clams and letting the soup rest overnight. That tenderizes the clams (they relax?), it's true, but it also allows the potatoes to thicken the liquid, so the chowder gets a rich feel in your mouth without a flour or cornstarch thickening.

SUPPER SUGGESTIONS: New Englanders eat their chowder with soda crackers. I prefer hot baking powder biscuits (page 164), which is what I grew up eating at Brooklyn's famous Lundy's seafood restaurant. In summer, corn on the cob and a tomato salad are perfect accompaniments, the tomatoes as an appetizer, the corn also as a course unto itself. A berry compote (page 201) or Karen's raspberry wedges (page 194) are great endings.

2 dozen large chowder clams, or 4 dozen cherrystones, in their shells, scrubbed and soaked (see page 136)
½ cup water
4 ounces salt pork, cut into ¼-inch cubes (about ½ cup)
2 medium onions, finely chopped (about 2 cups)
3 medium potatoes, peeled and cut into ½-inch cubes (about 3 cups)
2 cups water
½ teaspoon freshly ground white pepper
1 (13-ounce) can evaporated milk
2 cups heavy cream
Additional milk, if necessary

I. To steam and open the clams: In a large pot, combine the clams with the ½ cup water. Place over high heat, cover, and let steam until the clam shells open—no longer than 5 minutes.

2. Using tongs or a slotted spoon, remove the clams and shell them. Discard shells.

3. Strain the clam broth and measure. Add water, if needed, to make 2 cups.

4. Grind or chop the clams, preferably with a meat grinder or in a food processor. Set aside.

5. In a 6-quart pot, over medium heat, "fry out" the salt pork—let the fat render and the bits get brown.

6. Add the onions and sauté until limp.

7. Add the potatoes, 2 cups water, 2 cups of clam broth, and the pepper. Bring to a simmer over medium heat and cook gently, partially covered, until the potatoes are tender.

8. Stir in the evaporated milk, the cream, and the ground or chopped clams. Heat through but do not allow the chowder to come to a boil.

9. Let cool and refrigerate for at least 4 hours, preferably overnight.

10. Reheat over medium-low heat, never allowing the chowder to boil.

II. Serve piping hot in deep bowls, thinning with more milk if needed.

ADVANCE PREPARATION: The cooked chowder may be refrigerated for up to two days. Don't freeze.

A GRAND NEW ENGLAND CHOWDER

Serves 6

This is unquestionably a company dish, or at least one that is opulent and festive. It's obviously a takeoff on clam chowder. Think of it as a boiled seafood dinner.

SUPPER SUGGESTIONS: Hot baking powder biscuits (page 164) or really good French bread (possibly sourdough) are the bread choices, though it would also be nice to have a bread basket with a variety of loaves and/or rolls. For a gala dinner, put out several salads—coleslaw, platters of dressed vegetables, marinated mushrooms—and serve a crostata (page 194) or fruit tart for dessert. For a simpler dinner, a berry compote (page 201) is a refreshing ending, perhaps with cookies, too.

6 ounces salt pork, cut into ½-inch cubes
5 medium onions, coarsely chopped (about 5 cups)
4 tablespoons flour
5 cups fish stock, or half bottled clam juice, half water (see note)
3 large waxy potatoes, cut into 1-inch cubes (about 5 cups)
1 large bay leaf
½ teaspoon freshly ground white pepper
Big pinch of cayenne
¾ to 1 pound medium to large shrimp, shelled (see note) and deveined (if desired or necessary)

2 pounds white filleted fish (see note), such as cod, hake (whiting), monkfish, or grouper
18 littleneck or cherrystone clams, scrubbed and soaked (see page 136)
1½ cups heavy cream or half-and-half
Coarsely chopped parsley or dill

1. Bring a small saucepan of water to a rolling boil. Add the salt pork cubes and boil 3 minutes. Drain.

2. In an 8- to 10-quart pot, cook the salt pork cubes over medium-low heat until several tablespoons of fat are rendered and the cubes are lightly browned.

3. Stir in the onions, increase the heat slightly, and cook, stirring frequently, until the onions are beginning to brown, about 10 minutes.

4. Stir in the flour and let cook another 2 minutes, stirring constantly.

5. Stir in the fish stock, potatoes, bay leaf, pepper, and cayenne. Cover and bring to a boil. Reduce heat and simmer briskly for 15 minutes, or until potatoes are tender.

6. Add the shrimp and push them to the bottom of the pot. Make a layer of fish fillets. Place the clams at the top. Cover and bring to a boil. Let boil for 5 minutes or so, until clams have opened, without lifting the cover.

7. With a slotted spoon, remove the clams and fish from the pot. Place on a platter and cover with foil to keep warm for a few moments.

8. Carefully, stir the cream into the chowder and heat through.

9. To serve, ladle chowder with shrimp, then fish and clams into large flat or deep bowls. Sprinkle with chopped parsley or dill.

NOTE: The best base for this chowder is a homemade fish stock: Save the shells from the shrimp and combine them with bones and heads from the filleted fish—a total of about 2 pounds—in a large pot. Cover with about 2 quarts freshly drawn cold water. Cover, bring to a boil over high heat, reduce heat, and simmer briskly for 20 minutes. Strain through a cheesecloth-lined colander.

ADVANCE PREPARATION: Make the chowder base through step 5; refrigerate for up to two days. Bring the base back to a simmer before proceeding.

A GRAND MANHATTAN FISH CHOWDER

Serves 6 to 8

My grandfather was famous for his red clam chowder, which, at one time, he sold wholesale to restaurants that then served it as their own. This is modeled after his recipe.

SUPPER SUGGESTIONS: Because there is no cream in this chowder, you might have an ice cream-based dessert—say pound cake (page 192) or shortcake with berries (page 205) and ice cream or whipped cream. Coleslaw (page 179) is a good accompaniment to this chowder, too, but biscuits don't quite make it. Stick to a crusty long loaf.

¼ cup delicately flavored olive oil
5 medium onions, chopped (about 5 cups)
2 large celery ribs (with leaves), sliced ¼ inch thick (about 1½ cups)
1 large green bell pepper, chopped (about 1 cup)
3 large garlic cloves, finely chopped
2 large potatoes, cut into ¼-inch cubes (about 3 cups)
2 (28-ounce) cans plum tomatoes, with their juice, coarsely chopped (remove basil)
6 cups fish stock, or part bottled clam juice, part water (see note page 139)
¾ teaspoon dried thyme
1 large bay leaf
½ teaspoon freshly ground black pepper
¾ to 1 pound medium to large shrimp, shelled and deveined (if desired or necessary)
2 pounds white filleted fish, such as cod, hake (whiting), monkfish, or grouper
18 littleneck or cherrystone clams, scrubbed and soaked (see page 136)

1. In an 8- to 10-quart pot, warm the olive oil over medium heat and sauté the onions, celery, and green pepper until well wilted, about 10 minutes.

2. Stir in the garlic and sauté another minute.

3. Add the potatoes and stir them around to coat with oil.

(continued)

4. Add the chopped tomatoes, fish stock, thyme, bay leaf, and pepper. Cover and bring to a boil over high heat. Reduce heat and simmer briskly for about 20 minutes, until potatoes are tender.

5. Add the shrimp and push them down to the bottom of the pot. Make a layer of fish fillets, then clams.

6. Cover and bring to a simmer. Without removing the cover, cook 5 minutes, or until the clams open.

7. Serve piping hot in large wide bowls.

ADVANCE PREPARATION: Cook through step 4 and refrigerate for up to one day. Bring to a simmer before proceeding.

SHRIMP GUMBO

Serves 6 to 8

I know you want to make this. It's a great, classic Cajun-Creole dish, deeply flavored by a dark brown roux, a shrimp shell stock, the trinity of Cajun cooking—onion, celery, and green bell pepper—and the traditional battery of gumbo seasonings. But it looks daunting. Thirteen steps! Let's say I'm very specific. It's not hard at all. Just make sure to nurse your roux with a slow fire and frequent stirring.

SUPPER SUGGESTIONS: If you are not embellishing this with additional seafood

(see variations), then you might want to serve raw oysters or clams first. Otherwise, a leafy salad will do with this heavy dish. For dessert, bake a peach crostata (page 194) if the fruit is in season, the Swedish almond cake (page 192) or amaretti ricotta cheesecake (page 196) if it is not.

2 pounds medium or large shrimp in their
    shells
7 cups water
½ cup vegetable oil
1 cup flour
1 large onion, finely chopped (about 1½ cups)
3 large celery ribs, finely chopped (about
    1½ cups)
1 large green pepper, finely chopped (about
    1 cup)
3 large garlic cloves, crushed
1 (28-ounce) can plum tomatoes, cut into
    chunks, with their juice (discard basil)
1 teaspoon dried thyme
1 tablespoon Worcestershire sauce
2 large or 3 small bay leaves
¼ to ½ teaspoon cayenne
½ teaspoon freshly ground black pepper
1½ cups finely chopped scallions
1 tightly packed cup chopped parsley
    leaves
6 to 8 cups cooked long-grain white rice

1. Shell the shrimp, reserving the shells. Refrigerate the shrimp, well covered.

2. In a colander, rinse the shells briefly under cold running water. Place the shells in a pot with the 7 cups of water. Bring to a boil, adjust heat, and simmer briskly, partially covered, for 45 minutes.

3. Meanwhile, prepare the roux: In a 6- to 8-quart pot, combine the oil and flour over medium-low heat. Cook, stirring regularly, for about an hour, until the flour has turned a rich brown.

4. While the roux is cooking, chop all the vegetables.

5. Strain the shrimp stock. You should have about 6 cups; add water if necessary, or boil to reduce slightly if necessary.

6. As soon as the roux is the right color, add the onion, celery, and pepper. This will turn the roux a deep mahogany brown. Cover the pot and let the vegetables sweat for 10 minutes, stirring once or twice.

7. Add the crushed garlic and cook, covered, 2 more minutes.

8. Add the tomatoes, their juice, and the shrimp stock. Turn heat to high and stir until the liquid boils and is smooth, though it will still look a little granular.

9. Add the thyme, Worcestershire sauce, bay leaves, cayenne, and black pepper. Cover and simmer over low heat for 30 minutes.

10. Add half the scallions and half the parsley. Simmer another 30 minutes.

11. Before serving, heat the gumbo to the boiling point and add the shelled shrimp. Stir well and reduce heat to a simmer. Cook for about 10 minutes, partially covered and stirring occasionally, until shrimp are cooked through.

12. Either stir in the remaining scallions and parsley or garnish the bowls with them.

13. To serve, mound the rice in the center of a shallow soup bowl, then ladle the piping hot gumbo and shrimp around it. If using the parsley and scallions as a final garnish, sprinkle them over everything. Put a bottle of Tabasco or other Louisiana hot sauce on the table.

VARIATIONS: You can add more and/or different seafood, for instance scallops, crab, and of course crayfish. With additions, the base can be extended to serve 10 to 12.

ADVANCE PREPARATION: Cook through step 10, refrigerate for up to a day (or as long as you can keep the shrimp fresh), then proceed. The base may be made ahead and frozen, but fresh shrimp must then be available to finish the recipe.

CHAPTER 6

COLD SOUPS

Classic Andalusian Gazpacho
Eugene Jackson's Gazpacho with Kidney Beans
Gazpacho Ajo Blanco
Vichyssoise
Cold Roasted Garlic Soup
Cream of Broccoli Soup
Cold Cucumber Soup with Smoked Salmon, Potatoes, and Caviar
Schav
Creamy Borscht
Chlodnik

Also see: Paula Wolfert's Salmon Solianka

CLASSIC ANDALUSIAN GAZPACHO

Makes 2 quarts, serving 6 to 8

On my first visit to Spain a couple of decades ago on the occasion of the harvest (*vendemia*) in Jerez, I was invited to a midday garden party where gazpacho was served as the principal refreshment. There was plenty of other food and certainly the *fino* sherry flowed freely, but it was the gazpacho that restored the energy of the people mingling on the large, sun-baked lawn, all of whom had stayed out partying until dawn. Cooks were stationed at tables around the perimeter of the garden, each one with a huge basket of the necessary vegetables and a vast mortar and pestle with which to grind them into soup. The gazpacho was coarse and thick, just liquid enough to be able to drink it from a cup. As I remember, it was such a hot day that no one ventured too far from one of these gazpacho tables. Since most of us do not own mortars capable of grinding even a couple of quarts of vegetables, I've devised the following food processor method. Just be careful not to purée the mixture. It should be coarse. The addition of garlic-rubbed bread is an old-fashioned idea.

SUPPER SUGGESTIONS: Garlic toast (page 159) or great bread is a necessity. Follow with a cheese board and a green salad, then either fresh fruit or, more elaborately, berry shortcakes (page 205) with ice cream or whipped cream.

4 (¾-inch-thick) slices of stale or day-old Italian bread, 3 × 5 inches each (see note for microwave method to harden bread)
2 large garlic cloves, halved
2 pounds tomatoes (about 4 medium-large tomatoes)
1 (12-inch) European seedless cucumber
1 large red pepper, seeded and deveined
½ small hot cherry pepper
½ medium onion
⅓ cup extra-virgin olive oil (preferably Spanish)
½ teaspoon salt
Freshly ground black pepper
2 tablespoons sherry vinegar

1. Rub the slices of bread with the garlic cloves.

2. Place 3 of the tomatoes and the garlic in a food processor and purée. Remove to a large bowl, leaving some purée in the processor.

3. Purée the bread with the remaining tomato purée and place in the large bowl.

4. In the food processor, coarsely chop, a little at a time, the cucumber, pepper, cherry pepper, onion, and remaining tomato, adding some tomato purée for liquid if necessary.

5. Combine the chopped vegetables with bread and tomato purée in the large bowl.

(continued)

6. Stir in the oil, salt, pepper to taste, and vinegar.

7. Place, covered, in refrigerator to chill thoroughly, at least 4 hours or overnight.

8. Adjust seasonings to taste before serving.

NOTE: To harden bread in the microwave, place slices on a dish in the oven for 1 minute on HIGH. Turn over and cook on the other side for 45 seconds. Watch to make sure bread does not burn.

ADVANCE PREPARATION: Can be refrigerated for up to a day; do not freeze.

EUGENE JACKSON'S GAZPACHO WITH KIDNEY BEANS

Serves 6

My friend Bob Harned brought a container of this to me from work one day as an example of ideal gazpacho. "Rich," was my reaction. I said, "Get the recipe and let's see what's in it," although I could taste what was coming. Eugene Jackson, the chef in his firm's cafeteria, was happy to share the evident secret—such an enormous quantity of olive oil that you could use the mixture as salad dressing. I've reduced the oil by 75 percent and it's still a mouth-filling experience. Be my guest and replace some of it if you dare. I've also changed Eugene's soup by supplementing it with kidney beans. They make gazpacho a very filling dish and taste like a natural addition to me.

SUPPER SUGGESTIONS: A leafy salad and plenty of garlic toast (page 159) are all the accompaniments you'll want. For dessert, a peach crostata (page194) would make it seem like a really special meal.

24 ounces tomato juice
1 medium onion, finely chopped (about 1 cup)
2 small green peppers, finely chopped (about 1½ cups)
1 large garlic clove, finely minced
2 small ripe tomatoes, diced (about 1⅓ cups)
¼ cup extra-virgin olive oil, preferably Spanish
2½ cups cooked red kidney beans, drained (1 cup dry beans, cooked)
½ teaspoon salt
½ teaspoon hot sauce
¼ teaspoon freshly ground black pepper

1. In a 3-quart ceramic or glass bowl, mix together all the ingredients.

2. Cover with plastic and place in the refrigerator for 3 hours or overnight.

3. When thoroughly chilled, adjust seasonings and serve in deep or wide bowls.

ADVANCE PREPARATION: Can be refrigerated for up to a day; do not freeze.

GAZPACHO AJO BLANCO

Serves 4

Paula Wolfert's *Mediterranean Food* (Quadrangle, 1977) introduced me to this garlic-almond soup. At first, I thought peeling grapes as a garnish was a bit prissy. I was wrong. If you can muster the patience, peel them. Buy large ones so the job will be easier. But peel them. The cool, juicy surface of a sweet peeled grape against the rich garlicky broth is too much pleasure to give up.

SUPPER SUGGESTIONS: In the heat of July and August, the only time you would want to eat this soup, make it part of a summer vegetable feast—corn on the cob, sliced tomatoes, maybe some grilled peppers and eggplant. Don't forget the crusty bread. For dessert, strawberry shortcake (page 205), something substantial with the light soup, or blueberry apple crumble (page 203).

4 ounces shelled whole blanched almonds
2 large garlic cloves, finely chopped
1 teaspoon coarse sea salt
½ cup cold water
½ cup crustless French or Italian bread
cubes, soaked in water and squeezed to
extract excess moisture
⅓ cup olive oil
1½ teaspoons red or white wine vinegar
3 cups ice water
1 cup seedless green grapes, peeled (optional)
and halved

1. Place the almonds, garlic, salt, and cold water in a blender or food processor. Process until smooth.

2. Add the bread and a little more water, if necessary, and process again.

3. With the motor running, slowly add the olive oil in a thin stream.

4. Pour the mixture into a large bowl. Whisk in the vinegar, then gradually stir in the ice water. Taste and correct seasonings. Refrigerate until well chilled, at least 3 hours.

5. To serve, ladle into deep bowls and garnish with green grapes.

ADVANCE PREPARATION: Can be refrigerated for up to a week; freezes perfectly.

VICHYSSOISE

Serves 4

Is it French or American? A Frenchman, chef Louis Diat, created it in 1910. But at the time he headed the kitchens of the Ritz Carlton Hotel in New York City. According to Waverley Root and Richard de Rochemont in *Eating in America* (Morrow, 1976), it wasn't even known in France until after World War II, when touring Americans encouraged it onto menus by asking for it, thinking they were going to get a French delicacy on home ground. The name innocently refers to the then-fashionable resort city of Vichy, where Diat was born. Still, according to Evan Jones in *American Food* (Dutton, 1975), "it just missed entering history as 'crème gauloise' in 1941 when a group of chefs in America voted to change the name because they were offended by the wartime Vichy government."

SUPPER SUGGESTIONS: It's a rich but relatively insubstantial soup, even with a crusty roll or loaf, so start with a filling potato and shrimp salad (page 186) and finish with strawberry shortcake (page 205) or blueberry apple crumble (page 203).

2 tablespoons butter
6 medium leeks (white only), washed and
*   sliced (about 2 cups)*
3 medium potatoes (about 1½ pounds),
*   quartered*
6 cups water
1 teaspoon salt
½ teaspoon freshly ground white pepper
2 cups half-and-half
Chopped chives

1. In a 3- to 4-quart pot, warm the butter over medium-low heat and sauté the leeks until well wilted, about 5 minutes.

2. Add the potatoes, water, salt, and pepper. Cover and bring to a boil, reduce heat, and simmer steadily, partially covered, until the potatoes are very tender.

3. Let the soup cool slightly, then purée in a blender or with an immersion blender. Do not use a food processor—it makes the potatoes pasty.

4. Chill very well.

5. Stir in the half-and-half. Taste and correct seasoning with salt and white pepper.

6. Serve very well chilled, sprinkled with chopped chives, in deep or flat bowls.

ADVANCE PREPARATION: Can be refrigerated for up to a week; do not freeze.

COLD ROASTED GARLIC SOUP

Makes 6½ cups, serving about 4

This was a prizewinner at the annual Festival of the Stinking Rose in Gilroy, California, which is the garlic-growing capital of the country. It is nothing more than a garlic-flavored leek and potato soup, but for lovers of the Stinking Rose, that is quite enough.

SUPPER SUGGESTIONS: If it's cold soup, we're assuming summer. Start with a tomato salad or a huge mixed vegetable salad (page 173), or corn on the cob. For dessert, a berry compote (page 201) or strawberries in two liqueurs (page 200) or blueberry apple crumble (page 203).

2 cups garlic cloves (about 3 large heads)
1½ tablespoons vegetable or light olive oil
2 medium potatoes, diced (about 3 cups)
2 cups sliced leeks (white only)
4 cups light chicken broth (half canned, half
*   water)*

½ cup heavy cream
Finely chopped parsley or dill

1. Preheat the oven to 325 degrees.

2. Measure out the garlic and pour on the oil while the garlic is still in the measuring cup. Spread out oil-coated garlic on a baking pan and bake in the oven for 25 minutes, until garlic is tender. When cool enough to handle, peel the garlic and discard the skins.

3. In a 3-quart saucepan, combine the potatoes, leeks, and broth. Bring to a boil and cook 20 minutes.

4. Add the roasted garlic and purée the whole mixture in a food mill, blender, or with an immersion blender.

5. Stir in the cream and chill well.

6. Serve in deep or flat bowls, sprinkled with parsley or dill.

ADVANCE PREPARATION: Can be kept refrigerated for up to a week; do not freeze.

CREAM OF BROCCOLI SOUP

Serves 4 or 5

This is a very simple and marvelously thick soup that is delicious either hot or cold, although somehow it tastes better when eaten well chilled on a hot day—perhaps because the recipe is a souvenir of a trip to Puerto Rico, where it was served poolside at a fancy hotel.

SUPPER SUGGESTIONS: Potato and shrimp salad (page 186) is a good first course. Plain French bread is a satisfactory accompaniment, but fettunta (page 159) or Parmesan aioli toast (page 160) is better. Dessert, especially in midsummer, could be store-bought cookies with either berry compote (page 201) or strawberries in two liqueurs (page 200), or, for more substance, strawberry shortcake (page 205) or blueberry apple crumble (page 203).

1 bunch broccoli (about 2 pounds)
6 cups chicken broth
1 large potato, peeled and roughly cut up
    (about 1½ cups)
1 large celery rib, roughly cut up (about ¾ cup)
1 medium leek (white part only) or onion,
    coarsely chopped (about 1 cup)
1 small bay leaf
1 cup heavy cream, light cream, or half-and-
    half (approximately)
Coarse sea salt
Freshly ground pepper
Chopped chives

1. Cut the stems off the broccoli, peel, and cut into 1-inch pieces. Break the tops of the broccoli into small florets.

2. In a 4- to 6-quart saucepan, combine the broth, broccoli, potato, celery, leek, and bay leaf. Bring to a boil, reduce heat, cover partially, and simmer steadily for about 35 minutes, until the vegetables are very tender. Remove the bay leaf.

3. In a blender, or through a food mill or with an immersion blender, purée the soup.

4. Stir in the cream. Taste and correct seasoning with salt and pepper, oversalting slightly because flavors diminish when cold.

5. Chill thoroughly, preferably for at least 12 hours.

6. Just before serving, check the seasoning again and, if necessary, thin the soup with more cream or some milk.

7. Serve in deep or flat bowls or mugs, sprinkled with chopped chives.

ADVANCE PREPARATION: May be kept refrigerated for up to a week; it freezes perfectly for up to a year.

COLD CUCUMBER SOUP WITH SMOKED SALMON, POTATOES, AND CAVIAR

Serves 6 to 8

This is a lushly textured and luxurious soup created by chef John Schenk of West Broadway, a restaurant in the SoHo section of Manhattan. He serves it as a first course, but on a hot summer day it is substantial enough to be a glorious, even glamorous, soup supper.

SUPPER SUGGESTIONS: Slices of tomatoes and sweet onion dressed with torn basil and a drizzle of olive oil to start, not forgetting the crusty bread; a red berry compote (page 201) *and* sorbet for dessert.

2 large celery ribs, chopped (about 1 cup)
1 medium onion, chopped (about 1 cup)
½ cup sliced leek greens
8 garlic cloves, thinly sliced
1 medium Idaho potato, peeled and thinly sliced
4 tablespoons butter
6 small cucumbers, peeled and sliced (4 English cucumbers can be substituted)
1 tablespoon coarse sea salt
1 teaspoon freshly ground white pepper
Skin of half a side of smoked salmon
3 bay leaves
3 cups chicken stock, homemade or canned
1½ quarts heavy cream
Big pinch of cayenne

FOR THE GARNISH:
10 red new potatoes, boiled and sliced
1 medium cucumber, thinly sliced
½ pound smoked salmon, cut into
   ¼-inch cubes
4 ounces salmon roe
2 tablespoons snipped chives
1½ teaspoons chervil leaves

I. In a 6-quart stainless steel or enameled cast iron pot, combine the celery, onion, leek greens, garlic, and potato with the butter and sauté over medium heat, stirring occasionally, until the onion is soft and transparent, about 10 minutes.

2. Add the cucumbers and sprinkle with salt and pepper. Cover and continue to cook over medium heat, stirring occasionally, until the cucumbers have released their liquid and are quite soft, about 20 minutes.

3. While the cucumbers are cooking, tie the salmon skin and bay leaves in a cheesecloth sachet.

4. Add the sachet and the chicken stock to the vegetables and simmer gently for 10 minutes.

5. Add the cream and cayenne and return to a gentle simmer. Remove from heat.

6. Remove the sachet and purée the soup in a food processor. Taste and correct seasonings.

7. Pass the soup through a fine sieve into a bowl. To speed up the chilling process, place the soup in a large bowl of ice and stir to bring down the temperature; or simply let the soup cool and then place it, covered, in the refrigerator for at least 3 hours.

8. To serve, distribute the potatoes, cucumber, and salmon evenly among chilled, wide, preferably flat bowls. Ladle on well-chilled soup, then spoon rounded teaspoons of the roe on top of each bowl and sprinkle with chives and chervil.

ADVANCE PREPARATION: The soup can be kept refrigerated for up to two days. It does not freeze well; it becomes grainy.

SCHAV

Serves 8 to 10

This, a Russian soup, and beet borscht were the only cold soups I knew as a child, but they were a regular part of my mother's repertoire. The borscht she bought. The schav my grandmother made from scratch, which meant ordering enormous bunches of large-leafed sorrel—what she called "sour grass"—from her fruit and vegetable man. These days I see tiny bunches of tender sorrel for several dollars each and I laugh. I wait until I see older, tougher sorrel at a farmer's market, which I always do. It is also an easy perennial to grow.

SUPPER SUGGESTIONS: The way this is made into a main course is to chop into it garden vegetables and serve it with a boiled potato and a big spoonful of sour cream or thick yogurt. The corned rye (sour rye), called corn bread in New York, is the perfect loaf to have, though any rye bread is good. For dessert, serve a fruit salad; this is a light, late-summer family meal.

4 pounds sorrel
4 quarts water
Coarse sea salt and freshly ground black
    pepper
Lemon juice (optional)
4 eggs (optional)

FOR THE GARNISH:
Sour cream or yogurt
Chopped cucumber
Chopped scallions
Chopped red radishes
8 to 10 medium boiled potatoes

1. Pick over and wash the sorrel well. Remove the tough stems, then chop the leaves fine.

2. In a 5- to 8-quart enameled or stainless steel pot, bring the water to a rolling boil. Drop in the sorrel and boil for 10 minutes. Remove from heat. Season with salt and pepper to taste. Taste, and if a slightly tarter edge is desired, add a little lemon juice.

3. To enrich the soup with egg, beat the eggs well in a small bowl. Bring the soup to a boil, remove from heat, then beat the eggs into the hot soup. (Don't add eggs if you plan to store the soup longer than a week.)

4. Pour schav into clean quart jars and refrigerate.

5. Serve very well chilled in deep or flat bowls with a hefty dollop of sour cream or yogurt floating in the soup or beaten into it. Add chopped cucumber, scallions, and radishes, plus a boiled potato.

ADVANCE PREPARATION: Without eggs, the schav should keep well in the refrigerator for about ten days. With eggs, do not keep longer than three days. Do not freeze.

CREAMY BORSCHT

Serves 3 or 4

This is another Russian specialty. If you can get very thick yogurt, it's all the better. To thicken typical commercial yogurt, pour the yogurt into a strainer lined with a coffee filter or rinsed cheesecloth and let drain over a bowl, in the refrigerator, for several hours or overnight.

SUPPER SUGGESTIONS: Rye bread or black bread is the loaf. Start with either Roumanian eggplant salad (page 185) or potato and shrimp salad (page 186). For a sweet, serve cookies and fresh fruit.

2½ pounds (without tops) beets
4 cups water
1 tablespoon salt
1 medium onion, peeled
1 large garlic clove, peeled
Juice of ½ lemon
2 eggs

2 cups plain yogurt
Sugar (optional)
12 steamed new potatoes (hot and freshly
    cooked)
1 to 2 tablespoons chopped fresh dill

1. Preheat the oven to 400 degrees. Scrub the beets and wrap them in aluminum foil. Place in the oven for about 1 hour, or until tender. Use a skewer, poked right through the foil, to test for doneness. Peel the beets and shred them on the coarse side of a grater.

2. In a 3-quart pot, combine the water, salt, whole onion, whole clove of garlic, shredded beets, and lemon juice. Cover, bring to a simmer, and adjust heat so that it simmers gently for 45 minutes, or until the whole onion is soft. Remove the onion and garlic.

3. In a small mixing bowl, lightly beat the eggs, then beat in some of the hot broth. Pour egg mixture into remaining soup and stir well. Chill thoroughly.

4. Just before serving, beat in the yogurt. Taste and correct seasoning, adding more salt, sugar if needed, and/or lemon juice, as desired.

5. Serve very cold in flat bowls with hot new potatoes; the contrasting temperatures add interest. Sprinkle with dill.

VARIATION: For a richer soup, substitute sour cream for part of the yogurt.

ADVANCE PREPARATION: Can be kept refrigerated for up to a week, but no more than three days once the eggs have been added; do not freeze.

CHLODNIK

Serves 4 to 6

This iced Russian soup is from my editor Susan Friedland's book *Caviar* (Scribner's, 1986). The ingredients approximate *kvas*, the fermented barley drink that is the key ingredient in the Russian version. Salmon roe is Susan's creative addition.

SUPPER SUGGESTIONS: A platter of tomatoes, avocado, and onion (page 187) is a good beginning. For dessert, pound cake (page 192) topped with strawberries in two liqueurs (page 200) is as elegant as the soup.

4 cucumbers
Coarse salt
1 pound bulk or packaged sauerkraut (don't
    use canned), to yield ½ to ⅔ cup juice
2 cups sour cream
5 cups buttermilk
½ cup aquavit
2 teaspoons ground fennel seeds
¾ pound medium shrimp
8 to 10 tablespoons minced dill
4 hard-cooked eggs, sliced
8 tablespoons salmon roe

1. Peel, seed, and dice the cucumbers. Put in a colander and sprinkle with coarse salt. Let sit for 30 minutes.

2. Put the sauerkraut in a sieve over a bowl and press down hard with a wooden spoon to extract the juice. Save the sauerkraut for another use.

(continued)

3. In a large bowl, combine the sour cream, buttermilk, aquavit, sauerkraut juice, and fennel seeds. Stir well.

4. Run the cucumbers under cold water, drain, and pat dry with paper towels.

5. Add the cucumbers to the soup and chill for at least 8 hours.

6. In an uncovered saucepan, cook the shrimp in boiling salted water to cover for 3 minutes. Turn off the heat and let the shrimp cool in the liquid. Shell, devein (if desired), and cut into ½-inch pieces if the shrimp are large. Refrigerate until ready to serve.

7. Serve the soup in chilled, wide, shallow bowls. Sprinkle each portion with a generous tablespoon of dill. Place an egg slice in the center of each bowl and surround with shrimp. Garnish either the egg or the soup itself with salmon roe.

ADVANCE PREPARATION: May be kept refrigerated for several days; do not freeze.

CHAPTER 7

BREADS

BREAD AND TOAST
CROUTONS AND CROSTINI
TOASTED CROUTON CUBES
FETTUNTA OR GARLIC TOAST
BRUSCHETTA
PARMESAN AIOLI TOAST
FOCACCIA
SCHIACCIATA
BLUEGRASS COUNTRY COOKING'S CLASSIC SOUTHERN CORN BREAD
BAKING POWDER BISCUITS
POPOVERS
WALNUT ONION MUFFINS

BREAD AND TOAST

Good bread is particularly important when the rest of your menu is as simple as a salad, soup, and a fruit dessert. Bread can make or break a soup supper.

Explore all your local possibilities for buying bread—supermarkets, bakeries, farmer's markets. Look for sturdy loaves, chewy loaves, living loaves (not chemically embalmed loaves) that, aside from novelty loaves like raisin breads and nut breads, are made with only flour, water, and yeast. Artisan baking is a New Age American craft. There are young bread bakers all over the country and they're looking for people who understand how much the staff of life their product really is.

Or try baking a few loaves yourself. Many people find satisfactions in baking bread that they don't get from other kinds of cooking.

If all else fails, make toast. Even supermarket bread, sweet as it is, gains character when it's dried and crisped. Of course, the better the bread, the better the toast.

CROUTONS AND CROSTINI

Pieces of dried, toasted, or fried bread are called croutons in French whether they are small cubes of bread, which is what Americans usually mean by croutons, or full slices of bread that may be used as a sop (as in French onion soup, page 31, or egg bouillabaisse, page 48), or as a soup or salad accompaniment (as with Tuscan bean soup, page 58, and Italian mushroom soup with Parmesan, page 30).

Crostino—crostini in the plural—is the literal Italian translation of crouton. Both croutons and crostini are often served with toppings as snacks, appetizers, or accompaniments to salads and soups. Bruschetta (page 160) is a particular kind of crostini. Fettunta (page 159) is what Tuscans call grilled slices of bread rubbed with garlic and dressed with extra-virgin olive oil. Southern Italian *friselli* or *frisedde* (available from Italian bakeries and at some supermarkets), which are twice-baked bread slices or small rolls hard enough to be cause for dental work, are meant specifically for sopping up the juices in the bottom of a bowl (as in zuppa di cozze or zuppa bianca di vongole, pages 133 and 136). That's when they become edible.

When serving croutons/crostini as either an appetizer by themselves or as a salad or soup accompaniment, think of these possible toppings, all available at specialty stores and in jars or cans:

1. flavored olive oil

2. tapenade

3. olive paste

4. anchovy paste or butter

5. sardines

6. a thin smear of imported tomato paste, possibly with freshly ground black pepper, or a few red pepper flakes

7. cheese or a cheese spread

8. prosciutto or salami

9. smoked salmon

10. smoked turkey or chicken

11. smoked mackerel, trout, or bluefish

Also see eggplant salad (page 185), baked eggplant and garlic (page 184), tomato and red onion salad (page 180), and marinated mushrooms (page 177).

TOASTED CROUTON CUBES

About 1½ cups

These are good when you want the crunch but not the bulk of bread, as a soup or salad fillip. Baking cubes of fresh bread into croutons takes only minutes and doesn't require using oil or butter,

a fat savings from old-fashioned fried croutons. Feel free to make toasted croutons out of any kind of bread, remembering that each will require a slightly different baking time. Rye bread croutons are welcome in some split pea soups (pages 66 and 68). Toasted, coarse-grained, whole wheat bread croutons are an excellent substitute for classic white bread croutons in a Caesar salad (page 173). Other soups that might go with these kinds of croutons are black bean soup (page 62), lentil soup with fennel and sun-dried tomatoes (page 66), eggplant soup with frittata noodles (page 26), and fresh tomato soup (page 38).

4 slices firm supermarket white bread.

1. Preheat the oven to 350 degrees.

2. Keep the bread stacked as it comes from the package and, using a long-bladed, serrated-edge bread knife for all the cutting, cut the crusts off the bread. (The crusts can be cubed and toasted separately, but it is best not to mix them with the center of the bread because they brown more quickly.)

3. Still retaining the stack, cut the bread into ½-inch strips.

4. Cut the strips into ½-inch cubes.

5. Spread the bread cubes on a baking sheet and bake for 4 to 5 minutes, until the cubes are just beginning to brown.

6. Using a hamburger turner, toss the cubes around. Return them to the oven for another 4 or 5 minutes, tossing the cubes about every 90 seconds, until most are lightly browned and the brownest have not burned.

VARIATIONS: To fry croutons, heat 2 tablespoons olive or vegetable oil in a medium skillet until you see the vaguest, first sign of smoke. Immediately add all the bread cubes and toss around. Toss constantly until as evenly browned as you can get them. Immediately turn the croutons out onto a baking sheet to get them out of the hot pan.

For fried garlic croutons, add 3 whole, slightly smashed garlic cloves to the pan with the oil and cook over low heat until the garlic cloves are lightly browned. Remove the garlic, increase heat to medium, and proceed with the recipe.

For fat-free toasted garlic croutons, keep the bread slices whole and toast on both sides; rub with a cut clove of garlic and then cube. Or, if fat is not a consideration, brush fresh or days-old bread slices with a blend of crushed garlic and olive oil, or spread with garlic or other seasoned butter, cut the bread into cubes, then toast as in main recipe.

To add herb or spice seasoning to croutons, use dried herbs, powdered in a mortar with a pestle. Place the herbs in a paper bag and shake freshly made croutons in them.

ADVANCE PREPARATION: Toasted croutons can be kept for several months in a plastic bag, a jar, or a tin. Fried croutons can be kept for several weeks.

FETTUNTA OR GARLIC TOAST

When its green, peppery, eucalyptus-scented olive oil is freshly pressed, Tuscany exults in this simple pleasure—thick slices of its treasured salt-free bread, grilled over charcoal, rubbed with garlic, lavished with the new pungent oil, and sprinkled with sea salt and freshly ground pepper. At any time of year, however, and even made in an American kitchen broiler with any kind of high-quality extra-virgin olive oil, this is food of the gods.

I like to use a crusty, heavy, dark whole wheat bread for fettunta and bruschetta (see following recipe), but a dense white loaf with a thick crust is excellent, too. Light white breads usually cannot tolerate the garlic rub—they break or compact.

Bread, fresh or days old, but not hard
Garlic cloves, peeled and cut in half
Extra-virgin olive oil
Coarse sea salt
Freshly ground black pepper

I. Cut the bread into ½- to ¾-inch-thick slices. Cut long loaves slightly on the diagonal to create slices with more surface area. Depending on their size, cut round loaves into either half-loaf slices or quarter-loaf slices. (A good way to cut large rounds of bread is to cut them in half, then place each half cut side down and cut down through the crust to form quarter-loaf slices.)

(continued)

2. Arrange the bread directly on an oven rack or on a baking sheet and place under the broiler, about 4 inches from the heat. Toast until nicely browned, then turn and toast the second side.

3. Immediately, while the toasts are still very hot, hold each one in a hand protected with an oven mitt or pot holder, and with the other hand rub one surface of the toast with a cut clove of garlic. Rub until the stub of garlic is too small to hold.

4. Arrange the warm toasts on a serving platter. Drizzle with olive oil, using 1 or 2 teaspoons (or more) for each toast.

5. Sprinkle with salt and pepper to taste.

6. Serve immediately.

ADVANCE PREPARATION: Must be made just before serving.

BRUSCHETTA

In America, bruschetta has come to mean a toast—garlic-rubbed or not—that is topped with a chopped tomato salad. In Italy, bruschetta is simply the more nationally known word for fettunta and, like fettunta, it may have no more embellishment than oil, salt, and pepper.

To make bruschetta (pronounced brew-sket-tah, with the accent on the middle syllable), follow the directions for fettunta (see preceding recipe), then top with the tomato and red onion salad on page 180. Another extraordinary treat to serve as an appetizer or soup accompaniment is a slice of garlic-rubbed bruschetta topped with either Roumanian eggplant salad (page 185) or baked eggplant and garlic (page 184).

ADVANCE PREPARATION: Must be made just before serving.

PARMESAN AIOLI TOAST

Serves 3 or 4

This recipe is inspired by the toast served at James O'Shea's West Street Grill in Litchfield, Connecticut. It's one of the little things that hooked the local gentry into making this *the* place in the county. The toast dramatically dresses up a salad.

4 or 5 garlic cloves, crushed
1 cup mayonnaise
½ cup freshly grated Parmesan cheese
6 to 8 large, ½-inch-thick slices from a
  round, dense, crusty bread, lightly toasted
  on both sides.

1. In a small bowl, blend together the garlic, mayonnaise, and cheese.

2. Generously slather each slice of bread with the mayonnaise mixture and place them on a baking sheet.

3. Place under the broiler, about 4 inches from the heat, until the mayonnaise puffs slightly and browns lightly.

4. Serve immediately with salad or soup.

ADVANCE PREPARATION: The mayonnaise mixture can be kept in the refrigerator for a day or two. With longer storage, the garlic gets an acrid edge and the Parmesan flavor fades.

FOCACCIA

**Makes two 9-inch rounds,
serving 8 to 10**

Focaccia, which is less a specific bread than a generic Italian word for flat bread, is best hot out of the oven, which is why this is the only time-consuming yeast bread recipe I give in this book. To learn to make focaccia—after having tried numerous recipes from all sorts of sources—I turned to a local focaccia baker whose bread I admire. All he would say is: "Play with your dough." In other words, there is no recipe for focaccia that can promise perfection. What is generally thought of as focaccia in this country is the following fairly light, olive-oil enriched flat bread. If you want it chewier, "play with your dough"—add more olive oil, knead in extra flour, don't let it rise twice, refrigerate the dough overnight before letting it rise. Although

mixing and kneading take minutes to do, allow several hours to make focaccia, depending on how long it needs to rise.

FOR THE SPONGE:
2½ teaspoons active dry yeast (1 package)
½ cup warm water
3 tablespoons flour (preferably high-gluten bread flour, but all-purpose is fine)

FOR THE DOUGH:
3½ cups flour (high-gluten or all-purpose is fine), plus ¾ cup for kneading
1 teaspoon salt
5 tablespoons extra-virgin olive oil
1½ cups warm water
Olive oil
Coarse sea salt

1. For the sponge: In a small bowl, mix the yeast, water, and 3 tablespoons of flour. Cover with plastic wrap and set aside in a warm place until it bubbles, 5 to 10 minutes.

2. For the dough: In a large bowl, mix the flour and salt. Make a well in the center of the flour and pour in the sponge, the olive oil, and the warm water.

3. With a fork, beat the liquid ingredients together, blending in some of the flour until a dough starts to form.

4. Continue blending with your hands until most of the flour is incorporated and the dough is workable on a board.

5. Spread a board or other kneading surface with an additional ½ cup flour. Turn out the dough and any remaining flour in the bowl. Knead the dough for 10 to 12 minutes, until silky and elastic.

6. Place the dough in a lightly oiled bowl. Turn to coat with oil. Cover with plastic and set aside until doubled in bulk, from 45 minutes to 2 hours, depending on the temperature of your kitchen. Try to find a cool place where the dough will take the longer, not shorter, time to rise.

7. Punch down the dough and turn it out onto a lightly floured board. Knead again for 5 minutes.

8. Return the dough to the oiled bowl and let rise, covered with plastic wrap, for another hour.

9. Preheat the oven to 400 degrees.

10. Punch down the dough and, with a sharp knife, divide it in half.

11. On a lightly floured board, roll out each half to a 9-inch round between ¼ and ½ inch thick. Cover one half with plastic or a cotton towel while baking the other.

12. Before placing focaccia in oven, dimple the surface with your fingertips, brush lightly with olive oil, and sprinkle with about ½ teaspoon salt.

13. Bake for 15 minutes. Bread will be a light golden color.

VARIATION: Add to the dressing of oil and salt any herb, preferably fresh, and if dried, crumbled between your fingers. Rosemary or sage is traditional. Or top with bits of pitted olive or olive paste, or anchovies or anchovy paste, or either thinly slivered raw onion or thinly sliced onion sautéed until golden.

ADVANCE PREPARATION: The focaccia is best when still warm from the oven and for the following few hours. With some loss in quality, it can be refreshed in a 300-degree oven if baked the day before it is served, or if frozen (defrost it first). Alternatively, the dough can be prepared through step 7 and kept refrigerated for 24 hours. Punch down and continue with step 8.

SCHIACCIATA

Makes 2 10 × 14-inch sheets, serving 6 to 8

Schiacciata means "pressed" or "flattened," and that's exactly what you will have to do to focaccia dough to form this crackerlike bread dressed with coarse salt and oil. It used to be popular in the trattorias of Trastevere, in Rome.

1 recipe focaccia (see preceding recipe)
Olive oil
Coarse sea salt

1. Prepare focaccia dough.

2. Instead of letting it rise twice, punch down the dough after one rising and divide it in half.

3. Preheat the oven to 500 degrees.

4. On a lightly floured board, roll out each half of the dough into a very thin roughly shaped oval. Place on a lightly oiled baking sheet.

5. Press the dough down with your fingertips, making indentations in the dough. Brush lightly with olive oil. Sprinkle lightly with coarse salt.

6. Bake until lightly browned and crisp, 10 to 12 minutes. Remove before the thinnest parts burn.

7. Serve hot, broken—not cut—into large pieces.

ADVANCE PREPARATION: As with focaccia, the dough can be prepared through step 7 and kept refrigerated for 24 hours. Punch down and continue with step 8. However, do not freeze or reheat.

BLUEGRASS COUNTRY COOKING'S CLASSIC SOUTHERN CORN BREAD

Serves 4 to 6

This is out of this world when it comes from the oven—an astoundingly light crumb encased in a strikingly crisp crust. It is still an excellent bread when freshly baked and warm, but it turns to something like sawdust when baked and held for a few hours or overnight. It is so good when hot, however, you shouldn't have to be concerned about leftovers. The recipe comes from Curtis Balls and James White, both originally of Kentucky and now caterers specializing in southern food in New York. Bluegrass Country Cooking is both the name of their company and of their public-access cable television show. For maximum crispness, use a cast iron skillet, or at least a very heavy one.

1½ cups cornmeal, preferably stone-ground,
either white or yellow
½ cup unbleached all-purpose flour
2 teaspoons baking powder
½ teaspoon baking soda
1 teaspoon table salt
1 egg
1 cup buttermilk
¼ cup vegetable oil or melted bacon fat

(continued)

1. Preheat the oven to 425 degrees.

2. In a large bowl, combine the cornmeal, flour, baking powder, baking soda, and salt. Mix well.

3. In a small bowl, beat the egg lightly, then beat in the buttermilk.

4. Pour the oil into a 9-inch skillet or metal baking pan. Place in the oven until the oil is very hot but not smoking, about 10 minutes.

5. Just before the oil is hot enough, stir the liquid ingredients into the dry ingredients with a wooden spoon, but not thoroughly.

6. Being careful to use a heavy potholder to handle the skillet, remove the skillet from the oven and pour about half the oil into the batter. Stir until the oil is entirely incorporated into the batter. It should not take more than a dozen strokes or so.

7. Pour the batter into the hot, oiled skillet and return to the oven for about 20 minutes, until the top of the bread is golden.

8. Serve immediately, warm or at room temperature, with butter if desired.

ADVANCE PREPARATION: Not advisable. See introduction to recipe.

BAKING POWDER BISCUITS

Makes about 2 dozen biscuits

Some soups call out for freshly baked biscuits. At Lundy's, a long-gone famous fish house in Sheepshead Bay, Brooklyn, the tiny baking powder biscuits were as much an attraction as the steamers, lobsters, and gargantuan shore dinner. Anyone who ever ate there probably cannot to this day order a bowl of Down East clam chowder (page 136), which at Lundy's was called clam bisque, without thinking of those quarter-sized hot breads. Biscuits are also an ideal accompaniment to corn chowder (page 24), a good one for kidney bean gumbo (page 56). They are even a decent substitute for challah to dunk into chicken fricassee (page 110).

1¾ cups all-purpose flour
½ teaspoon salt
1 tablespoon baking powder
4 tablespoons cold butter, cut into small
  pieces
¾ cup milk (may be skim or low-fat)
Milk or melted butter for brushing the tops of
  the biscuits

1. Preheat the oven to 450 degrees.

2. Into a large mixing bowl, sift together the flour, salt, and baking powder.

3. Add the butter to the dry ingredients and, using your fingertips or a pastry blender, cut in the butter until the mixture is the consistency of coarse meal.

4. Add the milk and, with a fork, stir gingerly until the dough clings together. Work the dough as little as possible.

5. Turn the dough onto a lightly floured board. Knead it gently and quickly for about 30 seconds, just until it is no longer lumpy or sticky.

6. On a lightly floured board, with a lightly floured rolling pin, roll the dough to about a ⅓-inch thickness. Or pat the dough out on a floured board, using hands that have also been lightly floured. (The less you handle the dough the better.)

7. Cut rounds with a biscuit cutter dipped in flour, making sure you don't twist the cutter. The twist crimps the dough and inhibits rising.

8. For a brown top, brush the biscuits with milk or melted butter.

9. Place the biscuits on an ungreased baking sheet about 1 inch apart.

10. Bake until lightly browned, 12 to 15 minutes.

NOTE: Trimmed dough can be gathered together and rolled out again, but these biscuits will be less tender than the first cuts.

ADVANCE PREPARATION: Not advisable.

POPOVERS

Makes 9 popovers

Airy and eggy, this elegant Anglo-American classic should be served with delicate soups, like sweet pea soup (page 34) and cold cucumber soup with smoked salmon (page 150).

2 tablespoons butter
Freshly grated Parmesan cheese
    (approximately ¼ cup)
1 cup whole milk, at room temperature
1 tablespoon butter, melted
1 cup all-purpose flour, at room temperature
¼ teaspoon salt
2 eggs, lightly beaten, at room temperature

1. Preheat the oven to 450 degrees. Using the 2 tablespoons butter, grease muffin or popover tins *not* made of nonstick material. If you have only nonstick tins, sprinkle the buttered surface with grated Parmesan cheese. (For flavor, you may want to do this anyway.)

2. Combine the milk, melted butter, flour, and salt in a mixing bowl. With a whisk, beat just until smooth.

3. Add half the eggs to the batter and beat in until just mixed. Do the same with the remaining eggs. The batter should be about the consistency of heavy cream.

4. Fill the buttered baking cups three quarters full.

5. Put into the hot oven immediately. After 15 minutes, lower the heat to 350 degrees and bake about 20 minutes longer.

6. To test for doneness, remove a popover and test. As soon as they are removed from the oven, remove from pan and use a skewer to poke a few holes in the bottom of each.

7. Serve immediately.

ADVANCE PREPARATION: Not advisable.

WALNUT ONION MUFFINS

Makes about 48 miniature muffins

These started out as a recipe from the Hudson River Club, the marvelous restaurant with a view of the Statue of Liberty in downtown Manhattan. However, they have evolved somewhat since chef Waldy Malouf first gave me the recipe. I should especially note that a friend, the food writer Suzanne Hamlin, is responsible for the addition of Parmesan cheese, which truly takes these into the outer stratosphere of savory muffins; excellent accompaniment to green and mixed salads and some soups, for instance tomato rice soup (page 39), or mushroom soup with wild rice and brown rice (page 29).

I've tried baking these in standard-sized muffin tins, but they really must be baked in tiny tins to achieve the right texture. In larger tins, they brown and dry too much on the outside by the time the inside is baked.

10 tablespoons (1 stick plus 2 tablespoons)
  butter, melted and cooled
1 large onion, or more if needed to make
  1 cup purée
2 eggs, lightly beaten
1 teaspoon salt
1½ teaspoons baking powder
½ to ¾ cup freshly grated Parmesan
  cheese
1½ cups all-purpose or bread flour
1 teaspoon black pepper
1½ cups walnut meats, toasted lightly,
  chopped fine, but not powdered

1. Preheat the oven to 375 degrees. Butter the miniature muffin tins with 2 tablespoons of the butter.

2. Cut the onion into quarters and purée in a food processor. Measure the purée and increase or decrease the amount to make 1 cup.

3. In a large mixing bowl, whisk together the remaining butter and eggs until well blended. Beat in the puréed onions.

4. With a wooden spoon, gently stir in the remaining ingredients in the order given, mixing thoroughly but being careful not to overwork the batter.

5. Fill the muffin tins two thirds full (about 1 heaping tablespoon).

6. Bake for 35 to 45 minutes, or until the muffins are well browned.

7. Serve warm, but not hot from the oven.

VARIATIONS: Add a pinch of freshly grated nutmeg, ¼ cup pesto sauce (page 44), or finely chopped basil.

ADVANCE PREPARATION: The muffins can be kept for several days in a tin or plastic bag, or frozen and then reheated in a 300-degree oven.

CHAPTER 8

SALADS AND APPETIZERS

GREEN SALAD
MIXED SALAD
MOCK CAESAR SALAD
CELERY AND PARMESAN SALAD
CELERY ROOT RÉMOULADE
FATOUSH
MARINATED MUSHROOMS
GRILLED PORTOBELLO MUSHROOMS
COLESLAW
ENDIVE WITH WALNUTS AND BLUE CHEESE
CREAMY BLUE CHEESE DRESSING
TOMATO AND RED ONION SALAD
INSALATA CAPRESE
ASPARAGUS
ROZANNE GOLD'S GREEN PEPPERCORN DIPPING SAUCE
BOILED ARTICHOKES
BAKED EGGPLANT AND GARLIC
ROUMANIAN EGGPLANT SALAD
POTATO AND SHRIMP SALAD
TOMATO, AVOCADO, AND ONION SALAD
STRING BEANS WITH GARLIC AND SESAME OIL

GREEN SALAD

Preparing and tossing a salad is the fastest and easiest part of putting a soup supper on the table. Still, there's plenty of room for a salad to go wrong. The greens must be well chosen, meticulously washed, thoroughly dried, and dressed at the last moment with an appropriate dressing, which, to my mind, never means anything from a bottle, and most of the time means some version of great olive oil and wine vinegar.

TO CLEAN SALAD GREENS, YOU HAVE THREE OPTIONS:

1. Use the type of salad spinner into which you can run water as well as dry the greens. Do not crowd the spinner, and after rinsing the leaves once, open the spinner, rearrange the leaves, and rinse again. And rinse again, if they are not free of every speck of sand and dirt.

2. Or fill your (immaculately clean) kitchen sink or a very large bowl or basin with cold water. Swish the leaves around, dislodging any dirt, rubbing it off if you need to. Let the leaves float on top of the water for a few minutes. The sand and dirt will settle to the bottom of the vessel. Remove the leaves by lifting them from the surface of the water. Repeat this at least one more time, until the salad greens are perfectly clean.

3. Or rinse every leaf individually under cold running water.

DRYING SALAD GREENS is equally important. There are few foods as unappealing as a soggy salad. And after you've gone to the trouble of making a well-balanced dressing, you don't want it diluted by the water left clinging to the greens.

Salad spinners are handy for drying the salad, but they don't do a perfect job. After spinning the leaves dry, place them on a clean kitchen towel or on a few squares of paper towel and dab them dry, then roll them up in the towel loosely. Well-dried leaves, wrapped thusly in a towel, will remain fresh and crisp in the refrigerator for several days. If you don't have a salad spinner, dry the leaves well by shaking them in a large, absorbent bath towel: Place the leaves in the middle of the towel, gather the edges to enclose the leaves totally and to form a sort of bag, then shake, shake, shake.

NOW THE DRESSING: Its taste is up to you. The classic proportions for a French-style vinaigrette are three parts oil (olive preferred these days, but peanut was) to one part vinegar (plain, good red wine vinegar preferred) with, sometimes, a very small amount of Dijon mustard for flavor and to bind the oil and vinegar together, plus salt and pepper.

Over the years I have personally come to appreciate a more vinegary, less oily dressing. Half and half is a pleasant proportion, especially if you are using an assertive olive oil. The opposite of the classic proportion—three parts vinegar to one part oil—is a healthful goal and has a bright taste that can grow on you.

There are two basic ways to make a simple oil and vinegar dressing, which is all that *vinaigrette* is. You can prepare the dressing directly on the salad, or prepare it apart from the salad.

To make a dressing on the salad, which is more Italian style than French, have all the salad ingredients in the salad bowl. Measure out the necessary amount of oil. I do this directly into the large salad spoon that I use to toss the salad. Toss the salad with the oil. Now measure out the necessary amount of vinegar, again using your salad spoon as a guide. More because it is fun to do and good showmanship than because it is necessary, I dissolve the salt in one of the spoons of vinegar, stirring the mixture with the salad fork. Naturally, the vinegar splashes onto the salad as you beat it to dissolve the salt. That's the point. Now toss again. Grind on pepper. Toss once more.

You can make a dressing apart from the salad either in a small bowl or cup, or directly in the salad bowl, which is more French style than Italian. (For advance preparation, make the dressing in the bowl and pile the cleaned greens on top, tossing the two together at the last moment.) In this case, using a fork, beat the oil, drop by drop at first, into the mustard. Once all the oil and mustard have become homogenized, beat in the vinegar, salt, and pepper.

ABOUT DRESSING AMOUNTS: It's hard to say exactly how much dressing to put on a salad. Tastes vary on this. For a light dressing, I generally figure on about ¼ cup dressing (say 2 tablespoons oil and 2 tablespoons vinegar) for every 2 quarts of greens, which is enough for four generous servings.

DRESSING VARIATIONS can be achieved by using different vinegars, such as sherry vinegar, balsamic vinegar, white wine or white wine tarragon vinegar, herb vinegar or flavored vinegar. Dried oregano, marjoram, or tarragon is, for certain occasions, welcome in a salad dressing. Fresh herbs are a great addition almost any time: Whole leaves of parsley, basil, dill, coriander, chervil, and lovage are all excellent as salad greens or, chopped, as dressing additions. Use more mustard when the mood strikes. Or, when appropriate, add a spice to the dressing—cumin, coriander, curry powder, ground chilies, whole or ground caraway seeds, or fennel seeds.

ABOUT CHOOSING GREENS: Iceberg lettuce, though it has its place (see page 180), is the least interesting green for a tossed salad. Instead use one or more of these: crisp romaine, tender and buttery Boston and Bibb, which are all so-called head lettuces, and/or any of the tender leaf lettuces, and/or any green from the bitter chicory family, such as curly endive, Belgian endive, or *frisée,* the baby chicory. For flavor accent and dark green color, add peppery watercress or arugula, or mâche (also called corn salad), or raw *young and tender* spinach. Slightly bitter, tiny spring dandelion and chicory leaves, which grow wild almost everywhere, are a wonderful novelty in salad. However, radicchio, which is a red form of chicory, is, I think, too bitter for a tossed salad, trendy though it may be.

MIXED SALAD

When an exclusively leafy salad is not elaborate or varied enough, add vegetables to the bowl. Any diced or sliced vegetable is good in a salad, but not all are at their best raw: Broccoli, cauliflower, turnips, parsnips, snow peas, sweet peas, and asparagus taste best when they are cooked at least a few minutes. To stop their cooking and cool them for a salad, drain them immediately into a colander, then refresh them under cold running water.

Carrots cut into very thin rounds, or grated
Diced or sliced onions
Scallions, including the greens, cut into
    ¼-inch pieces
Peeled cucumbers, cut lengthwise into
    quarters, then sliced crosswise into
    ¼-inch pieces
Red or white radishes cut into thin rounds
Diced or thinly sliced celery
Diced bell peppers of any color
Tomatoes, in season, cut into chunks or
    wedges, or cherry tomatoes cut into
    halves or quarters

ADVANCE PREPARATION: Not advisable.

MOCK CAESAR SALAD

Serves 2 or 3

Caesar Cardini created his namesake salad at the end of the July 4th weekend, 1924, in his restaurant, Caesar's Place, in Tijuana, Mexico. Or so the legend goes. It was Prohibition and Caesar's Place was jammed with movie people who had gone south of the border to booze and party. The restaurant ran out of food, so Caesar sent his serving carts to the dining room with the fixings for this salad, all staples in his first-class kitchen—romaine lettuce, lemons, olive oil, red wine vinegar, garlic, eggs (coddled, or barely warmed through), Worcestershire sauce, imported Parmesan cheese—plus croutons made from not quite fresh bread. If the captains could make enough of a show of the salad preparation, no one would notice it was just salad. Or so the legend goes. No doubt, too, in the July heat of Tijuana before the days of air conditioning, a salad was about all anyone might want to eat, especially after consuming a certain amount of tequila.

Caesar Cardini insisted until his dying day that anchovies were not in the original salad. They came later when people tried to imitate the taste of the original, now the toast of Hollywood. Indeed, the taste of anchovies was in the original salad, but only because the salted fish are an ingredient in Worcestershire sauce.

For some reason, even though Caesar salad was created by an Italian in Mexico, it is considered American. Unfortunately, because of the salmonella contamination of our poultry, many Americans are now afraid to eat a true Caesar dressing, which gets its creaminess from nearly raw egg yolks. This recipe has all the original ingredients except the eggs. Instead, to bind the dressing and make it creamy, I've added a little Dijon mustard.

For maximum drama, make the dressing in the salad bowl, as the professionals do. To get the best emulsion, however, use a mortar and pestle.

3 or 4 large garlic cloves, smashed and finely
chopped, or puréed through a garlic press,
or whole
½ teaspoon coarse sea salt
½ teaspoon Dijon mustard
1 or 2 flat anchovy fillets (optional)
3 tablespoons extra-virgin olive oil
Juice of ½ lemon
2 tablespoons red wine vinegar
½ teaspoon Worcestershire sauce
Freshly ground pepper
Fine sea salt, if necessary
1 medium head romaine lettuce, washed and
dried, each leaf (except for the smallest)
torn into several pieces
⅓ cup freshly grated Parmesan cheese
½ to ¾ cup crouton cubes (page 158)
Diced anchovy fillets, to taste (optional)

1. If making the dressing in the salad bowl, use a fork to mash the pre-mashed garlic and salt together. Or use a mortar and pestle to work the whole garlic and salt together into a paste.

2. Add the mustard and beat it into the garlic very well, then mash in the anchovies, if desired. If using a pestle, work the mustard, anchovies, and garlic mixture into as smooth a paste as you have the patience to make.

3. Literally drop by drop, beat in or work in the olive oil. After the first tablespoon, the oil can be added a little faster. When all the oil has been incorporated you should have a thick emulsion.

4. Beat in the lemon juice, vinegar, Worcestershire sauce, and freshly ground pepper to taste. They will thin the dressing.

5. Taste and correct with lemon juice, vinegar, fine sea salt, and/or more freshly ground pepper.

6. Toss the romaine with the dressing, then with the grated cheese and croutons. If serving with additional anchovies, scatter them on top.

7. Serve immediately on plates. Pass the pepper mill.

ADVANCE PREPARATION: Not advisable.

CELERY AND PARMESAN SALAD

Serves 4

Here's an example of how common ingredients can be combined to make an unusual and uncommonly good dish.

6 large celery ribs, washed, dried, and
    trimmed of leaves (about 3 cups)
½ cup finely chopped parsley
½ cup finely chopped red onion
3 tablespoons extra-virgin olive oil
4 to 5 tablespoons freshly squeezed lemon
    juice
¼ teaspoon fine sea salt
¼ teaspoon freshly ground black or white
    pepper
Parmesan cheese, in one piece (or other
    grating cheese, such as Grana Padana,
    Pecorino Romano, or Asiago)

1. Slice the celery very thin on a sharp diagonal, to create pieces 1½ to 2 inches long.

2. In a mixing bowl, combine the celery, parsley, and onion. Toss with the olive oil, then the lemon juice, salt, and pepper. Taste and correct salt and pepper, if necessary.

3. Divide the salad among 4 salad plates. With a vegetable peeler, shave Parmesan cheese over each portion; 8 to 10 shavings, 1 inch long, ½ inch wide, are sufficient.

4. Serve immediately.

VARIATION: Instead of celery, use thinly sliced fennel bulb to make the same salad.

ADVANCE PREPARATION: You can cut the onion and celery ahead, but do not toss until the last moment.

CELERY ROOT RÉMOULADE

Makes 8 cups, serving 8 to 10

This is a standard appetizer in old-fashioned French restaurants, though a difficult recipe to find in French cookbooks written for Americans. Celery root, which is also called celeriac, has the crunch of celery and a delicate celery flavor, but the smoothness of a potato. It is very ugly—a pocked brown globe, often with many hairy roots still attached. It is not difficult to peel, however, and inside it is a beautiful creamy white. It appears in several soup recipes as a flavoring. Here it stars as a vegetable. When this salad is first prepared, the root is really too firm. Authentic French *céleri rémoulade* is limp but crisp. Make this at least twenty-four hours ahead to get the right texture. Or, if you'd like to make it at the last moment, boil the celery root pieces for about two minutes, then drain immediately and refresh under cold running water. That should soften the celeriac just enough.

(continued)

2 large or 3 medium celery roots
Juice of 1 lemon, or more to taste
1 cup mayonnaise
1 tablespoon red wine vinegar, or more to
taste
¼ cup Dijon mustard, or more to taste

1. To make them easier to peel and slice, cut the celery roots into quarters. With a sharp knife or vegetable peeler, peel off the skin, then cut each quarter into slices as thin as you can.

2. Stack the slices, then cut down through them to make matchstick pieces of root. (Alternatively, use a food processor or a mandoline.) In the end, you should have about 8 cups of celery root pieces. As you work, place the celery root pieces into a large bowl and squeeze on lemon juice. It flavors the vegetable and keeps it white.

3. In a small bowl, stir together the mayonnaise, vinegar, and mustard, then stir the mixture into the celery root.

4. Refrigerate overnight, or, even better, for a couple of days.

5. Just before serving, taste and correct vinegar and mustard. It should need no salt, and pepper is best ground at the table.

ADVANCE PREPARATION: Should be made twelve to twenty-four hours ahead. Can be kept refrigerated for up to five days.

FATOUSH

Serves 4 to 6

Start with a typical Middle Eastern chopped salad of tomato, cucumber, onion or scallions, olive oil, and lemon; flesh it out with lettuce, then embellish it with triangles of crisp toasted pita, plenty of garlic, fresh mint, dried mint, parsley, and powdered sumac (a sour and slightly peppery red spice), and you have this Lebanese masterpiece. I could make a meal of it alone, but follow it with a bowl of rashta or the other Lebanese lentil soup in this book (pages 63 and 64) and you have a perfect vegetarian meal. This version of the salad is from chef Riad of Byblos Restaurant in Manhattan.

4 6-inch pita loaves
4 to 6 large garlic cloves, crushed
½ cup olive oil
¼ cup lemon juice
½ teaspoon salt
1 large cucumber, cut in ½-inch cubes
(about 1½ cups)
2 medium tomatoes, cut into ½-inch pieces
1 large Bermuda or Vidalia onion, quartered
and sliced, then coarsely chopped (about
2 cups)
1 large or 2 small heads romaine lettuce, or
1 large head iceberg lettuce, chopped into
1-inch pieces
½ cup (firmly packed) fresh mint
1 cup (firmly packed) curly parsley leaves
1 tablespoon dried mint

1 to 2 rounded tablespoons sumac, depending on the potency of the sumac

1. Prepare the pita crisps: Preheat the oven to 400 degrees. Separate each pita into two full-round halves. Cut the bread into 1-inch pieces. Place the pita pieces on a baking sheet in the middle of the oven and bake until they are lightly browned and crisp, about 10 minutes. Set aside.

2. In a large bowl, whisk together the garlic, olive oil, lemon juice, and salt.

3. Add the cucumbers, tomatoes, and onion. Toss well.

4. Add the lettuce and toss well again.

5. Chop the fresh mint and parsley together, not too fine, then add them to the salad.

6. Sprinkle with dried mint and sumac. Toss again.

7. Taste and, if necessary, correct the dressing with a little more lemon juice and salt.

8. Add the pita chips. Toss well once more.

9. Serve immediately on plates.

ADVANCE PREPARATION: Not advisable. The pita chips must be crisp.

MARINATED MUSHROOMS

Makes about 3 cups, serving 4 to 6

These should be spooned over a buttery lettuce, such as Boston, or tossed with a bitter or peppery green, such as curly endive or watercress or arugula. For a pretty presentation, spoon the mushrooms onto leaves of endive arranged like spokes on a plate. Or use these as a bruschetta topping (page 160).

3 large garlic cloves, finely chopped or crushed
½ teaspoon coarse sea salt
½ cup freshly squeezed lemon juice
½ cup extra-virgin olive oil
12 ounces mushrooms, sliced as thin as possible

1. In a medium-sized bowl, with a whisk or fork, beat together the garlic, salt, lemon juice, and olive oil.

2. Toss the mushrooms in the dressing and let stand at room temperature for about an hour before serving. If they stand too long they will become dark and too limp and exude too much liquid.

3. Serve the mushrooms as the topping/dressing for greens, as suggested above, or make them part of a mixed antipasto plate.

ADVANCE PREPARATION: See step 2.

GRILLED PORTOBELLO MUSHROOMS

Serves 4

If, as it is said, mushrooms are the vegetarian's meat, then portobellos are prime sirloin—though not filet mignon, as one might say fatty-textured Italian porcini are. The impressively large caps of portobello mushrooms can, in fact, get dry and tough like steak if they aren't cooked ever so carefully. Short of having a charcoal fire on which to grill them (also like steak), I find this to be the most successful method.

Grilled portobellos are glorious on their own, served simply on a plate with some greens for garnish and counterpoint, or as the luxurious garnish for a larger, fully dressed salad. They always call out for sturdy bread, focaccia (page 161) or fettunta (page 159).

3 large portobello mushroom caps (about 1 pound with stems)
4 or 5 large garlic cloves, thinly sliced
4 to 6 tablespoons delicately flavored olive oil
¾ teaspoon fine sea salt
Freshly ground black pepper
3 tablespoons finely chopped parsley (or combination parsley and fresh mint)

1. Carefully break off the mushroom stems, then cut each cap into quarters or large chunks.

2. Place the pieces in a broiler pan, gill side up, or on a baking sheet with sides that can go under the broiler.

3. Scatter the garlic over the mushrooms and drizzle with about 3 tablespoons of the olive oil. Season with salt and pepper.

4. Place about six inches below the broiler's heat and cook 5 minutes.

5. Remove from the broiler and, using a hamburger turner for maximum efficiency, turn them over. Drizzle with the remaining olive oil.

6. Return to the broiler and cook another 5 minutes.

7. Remove, sprinkle with parsley, toss again, and cook another 5 minutes.

8. At this point, the mushrooms may be cooked through and tender. If not, toss again and return to the oven for another 5 minutes.

ADVANCE PREPARATION: Best served hot or warm.

COLESLAW

**Makes about 2 quarts,
serving 8 to 10**

People put all kinds of crazy things in their coleslaw, even sugar. As you can see, I'm a purist.

1 (1½-pound) head (or a little more) green cabbage, cored, quartered, and shredded as fine as possible
3 tablespoons cider, malt, or distilled white vinegar
¼ teaspoon salt
1 small onion, grated (optional)
2 medium carrots, grated
⅔ cup mayonnaise

1. In a large mixing bowl, toss the cabbage with the vinegar and salt.

2. Grate the onion directly into the bowl.

3. Grate in the carrots.

4. Add the mayonnaise and toss well.

ADVANCE PREPARATION: The slaw can be served immediately, but it is much better—more melded and tender—if allowed to stand, tossed occasionally, for several hours or overnight. It can be kept refrigerated for several days.

ENDIVE WITH WALNUTS AND BLUE CHEESE

Serves 4

This is not cooking. It's assembling and arranging. And in restaurants you pay a fortune for it.

6 heads endive
2 tablespoons peanut or walnut oil
2 tablespoons red wine or sherry vinegar
20 walnut halves
½ cup crumbled Danish blue cheese or Roquefort
Freshly ground black pepper

1. Prepare the endive in one of two ways: Either cut the heads crosswise into rings or separate the heads into individual leaves.

2. Divide the endive leaves among 4 salad plates.

3. In a small bowl or cup, beat the oil and vinegar together. (You won't need salt because the cheese is salty.)

4. Drizzle the dressing over each portion, then scatter on the walnuts and the blue cheese. Pass the peppermill or grate fresh pepper over each serving.

ADVANCE PREPARATION: Not advisable.

CREAMY BLUE CHEESE DRESSING

Makes about 1 cup

It must be written somewhere that all-American iceberg lettuce is grown mainly to be a foil for such thick, only-in-America salad dressings as this. Or vice versa. Actually, it's hard to find recipes for blue cheese dressing. I know, I've looked. Serve this dripping down a wedge of said head of lettuce. Who cares if it isn't politically or gastronomically correct? It's our heritage and it's delicious, especially before a bowl of tomato rice soup (page 39) or Senate bean soup (page 55).

⅓ cup cup sour cream (can be "light" or reduced fat)
⅓ cup mayonnaise (can be "light" or reduced fat)
1 tablespoon lemon juice, or a few drops more, to taste
⅓ to ½ cup crumbled blue cheese, preferably Roquefort
1 tablespoon milk (approximately)

1. Blend together the sour cream and mayonnaise with a fork.

2. Blend in the lemon juice.

3. Still using a fork, stir in the crumbled blue cheese, mashing it slightly, then stir in the milk to thin out the mixture.

4. Taste for lemon juice and add a few drops more, if desired. Stir in more crumbled blue cheese or, after dressing the lettuce, sprinkle it with more cheese.

ADVANCE PREPARATION: The dressing can be kept in the refrigerator for several days.

TOMATO AND RED ONION SALAD

Serves 4 as a salad or toast topping

Note that there is no vinegar or lemon juice in this salad. Add some if you wish—red wine or balsamic is the most appropriate—but when tomatoes are at their peak I think acidic dressings detract from the tomato's own acidity. Vinegar will also make the tomatoes mushy if they are left to marinate in it, so add the acid just before serving.

4 ripe medium tomatoes
1 small red onion
6 to 10 fresh basil leaves
1 teaspoon coarse sea salt
¼ cup extra-virgin olive oil, or more to taste
Freshly ground black pepper

1. Cut out the cores of the tomatoes, then cut each into 8 to 12 wedges. Place in a bowl.

2. Cut the onion in half through the root end. Cut off the root end, then thinly slice the onion the long way, through the root end. Add to the tomatoes in the bowl.

3. Tear the basil leaves into small pieces and add to the bowl.

4. Add the salt and toss well.

5. Pour on the olive oil, grind on the pepper, then toss again.

6. Let stand at least 30 minutes and up to 8 hours before serving.

VARIATIONS: Leave out the red onion and add 3 or 4 finely chopped large cloves of garlic, or use both onion and garlic. To make a chopped salad for bruschetta, dice the tomato into ¼-inch cubes and similarly dice the onion, if using. (The salad, preferably made with garlic and not onion, can also serve as an uncooked sauce for pasta.)

ADVANCE PREPARATION: The tomatoes will become mushy and the onions will wilt too much if the salad is kept longer than 8 hours.

INSALATA CAPRESE

Serves 4

Is it the romantic name that lets restaurants get away with charging big money for something as simple as sliced mozzarella cheese and tomatoes?

Do not bother to make this with the rubbery mozzarella that's so common in our supermarkets, nor with anything but vine-ripened tomatoes and fresh basil.

1 pound still moist, freshly made mozzarella
2 or 3 medium tomatoes
Full-flavored olive oil
8 basil leaves
Coarse or fine sea salt
Freshly ground pepper or red pepper flakes
Capers, anchovy fillets, black or purple olives
  (optional)

1. Cut the cheese into 8 or 12 slices.

2. Slice the tomato into 8 or 12 slices.

3. On a serving platter, alternate the tomato and cheese slices, slightly overlapping.

4. Drizzle with olive oil, the amount at your discretion (this is not a case where less is more).

5. Tear the basil leaves over the salad, then season with salt and pepper to taste.

6. If desired, scatter one or more of the optional ingredients over the salad.

VARIATIONS: If moist mozzarella is available but, because of the season, the tomatoes are not, substitute either roasted and peeled red peppers (not from a jar) or rehydrated and oil-plumped sun-dried tomatoes. A smear of imported tomato paste on each slice of mozzarella is another possibility instead of fresh tomatoes, but in that case definitely dress the salad with one or more of the optional ingredients.

ADVANCE PREPARATION: Not advisable.

ASPARAGUS

Steamed or boiled asparagus make a magnificent first course for any meal, from the most informal to the most elegant. As a veteran dieter, I can also attest that they are a great pleasure (and a diuretic) dressed with nothing but lemon juice and pepper, although in most circumstances you'll want a dressing, dip, or sauce. Olive oil and lemon are the simplest, especially if the asparagus are served at room temperature or cold. Or you can make a full-blown vinaigrette with mustard. Or use the dressing for mock Caesar salad (page 173), shaving on some Parmesan as a garnish. When the asparagus are hot, not much can beat a melting pat of butter.

I try to select medium-sized asparagus because they don't generally require peeling if you snap off the tough ends. I find that the very thin spears lack flavor and the heavy ones have tough skins that need to be pared.

To prepare asparagus for the pot (and you emphatically do not need a special one), break off the tough ends and wash them very well in cold water. (If you are frugal, the ends, except for the bottom inch or so, can be salvaged by peeling them deeply. These ends are excellent for making risotto, where they will cook for the full time with the rice, or you can freeze them and save them for a minestrone or vegetable broth.)

I find that a skillet large enough to accommodate the asparagus lying flat is the best pan in which to cook asparagus.

1. Place the asparagus in the pan, cover with cold water, then remove the asparagus.

2. Place the skillet of water over high heat and bring to a boil. Lightly salt the water, if desired.

3. When the water comes to a boil, add the asparagus. Boil for 5 to 8 minutes, depending on the thickness of the spears.

4. Remove the asparagus with tongs or a hamburger turner and drain on a clean cotton dish towel or paper towels.

5. Serve immediately at room temperature, or very slightly chilled.

VARIATION: An elaborate first course, almost meal-in-itself presentation, is asparagus Milanese: Arrange the asparagus like spokes around a fried egg, shave or grate on Parmesan cheese, then dress with melted or browned butter.

ADVANCE PREPARATION: Must be eaten the same day they are boiled.

ROZANNE GOLD'S GREEN PEPPERCORN DIPPING SAUCE

Makes 3 cups

This is a powerfully flavored dip for room-temperature or chilled asparagus, boiled or steamed artichokes, or any platter of steamed vegetables.

1½ cups mayonnaise
1 cup sour cream
½ cup Dijon mustard
¼ cup grainy Pommery mustard
3½ ounces green Madagascar peppercorns
    (1 small can or jar)

1. In a mixing bowl, beat together the mayonnaise, sour cream, and two mustards.

2. Drain the peppercorns, reserving the liquid, and stir the peppercorns into the sauce. Stir in a little of the reserved liquid to taste.

3. Cover and refrigerate for 24 hours before serving.

BOILED ARTICHOKES

Serves 2

Like asparagus, artichokes are an inviting beginning to almost any supper, informal through black-tie.

2 firm, large artichokes
1 lemon, cut in half
¼ teaspoon salt

1. Wash artichokes under cold water, making sure the water runs between the leaves.

2. With a sharp knife, cut off the stems at the base and remove the small bottom leaves and any discolored or particularly tough-looking outer leaves. As you are cutting, rub lemon juice over the cut surfaces to prevent them from discoloring.

3. With scissors, snip off the pointed ends of the outside leaves. With a sharp knife, cut off the top ½ to 1 inch of the artichokes. (This last step is optional.)

4. After each artichoke is prepared for cooking, put it in a large bowl of cold water to which you have added the juice of half a lemon.

5. Stand artichokes in a saucepan just large enough to hold them, snugly if possible. Add enough water to come 2 to 3 inches up the side of the pan. Add salt, cover, and bring to a boil.

6. Boil for 30 to 45 minutes, or until the bases can be pierced with a fork. If serving cold, undercook slightly. Remove from the saucepan and drain upside down.

7. To remove the inedible choke and prickly inner leaves, gently spread the leaves apart and pull out the cone of purple-tinged leaves. With a teaspoon, gently scrape out the choke hairs located on top of the meaty bottom. Serve warm or cold with a dipping sauce.

ADVANCE PREPARATION: Must be eaten the same day they are boiled.

BAKED EGGPLANT AND GARLIC

Makes about 1 cup, serving 3 or 4

Heady and unctuous are the best words to describe this nearly addictive purée. The idea, if not the specifics of the recipe, comes from M.F.K. Fisher, who, to my knowledge, never published a recipe for it but served it to a writer who was interviewing her during her last days. Mount the eggplant on large croutons (no garlic rub or oil necessary) and garnish with a few black, oil-cured olives, and a sprinkling of fresh mint, oregano, or basil, if you feel the need for a touch of green on the brownish purée. Or, for real color as well as a complementary flavor, top off the eggplant mound with a spoonful of chopped tomato salad (page 180). Either way, it's knife and fork food.

¼ cup (approximately) extra-virgin olive oil
2 whole heads fresh garlic, cloves peeled and
*   thickly sliced*
1 large eggplant, halved lengthwise

I. Preheat the oven to 400 degrees.

2. Pour the olive oil roughly corresponding to the shape of the eggplant halves in the center of a jelly-roll pan.

3. Arrange the garlic slices on the pan in patterns also corresponding to the shape of the eggplant halves.

4. Place the eggplant halves over the garlic slices, tucking any stray garlic slices under the eggplant.

5. Bake for about 40 minutes, or until the eggplant is very soft.

6. Turn off the oven and let the eggplant cool to room temperature. This could take as long as 2 hours.

7. Scrape the eggplant and garlic into a bowl, preferably a wooden one, and, using a wooden spoon, beat the eggplant and garlic together.

8. Serve mounded on bread or toasts, plain or topped with finely chopped parsley or basil, a diced tomato salad as for bruschetta (page 160), or with diced olives, or simply a whole olive or a few slivers of red onion.

ADVANCE PREPARATION: The purée is best when freshly made and slightly warm, but

it can be kept, if covered, at room temperature for several hours before serving. Or
refrigerate it overnight, bringing it back to
room temperature before serving.

ROUMANIAN EGGPLANT SALAD

**Makes about 1½ cups,
serving 2 to 4**

This is an old Roumanian recipe. I used
to know a lot of old Roumanians who
practically lived on it. If you can roast
the eggplants over charcoal, all the better.
The reason old Roumanians use only
wooden utensils is so the eggplant won't
discolor, which it does when in contact
with high-carbon steel or aluminum. I use
wooden utensils because it feels good, and
the dish looks so appealing served in a
wooden chopping bowl with its garnish
arranged around it.

1 large eggplant
3 tablespoons delicately flavored olive oil
Juice of ½ lemon
½ teaspoon salt
*1 small or large garlic clove, crushed or
    pressed (or to taste)*
Freshly ground black pepper
1 small onion, very finely diced
½ small green pepper, very finely diced
12 black or purple olives

1. Place the whole eggplant in a preheated
400-degree oven, directly on the oven rack
or on a baking sheet, and roast until it col-
lapses when you press it down, about 40
minutes. Remove and let cool enough to
handle.

2. Slit open the eggplant and, with a
wooden spoon or stainless steel knife,
scrape the eggplant off the skin into a
bowl, preferably a wooden chopping bowl,
or onto a wooden board.

3. With the same knife, coarsely chop the
eggplant. If it is not already in a bowl,
scrape it into one, preferably wooden.

4. Using a wooden spoon, beat and mash
the eggplant against the sides of the bowl
until it looks mashed, not chopped.

5. In a thin stream, start adding the olive
oil while beating the eggplant with the
spoon. Beat the eggplant well between each
tablespoon addition of oil.

6. When all the oil is incorporated into the
eggplant it should look like a rough purée.
Beat in the lemon juice, salt, garlic, and a
few grinds of black pepper.

7. Taste again and correct with more
lemon juice, salt, and garlic. Do not add
much pepper at this point.

8. With a rubber spatula, scrape the sides
of the bowl to neaten it, then garnish the
pool of eggplant with piles of diced onion,
green pepper, and dark olives.

9. Set out the bowl with a wooden spoon
and serve with bread or toasts on which to

spread the eggplant, garnished with diced vegetables to taste. Pass the peppermill.

SERVING VARIATIONS: Instead of serving the eggplant in the bowl it was mixed in, surrounded by the diced vegetables, blend the onion and pepper into the eggplant. Place a portion of the salad on a few lettuce leaves and garnish with olives and red radishes, a slice of red onion, or a scallion. As is, or possibly with a second clove of garlic, the eggplant is also excellent as a dip for crudités, or as a spread for crackers, lavosh, pita chips, etc.

ADVANCE PREPARATION: The purée is best when freshly made, but it can be kept, if covered, at room temperature for several hours before serving. Or refrigerate it overnight, bringing it back to room temperature before serving.

POTATO AND SHRIMP SALAD

Serves 6

A substantial salad like this is what you'll want to start off a soup supper featuring any of the gazpachos in the book (pages 145, 146, and 147), or any of the less substantial soups, such as zuppa pavese (page 120) or stracciatella (page 122).

2 pounds small new or waxy red potatoes, skins on

FOR THE DRESSING:
¼ cup extra-virgin olive oil, preferably Spanish
2 tablespoons sherry wine or red wine vinegar
1 rounded tablespoon drained tiny capers
1 rounded tablespoon finely chopped parsley
Salt and freshly ground pepper

FOR THE SALAD:
½ pound small shrimp, cooked and shelled, whole or cut in half lengthwise
12 to 15 small Spanish pitted green olives, halved
1 large red bell pepper, roasted, peeled, seeded, and cut into thin strips
Lettuce leaves

1. In a large pot, boil the potatoes in salted water until tender. Cool and quarter, leaving the skins on.

2. Meanwhile, in a large bowl, whisk together the dressing ingredients.

3. While the potatoes are still warm, add them to the bowl with the dressing and toss them with the cooked shrimp, olives, and roasted pepper strips.

4. Cover and set aside for at least 1 hour. Chill slightly if desired.

5. Serve on a bed of lettuce on salad or luncheon plates.

ADVANCE PREPARATION: Should be served within several hours of being assembled.

TOMATO, AVOCADO, AND ONION SALAD

Serves 2 or 3

Think of this as deconstructed guacamole. It's the same ingredients presented differently.

1 ripe Hass avocado
Juice of 1 lime
2 medium ripe tomatoes, halved and
*   sliced*
½ Bermuda onion, sliced
Whole coriander leaves
Sliced or diced red or green long hot chilies
*   to taste*

1. Cut the avocado in half and peel it. Immediately sprinkle it all over with juice from half the lime.

2. Place the avocado flat side down on a cutting board and cut it down into ¼-inch slices. Sprinkle the separated slices with the juice of the remaining lime half.

3. On a serving platter, arrange alternating slices of tomato, avocado, and onion.

4. Scatter coriander and sliced or diced chilies on top.

5. Serve at room temperature.

VARIATION: When tomatoes are not in season, substitute slices of orange.

ADVANCE PREPARATION: Do not prepare more than several hours ahead.

STRING BEANS WITH GARLIC AND SESAME OIL

Serves 6 to 8

Susan Friedland, the editor of this book, is famous for dragging home from Chinatown inordinate quantities of sesame oil. Her profligate use of it and garlic is what makes this recipe. Don't stint.

¼ cup toasted sesame oil
2 pounds string beans (ends snapped off),
*   washed and snapped in half*
12 to 15 large garlic cloves, finely chopped
½ teaspoon fine sea salt, or more to taste

(continued)

1. In a large skillet, over medium heat, heat the oil until very hot but not smoking—a test string bean should start to sizzle immediately. Add all the string beans and toss in the oil to coat.

2. Sauté for about 8 minutes, until the string beans begin to shrivel and are almost tender.

3. Add the garlic and salt. Continue to sauté, tossing almost constantly, until the garlic turns nutty brown. Remove from the heat immediately.

4. Serve hot or at room temperature.

CHAPTER 9

DESSERTS

Wacky Chocolate Cake
Norwegian Pound Cake
Swedish Almond Cake
Karen Howard's Raspberry Wedges
Peach Crostata
Plum Tart
Amaretti Ricotta Cheesecake
Oatmeal Lace Cookies
Forgotten Gianduia Meringues
Fruit Salad
Fresh Pineapple
Strawberries in Two Liqueurs
Red Berry, Red Wine Compote
Melon Balls with Rum and Brown Sugar
Cranberry Orange Sherbet
Blue Cheese and Honey
Blueberry Apple Crumble
Ruby Poached Pears
Old-Fashioned Strawberry Shortcake

WACKY CHOCOLATE CAKE

Makes one 9- by 13-inch sheet cake, serving 6 to 10

This is an eggless and milk-free chocolate cake that is also called "crazy cake," "cocoa cake," and "wet chocolate cake," though that last appellation is not at all descriptive of the final product. It is also a kind of "dump cake," which does indeed describe how it's made: All the ingredients are dumped into the pan *before* they're mixed. It couldn't be easier—or more dangerous!

A light, deeply flavored cake that appears to be a frugal Mennonite recipe, this particular version comes from a Lancaster County Mennonite church cookbook and was passed on to me by Sharon Opstbaum, one of my WOR radio listeners, formerly of Lancaster, Pennsylvania. Of the many "wacky cake" recipes sent to me after the subject came up on the radio, this one had the most cocoa, and you can taste it. Though it has no eggs or dairy products, please realize it does contain a normal portion of fat. Canola oil, "extra-light" olive oil, or other vegetable oils make a very fine cake, although it's better with butter.

3 cups all-purpose flour
2 teaspoons baking soda
2 teaspoons salt
⅔ cup cocoa
2 cups granulated sugar
2 teaspoons distilled white vinegar
2 teaspoons vanilla extract
⅔ cup melted butter, margarine, or vegetable oil
2 cups cold water

1. Preheat the oven to 350 degrees.

2. Sift into an ungreased 9 × 13 × 3-inch baking pan the flour, baking soda, and salt.

3. Combine the cocoa and sugar in a small bowl, then stir into the flour mixture.

4. Make three holes in the mixture. In the first hole put the vinegar, in the second put the vanilla, and in the third the melted shortening.

5. Pour the water over all and stir well with a fork. Use a rubber spatula to turn over the flour stuck in the corners and bottom of the pan.

6. Bake for 35 to 45 minutes, until a cake tester inserted in the middle comes out clean.

7. Cool thoroughly before serving. (Though who can resist a taste of warm cake?) Frost, if and as desired.

VARIATIONS: The ingredients can be halved for a smaller cake, in which case use a 9-inch square pan. It can be served plain, with powdered sugar or with a frosting on top, or with whipped cream or ice cream. Consider it a basic black cake, to be accessorized to suit the occasion.

ADVANCE PREPARATION: The cake keeps well for several days wrapped in aluminum foil and kept at room temperature.

NORWEGIAN POUND CAKE

Makes at least 12 servings

Fine-textured, light, with a buttery golden crust—this is the best pound cake I've ever baked. I've settled. I have no reason to look further for yet a better recipe. It's from Mike Eriksen of Bantam, Connecticut, a listener of my WOR radio show. To get perfect pound cake texture, make sure you sift the flour twice and beat the batter for the full twenty minutes. You'll see. It changes before your eyes.

2¼ cups sugar
6 eggs
¾ pound butter (3 sticks)
¾ cup milk
3 cups cake flour, sifted then remeasured, scooping the flour into the cup and leveling, then resifted with 1 tablespoon baking powder and ⅔ teaspoon salt
1 teaspoon vanilla extract
¼ teaspoon almond extract

1. Have all the ingredients at room temperature. Combine in a large mixing bowl and beat for 20 minutes at medium speed of an electric mixer, revolving the bowl and scraping down the sides regularly.

2. Preheat the oven to 350 degrees. Grease and flour a 10-inch tube pan with a removable bottom.

3. Pour the batter into the tube pan and bake for 1 hour and 20 minutes. Make sure to bake the full time. The cake will be a deep golden color.

4. Remove the hot cake from the tube pan, keeping it on the bottom for now. Cool on a rack, covered with a cotton kitchen towel.

5. When completely cooled, carefully draw a sharp knife under the bottom of the cake and very gently extricate the cake from the bottom of the tube pan.

ADVANCE PREPARATION: Will keep at room temperature for up to a week if wrapped in foil or stored under a cake dome. Toast lightly when the cake begins to get dry.

SWEDISH ALMOND CAKE

Makes two 9-inch cakes, serving 8 to 12

You can't buy cake like this. It is so buttery and toothsome, it's sort of a cake-confection, especially with its generous topping of roasted almond butter crunch.

FOR THE CAKE:
8 tablespoons (1 stick) butter
1½ cups sugar
4 eggs, separated
1 teaspoon vanilla extract
1½ cups all-purpose flour
1 tablespoon baking powder

FOR THE TOPPING:
½ cup sugar
8 tablespoons (1 stick) butter
2 tablespoons flour
1½ tablespoons milk
1 cup roasted almonds, coarsely chopped

1. Preheat the oven to 350 degrees. Lightly grease and flour 2 8- or 9-inch round cake pans.

2. In a large mixing bowl, cream together the butter and sugar. It will be grainy, not fluffy.

3. Add the egg yolks, one at a time, beating well between additions.

4. Beat in the vanilla.

5. Mix together the flour and baking powder, then sift the dry ingredients into the creamed mixture. Mix well. It will be a very stiff batter.

6. In another mixing bowl, beat the egg whites until stiff.

7. Fold the egg whites thoroughly into the batter. It will still be very stiff.

8. Divide the batter between the 2 pans, spreading it evenly with a rubber spatula. It will be too stiff to be smoothed out on top.

9. Bake for 22 to 25 minutes, until lightly browned and pulling away from the sides of the pan.

10. While the cake is baking, in the top of a double boiler (or in an improvised one), combine all the topping ingredients except the almonds. Stir constantly over boiling water until the mixture is smooth and thickened. Add the almonds and stir well. Keep over hot water until ready to use. It should be very loose, nearly liquid, when it goes on the cakes.

11. As soon as the cake layers are done, and while they are still in their pans, spread the topping mixture over the cakes. Place them a few inches under the broiler for a few minutes, just until the topping bubbles and browns. Watch them carefully so they don't burn.

12. Let cool slightly before serving, in wedges, hot, warm, or at room temperature, with whipped cream or vanilla ice cream, if you like.

ADVANCE PREPARATION: Store in the cake pans. The cake's texture will become heavy after two days, but it can be revived by warming it through, out of its pan, in a 350-degree oven for 5 to 10 minutes.

KAREN HOWARD'S RASPBERRY WEDGES

Serves 6

This is a bona fide convenience recipe—frozen pastry, a jar of preserves, and that's it. You'll love knowing about it and eating the wedges. They are a hot seller at Mother Hubbard's, Karen's cozy café in West Cornwall, Connecticut.

Frozen pastry for 2 single-crust pies
1 12-ounce jar raspberry preserves

1. Preheat the oven to 425 degrees.

2. Defrost the pastry and place one crust on a baking sheet. Pat it out so that it lays flat, mending any cracks by pushing them together with a bit of cold water.

3. Spread the entire jar of preserves evenly over the pastry, leaving a ½-inch border of exposed pastry.

4. Moisten the exposed border, then place the second pastry circle, also flattened out, over the bottom one. Press the edges together.

5. With a very sharp knife, cut a few slits in an attractive design in the top pastry.

6. Bake for 25 minutes, until the jam is bubbly and the edges of the pastry have browned.

7. Serve warm or at room temperature, plain, or topped with whipped cream or ice cream.

ADVANCE PREPARATION: Can be kept, if covered, at room temperature for several days. However, the pastry may lose its crispness.

PEACH CROSTATA

Serves 6

I always think of this as "beach crostata" because one August on Fire Island my housemates became addicted to it and I was forced to make it . . . all . . . the . . . time. I mean a couple every day. It was exhausting, and getting pretty boring. It says a lot for the pastry that I still look forward to making it every peach season.

2 cups all-purpose flour
1 cup sugar
½ teaspoon salt
8 tablespoons (1 stick) butter
5 or 6 medium peaches (preferably freestone),
*   peeled and halved*
Cinnamon (optional)
1 cup heavy cream, sour cream, or yogurt
2 eggs

1. Preheat the oven to 400 degrees.

2. In a mixing bowl, stir together the flour, ¼ cup of the sugar, and salt.

3. Cut in the butter, using the tips of your fingers, until the mixture resembles coarse meal.

4. Press the mixture evenly into the bottom and up the sides of a deep 9- or 10-inch pie plate. Make the top edge neat by pressing the side up with the side of your left index finger into the side of your right index finger (or vice versa).

5. Arrange the peaches over the crust and sprinkle with the remaining ¾ cup of sugar. Sprinkle lightly with cinnamon, too, if desired.

6. Bake for 15 minutes.

7. Meanwhile, in a small bowl, with a fork or whisk, beat together the cream and eggs until well blended.

8. After 15 minutes, remove the crostata from the oven, pour over the egg and cream mixture, then return to the oven for another 30 minutes.

9. Serve warm (not hot) or at room temperature. (The crostata is at its best if never refrigerated.)

VARIATION: Nectarines are a natural substitute for peaches.

ADVANCE PREPARATION: May be baked several hours ahead. Can be kept at room temperature for up to 24 hours.

PLUM TART

Serves 6 to 8

In 1989, in response to "repeated demands," Marian Burros ran a version of this recipe in the *New York Times* for the sixth and what she said would be the very last time. "It is beyond understanding why fans of the recipe do not just save it from year to year," she wrote. It is, indeed, a great recipe—easy and delicious—and no workaday file should be without it. Italian prune plums are generally in season from late August through the beginning of October. I also put them in my applesauce, both apples and plums with their skins, at a ratio of about one pound of plums to three pounds of apples. They not only flavor the sauce, but also give it a gorgeous color.

8 tablespoons (1 stick) butter
¾ cup sugar
1 cup unbleached flour
1 teaspoon baking powder
Pinch of salt (optional)
2 eggs
12 pitted purple plums, halved
Sugar, lemon juice, and cinnamon for topping

1. Preheat the oven to 350 degrees.

2. In a mixing bowl, cream together the butter and sugar.

3. Add the flour, baking powder, salt, and eggs. Beat well.

4. Spoon the batter into an 8-, 9-, or 10-inch springform pan. Place the plum halves, skin side up, on top of the batter. Sprinkle lightly with sugar and lemon juice, depending on the sweetness of the fruit. Dust with cinnamon, the amount depending on how much you like cinnamon, from ½ to 1 teaspoon.

5. Bake for 1 hour. Remove and let cool 5 minutes.

6. Remove the sides of the pan and let cool another 5 minutes or so before serving, plain or with whipped cream or ice cream.

VARIATION: To make an apple cranberry tart, follow directions for plum tart but peel, seed, quarter, and slice 2 or 3 large baking apples. Arrange ½ cup raw cranberries over the batter and top with the apple slices. Sprinkle generously with cinnamon; squeeze ½ to 1 tablespoon of lemon juice over the apples. Sprinkle with sugar. Bake as above.

ADVANCE PREPARATION: Prepare through step 4, then set aside at room temperature for several hours or refrigerate overnight. Bring back to room temperature before proceeding. Or prebake and reheat. To freeze, bake first; to serve, defrost and reheat briefly at 300 degrees.

AMARETTI RICOTTA CHEESECAKE

Serves 6

This is a light cake, actually a fallen soufflé, that is also marvelous served hot from the oven. Now, having called it a soufflé, I must add that it is extremely simple to make and very quickly prepared.

2 teaspoons butter
2 to 3 tablespoons sugar
8 double amaretti (16 individual cookies),
    processed to a powder in a blender
1 (15-ounce) container whole milk ricotta
Grated zest of 1 orange (optional)
5 eggs
2 tablespoons flour
⅓ cup sugar

I. Preheat the oven to 375 degrees. Thoroughly butter a 2-quart, 8- to 9-inch diameter soufflé dish. Pour in the sugar and rotate the dish to coat it thoroughly. Pour out the excess sugar and set the pan aside.

2. In a large mixing bowl, combine the powdered amaretti, the ricotta, and the optional orange zest. Mix well.

3. Separate 4 of the eggs and add the yolks to the ricotta mixture with the fifth whole egg. Mix well again.

4. Sprinkle on the flour and sugar. Mix well again.

5. In a large mixing bowl, beat the 4 egg whites until stiff.

6. Carefully fold the beaten egg whites into the cheese mixture, then pour the batter into the prepared pan.

7. Immediately place in the preheated oven. Bake for 40 minutes, or until the top is well browned.

8. Remove from the oven and let cool 5 minutes.

9. Place a serving dish over the top and—of course using oven mitts—turn the cake over to unmold it. The cake will have a light crust of caramelized sugar. Occasionally the crust sticks; cover it by sprinkling the cake with powdered sugar just before serving.

10. Serve hot in wedges, or let cool to room temperature, or chill well. As the cake cools it falls. When served hot, the texture is like a soufflé or light pudding. When cooled, it is more like a traditional Italian cheesecake.

VARIATION: Serve hot, spooned from the dish, with, if desired, a lightly sweetened berry purée as a sauce. A berry sauce is also excellent when the cake is cool and cut, in which case a fresh berry garnish is appropriate.

ADVANCE PREPARATION: Keeps very well for several days in the refrigerator, except that the caramelized surface will become soft instead of crisp.

OATMEAL LACE COOKIES

Makes about 2 dozen cookies

These are delicate, elegant cookies; ideal to serve with coffee after a fruit dessert, or with ice cream or sherbet. They are greasy straight from the oven, so make sure they drain thoroughly on absorbent paper. You can make these into *tuiles,* a name that refers to the curved roof tiles of France, by letting them cool draped over a thick rolling pin, or into cigarette shapes by rolling them around the handle of a wooden spoon, then filling them with a flavored buttercream or whipped cream. Warning: The latter takes considerable skill.

8 tablespoons (1 stick) butter, melted
½ cup sugar
2 tablespoons milk
¾ cup quick-cooking oatmeal
5 tablespoons all-purpose flour
1 teaspoon vanilla extract

1. Preheat the oven to 350 degrees.

2. In a mixing bowl, combine all the ingredients and mix well with a wooden spoon.

3. Drop one rounded spoonful of the mixture onto an ungreased baking sheet for a trial. Bake for 8 to 10 minutes, or until the cookie has browned without burning at the edge.

4. Cool for about 30 seconds, then remove and place on absorbent paper. If the cookie has spread and baked crisp and lacy, continue with the rest of the batter. If the batter spread too much, add another teaspoon of flour. If the batter is too stiff (unlikely), add another teaspoon of milk.

5. Proceed with the remaining batter, cooling the cookies on absorbent paper.

ADVANCE PREPARATION: Keep cookies in a tin.

FORGOTTEN GIANDUIA MERINGUES

Makes about 2 dozen

These small meringues are called "forgotten" because the original point was to put them into the oven after dinner, when it had just been turned off, then to forget about them until the next day when the oven was lighted anew. It was an energy-saving recipe, and not incidentally an indulgent way to use and not waste egg whites left over from a yolk-enriched soup, sauce, or dessert, foods not often eaten these days. Now we wonder what to do with leftover yolks after making all those egg-white omelets.

In reasonably dry weather and climates, these keep well in a tin for emergency situations. The combination of hazelnuts and chocolate is called *gianduia* in Italian.

2 egg whites
⅛ teaspoon salt
⅔ cup sugar
1 cup peeled and coarsely chopped hazelnuts
1 cup semisweet chocolate bits

1. Preheat the oven to 350 degrees for at least 20 minutes. Lightly grease and flour a baking sheet or line it with baking parchment.

2. In a perfectly clean and dry mixing bowl, beat the egg whites and salt with an electric mixer until thick and foamy.

3. Gradually add all the sugar, continuing to beat until stiff.

4. Carefully fold in the nuts and chocolate.

5. Drop by heaping teaspoonfuls onto the baking sheet.

6. Place in the oven and turn it off immediately. Leave in the oven overnight (at least 12 hours) without ever opening the door.

VARIATIONS: Substitute another kind of nut. Leave out the nuts or leave out the chocolate.

ADVANCE PREPARATION: In dry weather, meringues can be kept for several months in a tin.

FRUIT SALAD

Serves 6

This is more than a recipe. It is an all-purpose outline to all fruit salads. I could as much give a firm recipe for fruit salad as I could give an accurate report on the weather in the year 2001. Who knows what will be in season when you want to make fruit salad and find this reference in the index? I'll make a bet you can get oranges, apples, and bananas, but that's it. The rest is up to Mother Nature, your whim, and your budget.

1 to 1½ cups orange juice
1 red apple, peeled or not, as desired
1 large ripe pear, peeled or not, as desired
2 eating oranges, peeled
2 small or medium bananas, peeled
Sugar to taste
Mandarin or orange liqueur (optional)

1. Pour the orange juice into a large mixing bowl. You will cut the other fruits into the juice.

2. Core the apple and pear and cut them into ½-inch pieces. Put them into the juice.

3. Working over the bowl, segment the oranges and cut each segment into three or four pieces. Let them drop into the bowl.

4. Slice the bananas lengthwise in half, then into ¼-inch-thick half-round slices. Add them to the salad.

5. Mix well and refrigerate for at least a couple of hours before serving.

6. Taste and add sugar if desired. Stir in liqueur, if desired.

VARIATIONS: This is but a mere base to which any number of fruits may be added: grapes, kiwi, pineapple, cantaloupe or other melon, mandarins and tangerines, grapefruit, papaya, mango, and, in summer, soft fruits such as berries, peaches, and nectarines. Add berries at the last minute. Increase the amount of orange juice, or supplement it with cranberry juice, when you increase the amount of fruit. You might also add bruised mint leaves or minced crystallized ginger (which will melt into the syrup eventually), or a touch of vanilla extract, or a shot of Campari, both for flavor and color.

ADVANCE PREPARATION: Will keep nicely in the refrigerator for up to twenty-four hours. After that, the fruit loses its shape and attractiveness and the syrup created by the orange juice and bananas gets thicker. But it still tastes great.

FRESH PINEAPPLE

1 pineapple serves 4

A great pineapple—honey sweet and smelling like the tropics—is such a luxury that it needs no further adornment. It is almost sinful to do anything but cut it up in an attractive way. I think the following, dividing the pineapple into quarters with the leaves still attached, is the easiest and the prettiest, whether the wedges are going to be the centerpiece of a mixed fruit platter or served as individual portions.

1. With a long sharp knife (a serrated bread knife or ham knife will do if you don't have a large chef's knife), cut through the pineapple lengthwise. You should be able to cut easily through the leafy top.

2. Cut the pineapple halves in half.

3. With a small straight-bladed knife, cut off the section of hard pineapple core that forms the top point of each pineapple quarter. (This is unnecessary if you don't mind eating or serving to guests that woody section of the fruit.)

4. Next, cut the pineapple flesh free of the rind (a curved grapefruit knife is perfect for this), running the knife close to the rind under one side and to the middle, then the other side.

5. Finally, with the small straight-bladed knife, cut the pineapple wedges from top to rind every half inch. You now have the shell of the pineapple filled with pineapple wedges. If you want to get fancy, pull the wedges off center, alternating the wedges right and left.

6. If part of a platter, serve with toothpicks. If served as individual, plated portions, serve with a small fork.

VARIATION: Pineapple and rum is a natural combination, as both are born in the tropics. Either sprinkle each pineapple quarter with dark rum just before serving, or remove the pineapple wedges and place in a serving bowl. Douse lightly with rum and let macerate for an hour to several hours. Kirsch also complements pineapple; use it the same way.

ADVANCE PREPARATION: Should be served within a few hours of cutting.

STRAWBERRIES IN TWO LIQUEURS

Serves 2 to 3

I've yet to find an explanation for it. It was an accident that led to the discovery. But somehow the two unrelated liqueurs, crème de cacao and orange, amplify the flavor of strawberries. Eat these as is, or use them as a sauce for ice cream, crepes, or pound cake (page 192).

1 pint strawberries, hulled, washed, and dried
3 tablespoons sugar

2 tablespoons crème de cacao
2 tablespoons orange liqueur

1. Between 2 and 3 hours before serving, toss all the ingredients together in a mixing bowl. Let stand at room temperature and do not chill.

2. Serve in small bowls or cups or in stemmed glasses, with a spoon; or use as a topping for pound cake or ice cream, or top with a lemon or berry-flavored commercial sherbet.

ADVANCE PREPARATION: Should be served within a few hours of mixing.

RED BERRY, RED WINE COMPOTE

Serves 4 to 6

When berries are at their absolute peak, this simple treatment enhances them without overwhelming them.

2 to 3 tablespoons runny honey
1½ cups red wine
2 (½-inch) strips orange zest
1 pint strawberries, washed and hulled, at
    room temperature
½ pint raspberries

1. In a serving bowl, dissolve the honey in the red wine. You may need to let the honey sit for a while.

2. Add the orange zest and the berries. Let stand at room temperature for at least 30 minutes and no more than a few hours.

3. Serve in small bowls or stemmed glasses with a spoon to sip up all the wine.

ADVANCE PREPARATION: The berries become limp and less appealing after several hours.

MELON BALLS WITH RUM AND BROWN SUGAR

Serves 2 or 3

Here's a light but potent dessert.

1 medium melon of any kind
½ cup light rum
2 to 3 tablespoons brown sugar

1. Seed the melon and scoop the flesh out with a melon baller. Or cut the flesh off the rind and cube it. Place the melon in a serving bowl.

2. Toss the melon with the rum and sugar and let stand a few minutes before serving.

ADVANCE PREPARATION: Must be made just before serving.

CRANBERRY ORANGE SHERBET

Fewer and fewer fresh cranberries are coming to market because "dry harvesting," the technique that is necessary to produce whole fruit, is much more expensive than "wet harvesting," a technique that is fine only if the berries are to become juice. That's also why Ocean Spray, a growers cooperative that is the country's main marketer of cranberries, has created a national demand for cranberry juice products. Not that they're hard to like.

This recipe dates from the days when cranberries were sold in one-pound bags, as they were until 1980. Nowadays, in order to get the four cups of berries that are in a pound, one has to buy two 12-ounce bags, each of which holds three cups. What does one do with two extra cups of cranberries? They freeze perfectly for up to a year.

4 cups cranberries (there are 3 cups in a
*   12-ounce bag)*
3 cups water
3½ cups sugar
2 envelopes gelatin, softened in ½ cup water
½ teaspoon salt
2 teaspoons grated orange zest
½ teaspoon grated lemon zest
2 cups fresh orange juice
½ cup fresh lemon juice
2 large egg whites

1. In a 3-quart covered saucepan (not aluminum), cook the cranberries and water over medium heat, until the berry skins pop open, 6 to 8 minutes.

2. Sieve (or push through a ricer), the cranberries with their cooking water into a large bowl.

3. Except for the egg whites, add the rest of the ingredients in the order given. Mix well to fully dissolve the sugar and gelatin.

4. Pour the mixture into a shallow baking dish, lasagne pan, or roasting pan, preferably made of metal. One about $15 \times 10 \times 3$ inches is perfect. Place in the coldest part of the freezer.

5. When the mixture turns mushy—how long this takes depends on your freezer's efficiency; check it after 30 minutes—turn it into the large bowl of your mixer and whip in the egg whites until the mixture is a cotton candy pink, light, and fluffy.

6. Pour the mixture back into the pan. Return the pan to the freezer. Freeze to serving consistency—several hours.

7. If the sherbet separates into a light and dark layer, whip it up again before it gets too hard. Or allow the sherbet to soften slightly at room temperature, then whip again. Also, if the sherbet gets too crystalline it can be whipped again.

ADVANCE PREPARATION: It doesn't store as well as one might think. After several days in the freezer it will surely become icy. It can be brought back to a smooth consistency by whipping again, but after long storage it gets to a point of no return.

BLUE CHEESE AND HONEY

Salty and sweet, intensity on intensity, this combination sounds weird but it is divine. The two totally different and very assertive flavors have a synergism that is hard to believe.

1. Use any blue cheese, though creamy Gorgonzola Dolce and Roquefort, which is a sheep's milk cheese, are much better than crumbly Stilton or Danish blues. (Paula Wolfert introduced me to the combination of honey and white Greek sheep's milk cheese, which is hard to find but something like feta.)

2. Serve the cheese in a small portion, say a slab no more than 2 inches square and ¼ inch thick.

3. Pour on enough honey to cover the cheese. I prefer a dark honey here, but even a light supermarket brand is excellent.

4. Serve each portion on a separate plate, with a fork to eat it as is, and with plain water crackers (biscuits) to put the honey-drenched cheese on, if desired, and/or to clear the palate between bites.

ADVANCE PREPARATION: You could cut the cheese ahead, put the slices on plates, and keep them covered with plastic wrap at room temperature until serving time.

BLUEBERRY APPLE CRUMBLE

Makes 16 servings

Everyone should have a dessert for a crowd. This is devised for those who think ahead to winter parties and freeze some of summer's blueberries when they are at their peak and their least expensive. Like cranberries, which we also eat sugared and popped, blueberries earmarked for pies and cobblers freeze perfectly.

7½ cups frozen (not thawed) blueberries (1 pound)
7 cups peeled, chopped tart apples, such as Granny Smith (7 medium)
2 teaspoons grated lemon zest
1 tablespoon freshly squeezed lemon juice
½ cup all-purpose flour
½ cup sugar
¼ cup packed light brown sugar
1¼ teaspoons ground cinnamon

FOR THE TOPPING:
1 cup quick-cooking oats
⅓ cup all-purpose flour
¾ cup packed light brown sugar
Pinch of salt
2 tablespoons cold butter, cut into pieces
2 tablespoons canola or other vegetable oil, plus extra for preparing the pan

1. Preheat the oven to 400 degrees. Lightly oil two 11- × 8-inch (2-quart) glass or ceramic baking dishes and set aside.

(continued)

2. In a large mixing bowl, combine the blueberries, apples, lemon zest, and juice.

3. In a small bowl, stir together the flour, sugars, and cinnamon.

4. Stir the flour mixture into the fruit mixture and mix well. Divide the mixture evenly between the baking dishes.

5. Bake for 20 minutes. Stir and set aside. Leave the oven on.

6. To make the topping, combine oats, flour, brown sugar, and salt in a food processor.

7. Evenly distribute the butter over the oat mixture, then pulse just until the butter is incorporated. Add the oil and pulse until the mixture is the consistency of coarse crumbs. Do not overprocess or the ingredients will lump together. (To make the topping by hand, combine oats, flour, brown sugar, and salt in a large bowl. With a pastry cutter or your fingertips, cut in the butter. Stir in the oil.)

8. Sprinkle the topping evenly over the fruit. Return to the oven for 30 to 40 minutes, or until the tops are brown and the fruit is bubbly.

9. Remove the cobblers and let stand for 10 minutes on a rack before serving.

10. To serve, spoon into dessert bowls and, if desired, top with frozen yogurt, ice cream, whipped cream, or liquid sweet cream.

ADVANCE PREPARATION: Prepare through step 7. Store the blueberry mixture and the crumb mixture separately, covered, in the refrigerator for up to twenty-four hours.

RUBY POACHED PEARS

Serves 8

You always need to plan to eat pears at least three or four days ahead. Because they ripen off the tree they are rarely sold already ripe. And since pears bruise so easily when they *are* ripe, you, in fact, want it that way. Select your pears for their unblemished skins and uniform firmness. Be careful how they are handled by the supermarket checker, and how they are handled between store and home. Bruises get worse as the ripening proceeds. To ripen them with maximum rapidity, place them in a brown paper bag with an apple, at room temperature. For slower ripening—you may be able to shop on Tuesday and not need them until Sunday—leave them unwrapped at room temperature, but never in a sunny window.

8 dead ripe, blemish-free pears
Juice of 1 lemon
1 cup red wine
½ cup ruby port
2½ cups water
1¼ cups sugar
6 cloves
Zest of half a lemon, in strips
Zest of half an orange, in strips

1. Peel the pears and place them in a bowl of cold water with the lemon juice.

2. Combine the remaining ingredients in a saucepan just large enough to hold the pears and simmer 20 minutes to make a syrup.

3. Place the pears in the syrup and simmer very slowly for 20 minutes, or until tender. If the pears are not covered by the syrup, turn them while they are cooking.

4. Let the pears cool in the syrup, basting them while they are cooling if any sections are above the liquid level.

5. Serve at room temperature or chill well.

ADVANCE PREPARATION: Can be kept refrigerated for about a week.

OLD-FASHIONED STRAWBERRY SHORTCAKE

Serves 8

Shortcake is really a rich baking powder biscuit; in this case, a very rich drop biscuit. It's the high portion of butter and two egg yolks that makes this dessert old-fashioned. As they could gild a lily in the good old days, I suggest you butter the biscuits, too. You haven't lived until you've eaten shortcake this way—and, very important, straight from the oven with fragile local berries. These would thrill everyone at a summer party.

1 quart strawberries
3 to 4 tablespoons sugar
Kirschwasser or framboise liqueur to taste
　(optional)

FOR THE SHORTCAKE:
2 cups all-purpose flour
1 tablespoon baking powder
3 tablespoons sugar
½ teaspoon salt
6 tablespoons butter
¾ cup milk
2 egg yolks

FOR THE CREAM:
1 pint heavy cream
1 or 2 tablespoons sugar
½ teaspoon vanilla extract (optional)
Softened butter (optional)

1. To prepare the berries, wash, hull, and either cut them in half or slice them. Toss with the sugar and optional kirschwasser. Do not let them stand more than several hours.

2. Preheat the oven to 425 degrees.

3. To make shortcakes, sift together the flour, baking powder, sugar, and salt into a mixing bowl.

4. Add the butter and cut it in by rubbing the dry ingredients with the butter between the fingertips until the mixture looks like coarse meal.

(*continued*)

5. In a small bowl, beat the milk and egg yolks together with a fork.

6. Add the liquid to the dry ingredients and, still with a fork, mix gingerly until the dough binds together.

7. Onto a lightly greased or nonstick baking sheet, drop the dough off a large spoon, dividing the dough into 8 neat but irregular mounds. Space the shortcakes at least 2 inches apart.

8. Bake for about 15 minutes, or until the biscuits are tinged with brown.

9. In a large bowl, whip the cream and when it is starting to mount, add 1 or 2 tablespoons sugar and the optional vanilla. Whip just until the cream is thick but still loose enough to roll off a spoon.

10. To assemble: When the biscuits are done, let them cool a minute, then split them in half with a fork, as you would an English muffin.

11. Butter the shortcakes lightly, if desired, placing the bottom of each biscuit on a serving plate.

12. Cover with the berries and some of their juice, then the top halves of the biscuits.

13. Spoon the whipped cream over each shortcake and top with a few more berries.

ADVANCE PREPARATION: The berries must be macerated no more than a few hours, but the biscuits can be prepared and refrigerated on the baking sheet, covered with plastic wrap, for one day. The cream should be whipped just before serving.

INDEX

INDEX

INDEX

INDEX

INDEX

INDEX

INDEX